Fiduciary
Trust
International

GEORGE M. TABER

Tuesday, October 13, 2009
Washington, DC

IN SEARCH OF BACCHUS

Wanderings in the Wonderful World
of Wine Tourism

GEORGE M. TABER

*To Ken and Dee —
We share a love of wine
and traveling*

George M. Taber

SCRIBNER

New York   London   Toronto   Sydney

SCRIBNER
A Division of Simon & Schuster, Inc.
1230 Avenue of the Americas
New York, NY 10020

First Scribner hardcover edition October 2009

SCRIBNER and design are registered trademarks of The Gale Group, Inc., used under license by Simon & Schuster, Inc., the publisher of this work.

For information about special discounts for bulk purchases, please contact Simon & Schuster Special Sales at 1-866-506-1949 or business@simonandschuster.com.

The Simon & Schuster Speakers Bureau can bring authors to your live event. For more information or to book an event contact the Simon & Schuster Speakers Bureau at 1-866-248-3049 or visit our website at www.simonspeakers.com.

Manufactured in the United States of America

1   3   5   7   9   10   8   6   4   2

Library of Congress Cataloging-in-Publication Data

Taber, George M.
In search of Bacchus : wanderings in the wonderful world of wine tourism / by George M. Taber.
p. cm.
1. Wine tourism. 2. Wine and wine making. I. Title.
TP548.5.T68T33 2009
641.2'2—dc22
2009010147

ISBN 978-1-4165-6243-6
ISBN 978-1-4165-6249-8 (ebook)

PHOTO INSERT CREDITS

Photos courtesy of the author except as indicated. Page 1: Courtesy of Montes (*bottom left*). Page 2: Courtesy of Vergelegen (*top*). Page 3: Courtesy of Achaval-Ferrer (*middle*). Page 4: Courtesy of Chadwick (*top*); Courtesy of Leeuwin Estate (*middle*). Page 6: Courtesy of Vivanco (*bottom*). Page 7: Courtesy of Baumgart Winery (*middle*); Courtesy of Ruy de Brito e Cunha (*bottom*). Page 8: Courtesy of Castello Banfi (*top*); Courtesy of Banfi (*bottom*).

"Travel remains a journey into whatever we can't explain, or explain away."

—Pico Iyer, *Sun After Dark*

Contents

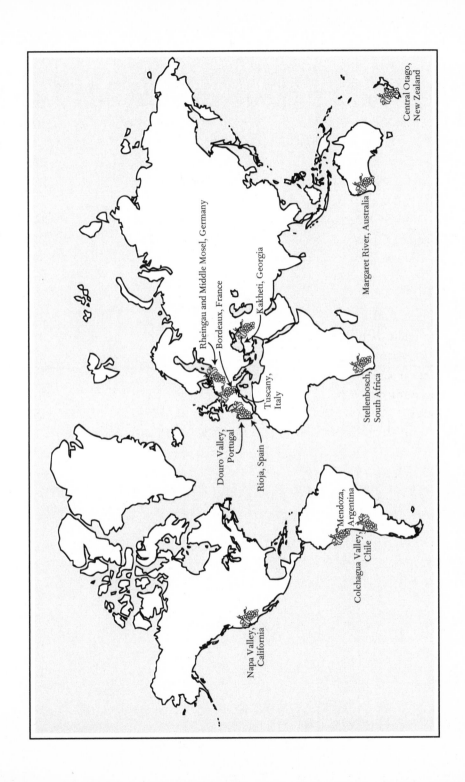

Rheingau and Middle Mosel, Germany

Bordeaux, France

Kakheti, Georgia

Tuscany, Italy

Douro Valley, Portugal

Rioja, Spain

Stellenbosch, South Africa

Margaret River, Australia

Central Otago, New Zealand

Napa Valley, California

Mendoza, Argentina

Colchagua Valley, Chile

Prologue

Ed Zimmerman, a classic Type A personality who hides it well behind a casual façade and lots of throwaway lines, doesn't do anything half-heartedly. Chairman of the Technology Group at Lowenstein Sandler, a law firm based in New Jersey and New York, he was described by clients in Chambers, the lawyer-ranking service, as "one of the best venture capital lawyers in the country—period." The primary focus of his law practice is working with companies raising venture capital and private-equity investments. Zimmerman's passion, though, is wine.

Wine was not part of Zimmerman's life while he was growing up poor in Brooklyn in the 1970s and 1980s. At times his father held down three jobs, primarily working for the City of New York, but supplementing the family's income by driving a cab, delivering pizza, and picking up odd jobs such as stuffing envelopes. Embarrassed that he couldn't afford to buy the shoes he needed to wear to a wedding, the father once declined to attend the celebration.

Zimmerman still remembers his first serious wine experience. It was in December 1990 at the Cape Cod house of Betsy Marks, a girlfriend he had met on her first day at Haverford College in Pennsylvania. He can't recall the vintage or the winemaker, but he's sure it was a Puligny-Montrachet Chardonnay from Burgundy. "It was an epiphany."

Although he has never been tested for it, Zimmerman may well be part of the 25 percent of the population that Dr. Linda Bartoshuk of the Yale School of Medicine classifies as "supertasters." "Supertasters live in a neon taste world; taste sensations are roughly three times as intense to them as non-tasters," writes Bartoshuk. Those people have an uncanny ability to remember wines and compare them to others they might have enjoyed years, if not decades, earlier. Zimmerman can recall in detail when, where, and under what circumstances he drank a memorable wine.

Zimmerman joined Lowenstein Sandler after graduating from the University of Pennsylvania Law School. He soon married Betsy Marks, and the combination of good food and wine became part of their lives. In September 1992, the couple took a one-week honeymoon to London so they could dine at La Tante Claire in the Berkeley Hotel, where master chef Pierre Koffmann was cooking. Money was tight, but they stretched their budget and took the sommelier's suggestion of a half-bottle of Guigal Châteauneuf-du-Pape wine to go with squab.

For Zimmerman, traveling to vineyards where his favorite wines are made and talking with the winemakers is as exciting as going to see Santa Claus at the North Pole would be for a big-eyed five-year-old. In 1995, he and Betsy made their first trip to France, visiting the Loire Valley and Burgundy wine areas. The couple planned their itinerary around Michelin-starred restaurants and stayed in inexpensive hotels so they could spend more money on food and wine. For one memorable picnic in Beaujolais they enjoyed local cheese, a loaf of bread, and an award-winning wine from the area while looking out at a spectacular countryside. "It was the ultimate French experience that every American tourist hopes to have," he recalls.

One night in South Africa in 1996, Zimmerman struck up a friendship with Christian Fins, the sommelier from Bosman's Restaurant in the Grande Roche Hotel, and the next day the two went out to visit some of Cape Town's smallest and best wineries. When traveling on business in California to see clients or law recruits at the University of California, Berkeley, Zimmerman routinely makes detours to visit the Napa Valley and dine at the homes of winemaker friends or at the famed French Laundry restaurant.

Getting to meet famous, but often reclusive, winemakers is no easy task, yet Zimmerman goes after them relentlessly. Colleagues at his law firm joke that he is so persistent in pursuing his targets that a winemaker will some day take out a restraining order against him. Zimmerman went after Austrian-born Manfred Krankl, the winemaker-owner of California's Sine Qua Non in Ventura, California, like a stalker. Krankl's winery is located in a shabby industrial park, but he makes California's most sought-after wines. Robert Parker's *Wine Advocate* regularly scores his wines in the high 90s and occasionally a perfect 100.

Zimmerman had been buying from Krankl since the 1996 vintage, and the two had struck up a friendship and enjoyed barrel tastings together. In 2004, Zimmerman thought it was time to get his hands dirty, by experiencing firsthand how wine is made. He e-mailed Krankl, asking if he could spend a week at Sine Qua Non during harvest. The lawyer said he would work for nothing, promised not to get in the way, and even offered to "mop the bathroom floor." In a series of e-mails, Krankl tried to discourage Zimmerman by detailing how unglamorous, exhausting, and busy the experience would be. Krankl feared that when things went wrong, he might lose a friend as well as a customer. Krankl also insisted on paying him, "so I can yell at you when you screw up." Zimmerman demurred at being paid, but said Krankl could make a donation to a charity the lawyer ran.

So in September 2004, Zimmerman, who earns several hundred dollars an hour as a lawyer, packed his grubbiest clothes, told his clients he would be gone for a while but not what he was doing, and flew off to California to do work for which migrant laborers might earn $9 an hour. During that week, Zimmerman did everything. He cleaned hoses, washed barrels, sorted grapes, pumped over fermenting grape juice. Living up to his promise, he even mopped the bathroom floor, though only once.

Maggie Harrison, Sine Qua Non's first employee and the assistant winemaker while Zimmerman was there, recalls him arriving at dawn, and staying late. "He knew he wasn't going to be leaning on a barrel, swirling a glass of wine and discussing whether the Syrah would be more like a Hermitage or more like a Côte Rôtie," she says. The only jobs the staff didn't ask him to do were manning the overnight shift and operating a forklift.

Sine Qua Non double-sorts grapes, first by bunches and then by individual grapes, while many producers don't hand sort in the winery at all. "Ed knew so much about wine when he arrived, but he had never had the experience of sorting grapes or understanding how important that is for the final wine," Harrison says. "Until you stand there doing it for a half day, as he did, you can't get what it's all about."

In August 2007, Robert Parker awarded the 2004 Sine Qua Non Poker Face, the Syrah on which Zimmerman had worked, a perfect 100 points. In his signature style, Parker wrote, "Fabulous texture, beautiful richness and purity, and a finish that lasts nearly a minute. It is a wine of enormous richness, multiple dimensions, and unreal purity."

Zimmerman also connects with winemakers by arranging unusual tastings. In early 2008, he invited a good friend to guest-lecture at his venture capital course at Columbia Business School. As he does with his many guest lecturers, Zimmerman decided to treat his friend and other wine lovers to dinner and some great wines after class. He and seven other wine geeks gathered at New York's Aureole Restaurant for a vertical tasting of ten of the best vintages of Château Margaux going back to 1961, with some bottles of Château Lafite Rothschild and Harlan Estate California Cabernet Sauvignon thrown in to make things more interesting. Zimmerman contacted Château Margaux in advance of the meal, and received a call back from Paul Pontallier, who provided tasting notes and recommendations on how to serve, decant, and organize the wines.

Zimmerman purchased the first release, a 1999 Cabernet Sauvignon, from a new Napa winery called Blankiet Estate and soon began e-mailing owner Claude Blankiet, asking him if he could visit. After a three-year campaign, Blankiet relented. At the end of several hours spent walking the mountainside vineyard and the construction site of Blankiet's new home, Zimmerman asked how frequently Blankiet gave tours. The amused Blankiet responded, "This is the first!"

On a subsequent visit to Blankiet's house, Zimmerman noticed a picture of Blankiet with a group of men in flowing red-and-gold robes and wearing funny hats. Blankiet explained it was a picture of his 1997 induction into Burgundy's Confrérie des Chevaliers du Tastevin, the world's most prestigious wine organization, whose home base is at the Clos de Vougeot winery. Blankiet, who had grown up in Burgundy, volunteered to sponsor Zimmerman for membership. The lawyer listened politely but dismissed the idea, thinking that he did not want to impose on his friend and knowing that it would be hard for an American to be inducted into the exclusive Clos de Vougeot chapter. This time, it was Blankiet who persisted, ultimately sending Zimmerman application materials. These included writing short essays on his love and knowledge of wines, particularly Burgundy, and getting endorsements from leading wine personalities, which Blankiet arranged. On the first weekend in June 2006, Zimmerman trekked to Burgundy's majestic Château du Clos de Vougeot where officials in those same red-and-gold robes inducted the tuxedo-clad group of some twenty mostly French wine insiders as Knights of the Tastevin. It didn't matter that Zimmerman couldn't understand most of the French ceremony. He was on top of the wine world.

Bacchus, the Roman god of wine and the theater, casts a magical spell on people such as Ed Zimmerman, who will travel far and wide to meet a winemaker and to taste his product in the place where its grapes were grown and it was made. This has become more and more common in recent years as the popularity of wine has spread from its roots in Europe. The most popular tourist destination in California today is Disneyland, the granddaddy of all theme parks. But the second most visited one is the Napa Valley, which each year welcomes more than 5 million travelers. Wines first enjoyed on distant shores seem to earn a warm spot in our remembrances of vintages past. British author H. Warner Allen wrote in *The Romance of Wine,* "Nearly every natural wine, though it be sour or course or rough in taste, has a singular attraction when it is drunk in its native place."

In January 2008, I set out in search of Bacchus: to explore wine tourism in twelve of the world's most interesting wine regions. This is the story of what I discovered.

CHAPTER ONE

Three Pioneers

Wine fans for centuries have traveled to the birthplaces of their favorite wines in order to enjoy the special pleasure of drinking them where the grapes are grown and the juice fermented. Here are just three—one from the seventeenth century, one from the eighteenth, and one from the nineteenth.

John Locke, the English political philosopher whose ideas had a major impact on the American Revolution, was one of the most influential thinkers in the Age of Enlightenment. Among Locke's revolutionary ideas were the concepts of "government with the consent of the governed" and "the rights of life, liberty, and property." The latter found its way into the Declaration of Independence as "life, liberty, and the pursuit of happiness."

Because of political setbacks at home and his problems with a chronic cough probably due to tuberculosis, Locke, a trained doctor, sought out a more temperate climate away from his home in London. In November 1675, he left for France with the intention of traveling as far south as Montpellier, a city with a major medical practice and where the weather would be much warmer. During his three and a half years in France, the philosopher wrote more than fourteen hundred pages of notes on what he saw and experienced.

While living in Montpellier, Locke made several trips to nearby wine regions. He carefully recorded how winemakers went about their craft, the quality of the wine, and the prices. Locke wrote that locals "seldom make red wine without the mixture of some sort of white grapes, else it will be too thick and deep colored." He also noted that peasants grew several varieties in the same vineyard and described in detail how farmers planted and pruned their vines.

The French taught Locke the importance of *terroir*, the untranslatable term for local vineyard growing conditions, and of blending different kinds of grapes. As he wrote in his notes, "The goodness of their wine to drink seems to depend on two causes besides the pressing and ordering the fermentation." These were "the qualities of the soil" and the "mingling a good quantity of white grapes with the red." Near Montpellier he noted with some perplexity, "Two vineyards, bounding one upon another, constantly produce the one good and the other bad wine."

Locke learned vines could be productive for "nay 100 years," and "the older the better" the wines. Young vines produced "commonly green *i.e.* sour" wine. He wrote that French wine was generally aged for many years in wooden barrels before it was drinkable, but winemakers had ways to speed up aging. "When they have a mind to have their wine fine sooner than ordinary, they put in a cask pretty good quantity of shavings of fir, and, in some places, of hazel, and with it they sometimes put some whole white grapes."

Many local viticulture practices clearly offended the Englishman: "[A]nd in all other parts of their making wine they are sufficiently nasty, according to their manner. The grapes are often rotten and always full of spiders. Beside that, they say they put often salt, men's dung and other filthiness in their wine to help, as they think, its purging."

When leaving Montpellier to return to Paris in March 1677, Locke decided to take a western route to see more of southern France. On Friday, May 14, he was in Bordeaux and rode a horse out of the city to what he described as "President Pontac's vineyard at Hautbrion," today's Château Haut-Brion. Locke had enjoyed wine in London, and now he wanted to see it at its place of origin. Although Locke by then spoke good French, he had trouble communicating with the working people at the winery because of his "want of understanding Gascoin," a dialect of the Occitan language spoken in southern France. Nonetheless, he wrote an insightful description of the vineyard: "It is a little rise of ground, lying open most to the west. It is nothing but pure, white sand, mixed with little gravel. One would imagine it scarce fit to bear anything."

Locke later wrote in a more detailed report of his visit to Château

Haut-Brion: "There is such a particularity point in the soil that the merchants assured me that the wine growing in the very next vineyards, where there was only a ditch between, and the soil, to appearance, perfectly the same, was by no means so good." That ditch, and the difference in the wines from the two vineyards, are still there today.

Locke stayed in Paris for a year before he and a student who had been placed in his charge returned to southern France in July 1678. The two again took a western route, going through Tours and the Loire Valley. They stopped at the home of Nicolas Thoynard, a fellow scholar who shared Locke's wide range of interests. The two men discussed the writings of the evangelists in the Bible, new forms of ammunition, and Thoynard's proposal for sealing bottles of wine with a glass stopper rather than a cork. They also shared "a large bottle of Muscat or Jenetine wine of Orléans stopped with a glass stopper."

As he traveled, Locke was shocked to see the drop in wine prices since he had been there only a year earlier. Wines were selling for one-third as much as before. The reason was a glut of wine precipitated by a war between France and Holland, which had severely reduced exports to both Holland and England. In Saumur he wrote, "The white wine here in this town is very good & wine so plentiful that they sell it for 18 deniers the pint at their boushons *i.e.* where people in private houses sell their own wine by retail." Locke also noted that ten deniers of that went to the king as excise taxes, while the vintner got only eight deniers. Later in Angers, wine was selling for one-fourth as much as before. In the port city of Rochelle, the price of wine was down 50 percent, with the exception of President Pontac's and "some others of particular note" that still sold for twice as much as the rest. While going through Bordeaux on his second trip, Locke did not revisit Haut-Brion.

Three months before leaving France in the spring of 1679, Locke wrote a treatise entitled *Observations Upon Vines* that brought together all he had learned about wine in France. Despite his long stay in the country, he had not become a great fan of the French, writing in the introduction, "The country where these observations were made hath vanity enough to over-value everything it produces." He recounted in detail when and how the French planted their vineyards. His preference for aged vines was clear: "The older the vineyard, the fewer the grapes, but the better the wine. Newly planted vineyards produce more, but the wine is not as good." Locke added that in the village of Galliac near Montpellier, "If a peasant there should use any but birds dung about his vines, his neighbors would burn his house because they would not have the wine of that place lose its reputation."

Locke recorded in his report the local belief that "a sheep's horn buried at the foot of a vine will make it bear well even in barren ground." But he quickly added, "I have no great faith in it, but mention it because it may so easily be tried."

In late April 1679, Locke boarded the *Charlotte* in Calais for the return trip home, and two days later, he landed at the Temple stairs, on the Thames, in London. John Locke never again returned to France.

A little more than a century later, Thomas Jefferson, on July 31, 1784, arrived in France to join Benjamin Franklin and John Adams as representatives of the new United States of America, which less than a year before had signed the Treaty of Paris, ending the American Revolutionary War. Although Jefferson was familiar with the political philosophy of John Locke, there is no evidence that he was aware of his writings on French wines. Nonetheless, Jefferson was to follow many of the Englishman's tracks across France's wine country, which he recorded in even greater detail.

Jefferson had already long enjoyed wine and had made unsuccessful attempts to grow wine grapes at his Monticello estate in Virginia, where he had a well-stocked cellar. Thus it was not surprising when, four days before he was to depart for France from Boston aboard the sailing ship *Ceres,* Jefferson bought four cases of German white wine from the Rhine to get him through the voyage that was to take twenty days. And less than two weeks after arriving in Paris, he purchased 276 bottles to start his new cellar there.

Jefferson's partners in the diplomatic mission were also fond of French wine. Benjamin Franklin had a Paris cellar of more than eleven hundred bottles with an emphasis on Champagne. John Adams had landed in Bordeaux in April 1778 when he first came to France and had seen some of the wine country there on his way to Paris. Jefferson, though, had a substantially stronger interest in wine and set out to learn more about topics such as Burgundy wines, which were almost totally new to him.

During his first years in Paris, Jefferson stuck to his work of learning French and observing the internecine world in the court of Louis XVI and his wife, Marie Antoinette. After two and a half years of diligent work, however, Jefferson, in early 1787, decided to tour France for several months. The explanations for the trip were many. The official reason was that he was going to look into the potential for exporting American tobacco and whale oil to southern France. The clandestine one was that he was going to meet a Brazilian revolutionary in Marseilles who was trying to get American support for a movement to drive the Portuguese out of his country. Another story was that he was going to Aix-en-Provence in hopes that its famous thermal springs could help heal his right wrist, which had been injured during some horseplay with Maria Cosway, his then romantic interest. Jefferson's overriding reason, though, was to visit vineyards and to buy wine directly from producers. Jefferson had grown suspicious of wine dealers and thought the only way to be certain of getting the real product, rather than a forgery, was to buy it on the spot. "Genuine wines can never be had but of the *vigneron*," he wrote.

Traveling at first incognito and with no servant in hopes of seeing what France was like outside the capital, Jefferson left Paris through the Porte d'Orléans on February 28, 1787, in a carriage pulled by three horses. He later recounted a detailed history of his travels in his report *Notes of a Tour into the Southern Parts of France, &c.* He recorded everything from the price of wine along the way to how long a farming family could live off a slaughtered hog, which was one year. He even offered tips for future travelers: "When one calls on the taverns for the *vin du pays* they give what is natural and unadulterated and cheap; when *vin etrangere* is called for, it only gives a pretext for charging an extravagant price for an unwholesome stuff."

When he arrived in Dijon, Jefferson hired a manservant to help him with the local dialects since he spoke only Parisian French. In his report, Jefferson noted that corn grew on the plains, while on the hillside, known as the Côte, vines were planted. In the red-wine towns of Pommard and Volnay he reported that the staple of the diet was "good wheat bread," but a little farther south in Meursault, where white wines were made, people ate rye bread. When he asked why, "They told me that the white wines fail in quality much oftener than the red, and remain on hand. The farmer therefore cannot afford to feed his labourers so well. At Meursault, only white wines are made, because there is too much stone for the red." He noted that the villages of Chambertin, Vougeot, and Vosne produced the best reds, but he also liked Volnay, which sold for only one-quarter as much as the others. On the white wine side, he looked again for value. Montrachet sold for the same price as a Chambertin, but a Meursault from the Goutte d'Or vineyard was one-eighth as much. Jefferson then placed a large order for Goutte d'Or.

Traveling south, Jefferson next ventured into the Rhône Valley. The best red wine, he wrote, is "produced at the upper end in the neighborhood of Ampuis," while the best whites came from "next to Condrieu." He was particularly fond of "the wine called Hermitage . . . made on the hills impending over the village of Tains." The Hermitage vineyard, he noted, is on a hill and added that the last hermit died in 1751. Jefferson became a great fan of white Hermitage, which was then slightly sweet. Among other white wines, Jefferson liked Viognier, sold by "Chateau Grillé [modern day Château Grillet] by Madame *la veuve* [the widow] Peyrouse." In the town of Nîmes he had high praise for the inexpensive "vin ordinaire, good and of a strong body."

On March 25, Jefferson arrived in Aix-en-Provence, where he stayed for four days and underwent extensive treatment at the thermal springs that seemed to do little good. Yet on March 27, he wrote in a letter to his private secretary William Short, "I am now in the land of corn, wine, oil, and sunshine. What more can man ask of heaven? If I should happen to die in Paris I will beg of you to send me here, and have me exposed to the sun. I am sure it will bring me to life again."

After a brief stop in Marseilles and other towns along the Mediterranean, Jefferson ventured into Italy on the back of a mule. He had originally hoped to follow the route Hannibal and his elephants had used for his invasion of Rome, but there weren't enough landmarks to follow. In Turin, Jefferson delighted in the discovery of a new wine: "There is a red wine of Nebiule [modern Nebbiolo] made in this neighborhood which is very singular. It is about as sweet as the silky Madeira, as astringent on the palate as Bordeaux, and as brisk as Champagne. It is a pleasing wine."

In Rozzano, Jefferson watched Parmesan cheese being made, recording the steps in great detail. Finally, he went to Genoa before returning to Nice via the Italian Riviera. Then he traveled through Provence and Languedoc, where he discovered Rochegude, a sweet white wine made near Avignon, and white and red Frontignan. They all became among Jefferson's favorites. He bought 250 bottles of Frontignan and had them shipped to Paris. Like a man on a mission, Jefferson pressed on toward Bordeaux.

From May 24 to May 28, Jefferson visited Bordeaux, staying at the Hôtel de Richelieu in the center of town. He traveled all around the wine capital of France, keeping records on viticulture practices as well as how much vineyard workers were paid, noting that men earned twice as much as women. Picking up an informal classification used in Bordeaux wine circles, Jefferson came up with the "4 vineyards of first quality" for red wines. They were: "Chateau Margau, La Tour de Ségur, Hautbrion, and Chateau de la Fite." He also gave the annual production and owner of each. With modern spellings they are Château Margaux, Château Latour, Château Haut-Brion, and Château Lafite-Rothschild. They were the top four wines in the French classification of 1855 and are still considered outstanding. He also listed wines in Second and Third Growths.

Just as Locke before him, Jefferson walked through the vineyards of Haut-Brion and wrote a similar description: "The soil of Hautbrion particularly, which I examined is a sand, in which is near as much round gravel or small stone, and very little loam." Jefferson, who had first enjoyed the wine at the table of Benjamin Franklin, always had a soft spot for Haut-Brion, writing to his man in Bordeaux in 1784 that it was "a wine of first rank and seems to please the American palate more than all the others that I have been able to taste in France."

Among the dry white wines, Jefferson noted that the three best came from the Graves region: Pontac, St. Brise, and De Carbonius, which he said Benedictine monks made and sold for twice as much as the others. The latter is now known as Château Carbonnieux, although the white wine vineyards are no longer the same. Jefferson wrote that sweet Sauternes were "more esteemed in Paris" than dry whites and that "the best crop belongs to M. Diquem," now Château d'Yquem. He cited two others, known today as Château Filhot and Château Suduiraut.

After his visit to Bordeaux, Jefferson left the city by boat, sailing down the Gironde Estuary past the great vineyards of the Médoc. He then skips rather quickly over the rest of the trip. He writes that wines "of good quality," but not up to the standards of Bordeaux, are made near Angers, only 185 miles southwest of Paris, that are "probably sold abroad under the name Bordeaux."

Jefferson finally returned to Paris on June 10, 1787, and only four days later wrote his new wine buyer in Burgundy to order a *feuillette*, a small oak barrel used mainly in Chablis that held approximately 36 gallons, of both Volnay and Meursault Goutte d'Or wines. In a postscript to the letter, Jefferson told his agent to list the wines as "*vins ordinaires*" and to have the driver enter Paris in a way that would not attract much attention from tax collectors. On June 19, Jefferson wrote of his travels to John Bannister Jr., a fellow Virginian, saying that he had "never passed three months and a half more delightfully."

It didn't take Jefferson long to do some more wine tourism. Less than a year later, on March 4, 1788, he left Paris by carriage heading toward Amsterdam. The ostensible reason for this trip was to see John Adams before he returned to the United States. After some negotiations with Dutch bankers about loans to the new American government, Adams left Amsterdam and Jefferson headed to the wine region of Germany, intending to go up the Rhine as far as Strasbourg. In his report *Notes of a Tour through Holland and the Rhine Valley*, Jefferson recounts his travels, though not in as much detail or with the same enthusiasm as he had for southern France. This may be due in part to the fact that he did not speak German and had difficulty communicating with people along the way. He wrote in his journal on

April 2: "There was not a person to be found in Duisberg who could understand either English, French, Italian or Latin. So I could make no enquiry."

Jefferson saw his first vineyard in Cologne, and a little ways south in Bonn, vines became plentiful. He noted a difference in the wines from grapes grown on the flatland and on the hillsides: "It is observed here, as elsewhere, that the plains yield much wine, but bad. The good is furnished from the hills."

On April 5, Jefferson was in Koblenz, where the Mosel River flows into the Rhine. He did not visit the Mosel wine region, but liked its wine a great deal. He said the best Mosel wines came from the "excessively mountainous country" 15 leagues (45 miles) back from the confluence of the rivers. He ranked Brauneberg the top, followed by Wehlen, Grach, Piesport, and Zelting. He cautioned, though, "These wines must be 5 or 6 years before they are quite ripe for drinking."

Jefferson was harsh in his views about Rhine reds: "The red wines of this country are very indifferent and will not keep." Later he was still more caustic, calling them "absolutely worthless."

On the other hand, he loved white wines from the Rheingau region. "It is only from Rüdesheim to Hochheim that wines of the very first quality are made." He particularly liked the wines of Johannisberg, calling them the "very first quality" and noting that they sold for "double the price" of similar wines. He attributed this to the fact that the vineyards face south and the soil was "a barren mullato clay mixed with a good deal of stone and some slate." He wrote that Johannisberg wines had "none of the acid of the Hochheim and other Rhenish wines." Farther south in the villages of Bodenheim and Nierstein, they were "second quality."

Jefferson's interest in local wines again picked up in Alsace, where he found the interesting *vin de paille* (straw wine) being made near Colmar. He recounted that vintners made it after leaving grapes harvested in the fall spread out on straw until the spring. "The little juice then remaining in them makes a rich sweet wine, but the dearest in the world without being the best by any means." He concluded that a much better wine of that style is southern France's Frontignan.

Jefferson could be brutal in his critiques. Traveling farther west near the town of Nancy, the capital of Lorraine, he wrote that there were "some small vineyards where a bad wine is made."

In a letter to his personal secretary William Short on April 9, 1788, Jefferson explained that when he left Alsace, he was going to return to Paris "a little circuitously, perhaps by the way of Reims in Champagne, so that I am unable to say exactly when I shall be at Paris." Given his love of Champagne, Jefferson couldn't pass up a chance to see where it was made. He was immediately impressed by the soil, writing, "The hills abound with chalk." He also reported, "Their red wines, though most esteemed on the spot, are by no means esteemed elsewhere equally with their white, nor do they merit it." Champagne then made both sparkling wines and still ones. Jefferson seems surprised when he writes, "The sparkling are little drank in France but are alone known and drank in foreign countries." He reported that sparkling wines sell for eight times as much as still ones. While Champagne today is known by such major brands as Hennessy or Taitinger, in Jefferson's day the wine's village of origin determined the quality, and so he gave a report on the various villages and included a map showing their locations. His favorite was Ay, and he names several producers "all of the 1st quality." He wrote that Monsieur Dorsay made the best. Jefferson also liked Champagne made by the monks in Hautvillers, where Dom Pérignon had been cellarmaster more than a half-century before, but wrote it was "hardly as good as Dorsay's."

Along with many visitors to Champagne both before and since, Jefferson was overwhelmed by the caves where wine was stored, writing that they extended "into ground in a kind of labyrinth to a prodigious distance" and concluded, "I have no where seen cellars comparable to these."

On April 23, and after visiting the Champagne village of Épernay, Jefferson went to Meaux, a village famous for its Brie cheese, and then turned west to return to Paris.

Only six months later, on October 23, 1789, Thomas Jefferson left France to return to the United States to become George Washington's secretary of state. He shipped 363 bottles of French wines with him. Despite his love of Bordeaux reds, he took only white wines, and the majority of those were sweet wines such as Château d'Yquem and Frontignan. He also packed away thirty-six bottles of Champagne.

While Locke and Jefferson traveled through the wine country of France, Robert Louis Stevenson, author of *Kidnapped* and *The Strange Case of Dr. Jekyll and Mr. Hyde,* visited the Napa Valley and wrote about it in his book *The Silverado Squatters,* which he published in 1883. Stevenson wrote his first story at the age of six and in his twenties was attracted to the bohemian life of artists in France. While living in an artist's colony in 1876 in Gerz, outside Paris, he met Fanny Osbourne, an aspiring artist who had left a philandering husband in California with three children in tow, to paint in France. Although eleven years his senior, she and Stevenson were soon lovers. But in August 1878, she left France to return to California for an attempted reconciliation with her husband. After that failed, she sent a telegram to Stevenson, the contents of which were never known. But somehow she convinced him to sail across the Atlantic to join her in America.

After Fanny's divorce was finally granted, the two married in San Francisco on May 19, 1880. Stevenson already suffered from lung disease, and the couple took the advice of friends and spent a two-month honeymoon in the dry mountain air on Mount Saint Helena above the spa town of Calistoga. Because they couldn't afford to stay in a hotel, a local shopkeeper pointed the couple toward the abandoned mining town of Silverado, where they stayed in an old bunkhouse. While he was there, Stevenson took copious notes that were the basis for *The Silverado Squatters.*

After a quick introduction to a land that he admits is "difficult for a European to imagine," Stevenson recounts tales of a strange mélange of local characters and customs. He devotes the third chapter to Napa wines, writing, "I was interested in California wines. Indeed, I am interested in all wines and have been all my life." Having lived in France when the phylloxera bug that devastated vineyards seemingly meant the end of French wine, he lamented, "Bordeaux is no more. Chateau Neuf is dead, and I have never tasted it; Hermitage—a hermitage indeed from all life's sorrow—lies expiring by the river."

Stevenson spent time with two winemakers, whom he identifies only by their surnames: Mr. Schram and Mr. M'Eckron. He wrote that Napa Valley vineyards were nothing "to remind you of the Rhine or Rhone." Instead, "all is green, solitary, covert." He first visited the Scotsman M'Eckron and clearly enjoyed meeting a fellow countryman and exchanging a "word or two of Scotch, which pleased me more than you would fancy."

More interesting from a wine point of view was Mr. Schram. While Mrs. Schram entertained Fanny on the veranda, the writer and the winemaker tasted wines in the cellar. "I tasted every variety and shade of Schramberger, red and white Schramberger, Burgundy Schramberger, Schramberger Hock, Schramberger Golden Chasselas, the latter with a notable bouquet, and I fear to think how many more."

Stevenson liked what he tried in Schram's cellar and elsewhere in the Napa Valley, but he thought local winemakers were just beginning to discover which grapes flourished best in their valley. "In this wild spot, I did not feel the sacredness of ancient cultivation," he wrote. "It was still raw, it was no Marathon, and no Johannisberg; yet the stirring sunlight, and the growing vines, and the vats and bottles in the cavern, made a pleasant music for the mind."

Californians, he wrote, are "still in the experimental stage" of wine-making. "So, bit by bit, they grope about for their Clos Vougeot and Lafite." Nonetheless: "The wine is bottled poetry."

Stevenson's brief foray into California wine country left him with hope for the future of wine that seemed to be dying in France. "The smack of California earth shall linger on the palate of your grandson."

CHAPTER TWO

Napa Valley, California

On summer weekends in the late 1960s, Michael Mondavi, who had just returned from military service and was working for his father's business, used to slowly drive his beat-up, off-white Chevrolet El Camino up California State Route 29 through the Napa Valley from the sleepy city of Napa, which was then best known as the home of the State Mental Hospital, toward Calistoga at the northern end of the valley. Soon a parade of cars would build up behind him on the road that was too narrow for anyone to pass. But even though drivers behind him honked in an attempt to get him to drive faster, Mondavi just poked along, oblivious to their anger.

Shortly after the caravan of cars passed the sign indicating that they had entered the unincorporated village of Oakville (pop. about 150), drivers would often see a man with a receding hairline and wearing a sport shirt out by the side of the road waving them to turn into his winery. The sign just before the driveway leading into the property was simple, but tastefully attractive, and identified this as the **Robert Mondavi Winery**. Behind it was a striking Mexican mission-style winery with a distinctive bell tower. Michael pulled into the winery, and soon others, who were tired of being on the road, followed him. He then hopped out of his car and started urging people to take a tour of the winery. If they were willing to go through the hour-long lesson on winemaking that Robert often gave, visitors would get a free sample of three Mondavi wines. Michael had done his job, and later he might head back to Napa, repeating his drive and bringing in even more tourists.

Located about 50 miles north of the San Francisco metropolitan area, Napa Valley has long been a paradise that attracts visitors who want to enjoy its natural splendors and mild climate. The valley stretches some 40 miles from American Canyon in the south to Calistoga in the north and is less than 10 miles wide. Mountain ranges stand along both the eastern and western sides of the valley, and the Pacific Ocean is only 40 miles to the west.

Invading Spaniards called the Indian tribes who had inhabited the region for centuries when Europeans arrived *guapo,* or courageous, and the name evolved into Wappo. The area was part of Spain until 1821, when Mexico achieved independence from Spain. There were about fifteen hundred Indians in the valley when the first Westerners arrived on June 28, 1823. José Altimira, a Franciscan priest who was looking to set up a new mission north of the one at San Rafael just above San Francisco Bay, led the group. First he came to a place local Indians called Sonoma, which he thought would make a good site for a new mission. Then he traveled to an area called Napa, after the Napato Indians. Altimira compared it to his native Barcelona and marveled at the broad fields where large numbers of elk, deer, antelope, and bear grazed. Indians were burning fields, which he thought was a warning to others of an invasion, but it was more likely the tradition of burning brush in June to avoid fires during the summer. Altimira noted the clumps of tall oaks and speculated that the fields might be good places to plant vineyards. After spending four days in the Napa Valley, Altimira traveled back to Sonoma and decided to build his new mission there because timber and water were more readily available than in Napa. In 1836, George C. Yount, a mountaineer nicknamed Captain Buckskin, received a land grant from Mexico of 11,814 acres in the heart of the valley that today makes up the towns of Yountville, Oakville, and Rutherford. He called the property Rancho Caymus in honor of Indians that were a subgroup of the Wappos, and planted the first vineyard.

Robert Mondavi did not invent Napa Valley wine tourism. But through myriad innovative marketing initiatives, including Michael's slow drives up Route 29, he took it to a whole new level. Soon, thousands of people a year were visiting his adobe winery in Oakville. And ever since it was built, winemakers from around the world have flocked to the Napa Valley to see how Mondavi did it and to determine what they might copy at their wineries from New Zealand to France.

Born into an Italian immigrant family in Minnesota, Robert Mondavi arrived in California's wine country in 1923 at the age of ten. The family's prized possession was the Charles Krug Winery, which his father, Cesare, bought in 1943. Robert and his younger brother Peter both went into the business and had a good working relationship as long as their father was around. Robert concentrated mainly on marketing, while Peter focused on winemaking. In the 1950s and early 1960s, most land in the Napa Valley was devoted to fruit orchards or cattle grazing, and there was no such thing as wine tourism. Few Americans then even drank wine.

Gradually, though, and with no active promotion, people from the San Francisco Bay area in the 1960s began to find their way to the valley both to enjoy the scenery and to taste the wines. Students and young professionals developed a standard plan for how to get the most tastings out of a trip. They drove up Route 29, stopping first at Beaulieu Vineyard in Rutherford, where they could taste four wines for free. A little farther north was the Louis M. Martini Winery, which made some twenty wines and whose staff was famous for having a heavy hand when pouring samples. Once through the town of St. Helena, the next place to visit was the Charles Krug Winery, which was noted for pouring rather skimpy portions. Then the intrepid tourist would cross the road and begin driving south, making a first stop at Greystone, a majestic building that looks like a French château and housed the Christian Brothers winery. Samples were again generous and included a sparkling wine they called Champagne. The next stop was the Beringer Vineyards Rhine House, a German-style mansion and winery that has magnificent wine caves dug by Chinese laborers in the previous century. The final tasting on the tour was back in Rutherford at Inglenook, then the most respected name in California wine.

After Cesare Mondavi died in November 1959, the smoldering sibling rivalry exploded between Robert and Peter that ended in a fistfight over a mink coat Robert bought for his wife to wear to a White House dinner. Following that, Mama Mondavi sided with Peter over Robert, and in November 1965, they ousted him from the family business. A man of driving ambition, Robert soon found financial backing for a new winery that he opened only a year later. At the time, there were about two dozen wineries in the Napa Valley, and this was the first major new one since Prohibition ended in 1933.

Wine tourism was part of the Robert Mondavi Winery from the beginning. He later wrote, "As I planned my own winery, I realized that . . . potential sites in Oakville along busy Highway 29 would be ideal for tourists and tasting. Imagine the concerts and other cultural events we could put on in the center of the valley; imagine the number of visitors we could attract." Mondavi purposely located the winery south of his competitors, so it would be the first one visitors would see driving north from San Francisco. The winery building, with its distinctive mission-style architecture and plenty of room for visitors, was designed to attract attention and tourists. It wasn't just a functional place where wine was made. In fact, some features, such as a dimly lit barrel room, were better suited for visits than winemaking. Mondavi wanted the winery to make a statement: *Visitors Welcome.*

Mondavi was going after tourists for hard business reasons. He wanted visitors to become ambassadors for his wines, not just drinking them but also recommending them to their friends. Some wineries in the valley were concerned that by selling wines at the tasting rooms they would be taking business away from their main customers: wine stores and restaurants. Mondavi disagreed and believed that a winery's real customer is not the wine trade but the wine consumer. An added bonus was that the winery earned 100 percent of the wine's price on whatever it sold there rather than the 50 percent it got after a wholesaler and retailer took their share. Soon 10 percent of Robert Mondavi sales were made at the winery.

Following the fistfight between the Mondavi brothers, the Krug staff divided into pro-Peter and pro-Robert factions, and the latter soon left. Among them was Swiss-born Margrit Biever, who was married to a former American military officer, had three children, and was living in the town of Napa. An energetic woman with a keen interest in art, music, and food, she had joined Krug after trying to organize a concert at a winery to support music in the Napa schools. Beaulieu, Martini, Inglenook, and Beringer all turned her down, but Robert Mondavi at Krug agreed. The event attracted a crowd of some four hundred, and in 1964, Biever began working part-time for $2 an hour at Krug giving tours and selling wine. She rapidly became the top salesperson in the tasting room and also started a series of music events that became known as the August Moon Concerts.

After leaving Krug, Biever spent her free time painting at a water tower across Route 29 from where Robert Mondavi built his winery. One day in the fall of 1967, she met a former colleague from Charles Krug who was already working for Robert. He showed her around, and a few days later called and asked her if she wanted a job. Vic Motto, an investment banker who has put together many Napa winery deals, says, "Margrit became Robert's food-and-art muse."

The excitement around the Mondavi winery in those days was intoxicating. Everything in the place was new, and Mondavi was always showing it off. Biever still remembers his philosophy: "If you think something will work, don't talk about it. Just do it." Her first job was giving tours just as she had at Krug and helping in the retail shop. Since Biever spoke French, Italian, and German, her native country's three official languages, she gave all the tours to foreigners. In addition, she became the winery's first chef, cooking meals for as many as fifty visitors from the wine trade.

Given her background in painting, it was not surprising that soon after starting work at the winery, Biever went to Mondavi and told him, "We have all these empty walls. Why don't we let some local artists bring in their work to show it off? They'll get some public exposure, and our walls won't be bare." She added that it wouldn't cost much money because they'd only have to throw a party at the opening of a new artist's show. Mondavi, who had little experience with the arts, agreed.

Mondavi hoped his tourism-oriented winery would immediately take off and thousands of visitors would be beating down his doors. Build it, and they will come. But they didn't come. As the first year dragged on, only a trickle of visitors was showing up. Young people intent on drinking were not happy when they had to go through a one-hour tour and lecture before the wines came out. Education, however, was crucial to Mondavi, and he would accept no shortcuts. The first year the winery lost money on the tours, and the summer of 1966 was a major disappointment. At one point the Mondavi staff wondered if there might be a day when there would be no visitors. But that never happened; the all-time low was three. As the winery headed toward the end of its second year, however, everything started to pick up and soon it was getting 250,000 visitors annually, often by the busload since there was a special parking spot for them. On some days the staff had to limit visitors to about fifteen hundred, which is as many as the winery could comfortably accommodate.

Many Europeans are big fans of American jazz, and Biever is one of them. So in 1969, the Robert Mondavi Winery launched a summer music festival. The first concert was a low-key affair with the musicians coming from the Napa Valley Symphony, where Margrit still had connections. Since the symphony didn't have a guitarist, Biever hired one for $25. Rouge et Noir cheese from nearby Marin County provided the cheese served at intermission, and four hundred people paid $3 each to attend. The winery made a $1,000 profit, and Robert set the money aside to pay for a band for the next year's concert. That turned out to be the famed Preservation Hall Jazz Band from New Orleans. In the third year, Ella Fitzgerald was the star attraction, and the summer concerts are still going strong.

When it came to food, the Napa Valley in the mid-1970s was a wasteland. Anyone interested in good cooking had to travel to Marin County for dinner. There was little more along Route 29 than Taylor's Automatic Refresher, a McDonald's-style hamburger stand in St. Helena. Nonetheless, Michael James and Billy Cross, who owned the Hi Tree Farm guesthouse in nearby Rutherford, inaugurated a series of cooking class weekends given by top chefs from around the world. The first one was Simone "Simca" Beck, a coauthor with Julia Child of *Mastering the Art of French Cooking*. Jean Troisgros, a three-star French chef, also taught one weekend. While James and Cross had fantastic ideas, they struggled financially, and by 1976 they were losing the lease on their guesthouse and were $120,000 in debt. Margrit had attended some of their events, and in early 1976, they came to her and asked if Mondavi might want to take over the program in exchange for paying off their debt. She knew Robert had long been talking about opening a small cooking school, so she thought he might be interested. He was and took the issue to his board of directors, who thought he was crazy but agreed to let him do it. The program moved to Mondavi and was renamed the Great Chefs of France. The first guest chef was

Paul Bocuse, then considered France's best, and such food luminaries as Gaston Lenôtre, Michel Guérard, and Alain Chapel followed. Each gave five classes on topics such as how to prepare *fois gras*. One of the added benefits was that this was a way to introduce Mondavi wines to the chefs, who had no experience with them. They often took the wines back to France, and some even put them on their wine lists. Later, Mondavi set up a separate program with American chefs that included Alice Waters of Chez Panisse in Berkeley, who invented California Cuisine, Paul Prudhomme, and Wolfgang Puck. Mondavi staffers still talk about how Waters cooked bouillabaisse in a giant copper pot in the Mondavi vineyards. Julia Child taught there three times, once with her French cooking friend Jacques Pépin. Some 70 percent of people who attended the Great Chefs programs were repeat visitors.

Chilean-born and American-educated Agustín Huneeus owns two wineries, Veramonte in Chile and Quintessa in the Napa Valley, and has spent a half-century at the top of the international wine business. Looking back over what Mondavi did at his winery in the late 1970s, he told me, "Bob understood the marketing of wines better than anyone else in the world had up to that point. He wasn't thinking of tourism, but of marketing his wine. He built a winery that combined all those hospitality elements with food and wine and art."

Robert Mondavi was also a generous person, always ready to help fellow winemakers if they had troubles with a grape crush or finding a new employee. He was an enthusiastic and boundless supporter of the Napa Valley; just like the Man of La Mancha, he would march into hell for a heavenly cause.

While most Napa Valley residents were happy to see the proud new Robert Mondavi Winery rise up out of the vineyards along Route 29 and prosper, not everyone was glad. Locals, whether old-timers or newcomers, have long had an ambivalence about economic development, anxious to enjoy the prosperity but also agonizing over preserving their treasured rural way of life. In addition, there has been tension between winemakers, often rich outsiders who made their millions in Hollywood or elsewhere, and less affluent people who stayed in the valley or came there because they liked the slower, simpler way of life. Tourism and development brought business to local merchants, but with it came traffic congestion on the county's narrow roads. The Napa Valley simultaneously hated tourism and loved it.

Those worried about losing their lifestyle didn't have to look far to see what had happened to similar areas. One of California's prime wine regions before and after World War II was the rich agricultural area of Santa Clara County to the south, where wine pioneers Paul Masson and Martin Ray had once tilled the soil and produced excellent wine. But starting in the 1960s and with increasing speed thereafter, farms where grapes once grew were paved over and turned into office parks. Santa Clara County morphed into Silicon Valley, an ugly, congested, concrete jungle of buildings and freeways. Creeping suburbanization of Northern California seemed to be inexorably moving out of San Francisco, as people bought weekend homes in the bucolic Napa and Sonoma valleys only an hour's drive north of the Golden Gate or Bay Bridge. Many Napa people looked at Santa Clara County in horror and began seeking ways to protect their valley from a similar fate. To them suburban development meant urban sprawl.

In the late 1960s, a group advocating the preservation of Napa's natural environment—the Upper Napa Valley Associates—tried to rally support for protecting farmland from urban development. Jack Davies, a newcomer who was just starting to restore the old Schramsberg Vineyards, spearheaded the efforts. The goal was to use the California Land Conservation Act of 1965, which permitted local government to make deals with local landowners to restrict the use of property for agriculture or open space. The landowners, in return, received property tax breaks. In an often raw and emotional political battle in late 1967, Napa politicians and the public argued about the merits of what was called the Agricultural Preserve that would set aside for farm use some 26,000 acres of land, mostly on the valley floor in unincorporated areas between Napa City and Calistoga. The region was later raised to 40,000 acres.

Farm families were deeply split over the issue, with one brother saying it would destroy his property rights and was socialism, while the other would say it was the only way to keep agricultural land out of the hands of speculators, who were going to divide the valley into small lots and build new Levittowns. Winemakers were equally split. Robert and Peter Mondavi both supported the Agricultural Preserve, as did the owner of Beringer Vineyards. At one point in the debate, Louis M. Martini, one of the most respected vintners in the valley, asked, "Do the citizens of Napa Valley really believe the future of our land is best served by destroying landmarks and vineyards and replacing them with subdivisions, bleak shopping centers, and highway strip developments?" But John Daniel, a valley patriarch who had recently sold the historic Inglenook Winery, strongly opposed it. The county Board of Supervisors in March 1968 finally approved the Agricultural Preserve plan. It was the first of several pieces of local legislation that would be passed over the years both to protect Napa's agricultural heritage and to restrict what kind of business wineries could conduct beyond winemaking. Agricultural Preserve battles, though, never seem to go away. In the spring of 2009, a fight developed over Will Nord's plans to divide his 83-acre Trio C Vineyards on the outskirts of Yountville into six parcels. He has three daughters and five grandchildren, and wants them to have a piece of the Napa Valley. He said he expects homes will be built on each lot, which has outraged neighbors who say that would be against the Agricultural Preserve. Nord received permission to split up the land under a state law that permits such action if surveys show the parcels existed before. He produced a 1926 map to support his plan. The county Board of Supervisors eventually approved Nord's request to reconfigure his property into six parcels, where homes will undoubtedly be built.

🍷 🍷 🍷

While the Robert Mondavi Winery was gathering strength in the early 1970s and the Agricultural Preserve was being adopted, another venture was getting started also with an eye toward Northern California wine tourism. The company was Moët & Chandon of France, whose extensive facilities for visitors near its headquarters in Épernay had impressed Mondavi and been a model for his own operation.

American John Wright was the inspiration for Moët's California dream. While serving in the U.S. Army in Germany in the 1950s, he learned about wine while in Geisenheim, the heart of the Rhine wine region and home to the country's leading wine research institute. After the army, wine became Wright's hobby as he held a variety of jobs, ending up with Arthur D. Little, a leading management-consulting firm. His homemade wine never won any prizes, but in 1969, when he moved to San Francisco with the company, he and some partners bought property in the Napa Valley and soon had a bad case of the wine bug.

Arthur D. Little regularly produced industry outlook reports that it sold to clients for high prices, and the authors of the studies often later consulted with those same clients. In mid-1970, Wright proposed doing a study on the American wine business, which was starting to grow rapidly. The title of the three-volume work that came out in March 1972: *Wine America*. Six clients bought the report for $20,000 each. They included Robert Mondavi and big companies considering investments in wine such as Philip Morris, H. J. Heinz, and Coca-Cola. The study focused on the trend toward higher consumption of dry table wines and declining sales for sweet wines, and backed up its conclusions with extensive statistics and market forecasts. Sparkling wines were not a significant part of the research.

Shortly after the report came out, Wright got a call from the head of the Paris office of Arthur D. Little saying that the Banque Nationale de Paris, France's largest bank, had engaged the consulting firm to help it select areas of interest to French companies looking to invest abroad, and wine was one of the fields. Wright wrote a Cliff Notes version of his longer report for the bank and a few months later met in Paris with Guy de la Serre, the top executive at Moët Hennessy, the owner of Moët & Chandon. French wine regulations limit the quantity of grapes that can be grown in a region such as Champagne, which restricted how much wine Moët could make there. As a result, Moët had begun to look abroad for new prospects and had already invested in Latin America.

Soon several Moët executives and an enologist were in California looking at both the business and the viticulture prospects of opening a winery in the Napa Valley that would produce sparkling white wine. From the beginning, the French insisted that the Americans could not call it Champagne, the appellation belonging only to wine from that region of France. After the enologist concluded that quality wines could be made there, the executives in March 1973 started an American subsidiary, later naming it **Domaine Chandon**.

French executives felt it was crucial to have the right person to head the American operation, and that meant Wright, who was stunned when the chairman of Moët Hennessy, Comte Robert-Jean de Vogüé, offered him the top U.S. job. With lots of help with the winemaking from France, the company moved quickly to start the Napa Valley operations, working for two years out of a nineteenth-century winery located just north of the city of Napa on Route 29 that Trefethen Family Vineyards owned. Moët Hennessy also helped the Trefethens revitalize and equip the winery. Domaine Chandon even bought grapes for its new sparkling wine from them, and Wright, already in the fall of 1973, produced the first vintage of sparkling wine.

Wright then quietly bought vineyard sites in several locations in the valley, but decided for tourism reasons to put the winery and tasting room adjacent to Yountville. During his many trips to Épernay, he had been impressed by Moët's visitor facilities that included a museum, a Michelin-star restaurant, and a luxury hotel. Those attracted thousands of tourists annually who then became Moët consumers, and Wright wanted to replicate that in the Napa Valley. Yountville was then little more than a village best known for its bars and a brothel, both of which got many of their clients from a nearby veterans hospital. Yountville's appeal to Wright was its location at the end of the freeway that brought people from San Francisco, which turned into a two- and three-lane road after that. Wright believed that a vigorous program for visitors was crucial to the marketing plan he envisioned for Domaine Chandon.

The first step in attracting tourists was a well-designed winery, and Wright built one that had plenty of rich stone and large windows looking out at the vineyards. The tasting room, which Chandon called the "tasting salon," broke precedent by becoming the first in the valley to charge for a tasting. No one before had dared do that, figuring it would discourage visitors. Sparkling wine, though, is considered a luxury item and the tax on it is more than three times higher than for still wines. Wright felt that because his product was more expensive going out the door, he couldn't just give it away. He also thought there would be a greater perceived value if someone were paying for the tasting. The fee was a modest $3 for trying three types of sparkling wines, but it set a precedent. The move worked, and Chandon drew good crowds. The only problem in the tasting salon was that it was losing a lot of glasses. Domaine Chandon had introduced a new type of glass for sparkling wines, the now common flutes, and tourists were walking off with them. Most Americans were then used to old-fashioned Champagne glasses, which look something like a saucer on a stick. Staff behind the bar tried to keep an eye out for people pilfering the flutes, but they couldn't stop all of the glass thieves.

Another Chandon innovation that has since been copied by wineries not only in the Napa Valley but also around the world was the wine club. Visitors who signed up for Club Chandon would periodically receive a case of wine. America's complex liquor laws made it impossible to send wine to most states, but the program worked for more than a dozen states and the number of club members started growing. People could cancel their membership at any point, but not many did. The club became a huge success and by the late 1980s had 100,000 members and accounted for 25 percent of Chandon sales. The club also began holding special receptions around the country to further cement the relationship between the winery and members outside California.

Wright also decided to build a museum near the tourist entrance similar to the one at Moët in Épernay. When he heard that one of his vineyard workers had a master's degree as a museum curator, she got the job of coming up with the plans for the small museum. The goal was to educate visitors about the special procedures used to make sparkling wines as well as to reinforce Chandon's connection to the biggest and most respected Champagne company in the world. Displays showed how corks for its bottles are different from those in regular wine bottles, how bottles are rotated during aging, and old vineyard photos from Champagne. It was all a subtle way of telling Americans that Domaine Chandon must be pretty good since it was associated with such a prestigious French company.

Next came a restaurant, which at first was called simply the Restaurant at Domaine Chandon but was later named Étoile in honor of the winery's top sparkling wine. Since the Moët-owned restaurant in Épernay had a prized Michelin star, the executives in France set high standards for the one in the Napa Valley, reminding Wright that the parent company has a long history and image to protect. They didn't want it compromised by a second-class restaurant in Yountville.

Despite Mondavi's Great Chefs programs started the year before, there still wasn't a really good restaurant in the Napa Valley. But first Chandon had to get around the recently adopted Agricultural Preserve legislation, which did not permit a restaurant at a winery. Wright asked Michaela Rudeno, who says she got her job at the winery because she had a master's degree in French literature from the University of California, Davis, to try to persuade the Napa County planning board to change the rules and allow a restaurant at Chandon. It was a tough sell, but both the county Planning Commission, the group that handles all building and land-use issues, and the higher-level Board of Supervisors approved the proposal because they wanted the valley to have at least one decent restaurant. The way around the rule was to approve carving a special "planned development zone" out of Chandon's 300 acres just off Route 29. This violated the spirit, if not the letter, of the Agricultural Preserve, but it was the county's solution and it passed.

Again with help from France, Domaine Chandon satisfied the wishes of Épernay and built a restaurant that was beyond anything in the Napa Valley. The first chef was Udo Nechutnys, a young German who had studied under Paul Bocuse, and the sous-chef was Philippe Jeanty, a *champenois* who cooked for Moët in France. A big opening celebration was held in April 1977 that included Bocuse, putting the stamp of approval on the Napa venture. Naturally there were some start-up problems, such as the fact that the kitchen was too small and was initially located in the basement, which made food service difficult. But those issues were worked around or eliminated, and the restaurant almost instantly had a long waiting list. The Napa culinary desert finally had a quality restaurant, and people flocked to it just as they had to the tasting salon. The restaurant also had the minor problem of customers stealing Champagne flutes, but eventually that went away as they became more common in the United States.

Soon other *haute cuisine* restaurants began opening in the valley. Just a year later, Don and Sally Schmidt started a restaurant in a building that had once been a brothel in downtown Yountville. They called it The French Laundry, since, in the 1920s, the building had housed a French-style steam laundry. The restaurant served simple, but tasty, fresh American food and had a good wine cellar near the front door. Sally did the cooking, and Don handled the door. The French Laundry soon became a favorite of the valley's winemakers and visitors. In 1994, the Schmidts sold the restaurant to chef Thomas Keller, who kept the name and turned it into perhaps America's highest temple of *haute cuisine*.

Throughout the 1980s, the tug-of-war between tourism and tradition continued to be fought out in the Napa Valley over issues small and large, often pitting winery owners against grape growers and both against real estate developers. One of the small things that had a big impact was the television soap opera *Falcon Crest*. In more than two hundred episodes from December 1981 to May 1990, the saga recounted the infighting among members of the wealthy Channing and Gioberti families of winemakers, set in "Tuscany Valley," which everyone knew was Napa Valley. *Falcon Crest* became a weekly celebration of the Napa Valley on prime-time television, and tourists poured in to see where the action took place. Spring Mountain Vineyard, a Victorian structure where many scenes were filmed, was a star of the show and a must-see winery for tourists to visit.

Another major development of wine tourism was the Napa Valley Wine Auction, which also started in 1981. The idea again came from the fertile marketing minds of Robert Mondavi and Margrit Biever, who had become Margrit Biever Mondavi with their May 1980 marriage. A friend asked Margrit if she would help stage a wine tasting to raise money for the St. Helena Health Center. The idea grew and grew until the Mondavis suggested that the Napa Valley should have its version of the Hospices de Beaune auction in Burgundy, which has been raising money for charities since 1859. The first Napa Valley Wine Auction raised $324,142 for local charities and attracted visitors from all over the country. The event expanded quickly as winemakers tried to outdo each other in offering spectacular gifts of wines and trips, and by the end of the decade annual proceeds were up to nearly $1 million.

In 1983, a group of investors led by wealthy Vincent DeDomenico came up with plans to start the Napa Valley Wine Train for visitors that would wind its way up the valley, while serving passengers good food and wine. Everything was already in place. The railroad tracks existed, and the Southern Pacific Railroad planned to discontinue service on the line. DeDomenico bought six vintage 1915 rail coaches that had previously been used in Colorado as a ski train and painted them an appropriate burgundy color. The path would parallel Route 29 from downtown Napa to the city limits of St. Helena, which refused to let the train pass through. The plan was for the train to stop at several wineries along the way to let travelers off for vineyard and cellar tours. For nearly a decade, however, Napa Valley residents fought over the concept. Proponents argued it would reduce car traffic on already crowded roads, while opponents said it would bring in more tourists. Eventually the fight went all the way to the federal Interstate Commerce Commission, which tossed the issue back to California regulators who approved it. The Wine Train finally went into operation on September 16, 1989, and soon attracted big crowds.

In the middle of the 1980s, wineries were being started as quickly as pastureland could be turned into vineyards. The number reached two hundred, and there were no signs of slowing down as American wine consumption continued to climb. Locals lamenting the end of their Eden were terrified when they read projections that the population of Napa City, which in 1970 had 79,650 residents, would have 200,000 by 2000. More and more private homes were being turned into B and Bs, and new hotels were going up. There were now restaurants for every taste and pocketbook. All sorts of tourist services from hot air balloons and bus tours to wedding planners and health spas were started or expanded. There was even talk of having elephant rides in the vineyards, but officials nixed that idea.

Following the standard set by the Robert Mondavi Winery, the style of winery was also changing, from being purely functional wine-production factories to sprawling tourist centers. And while the Agricultural Preserve had safeguarded vineyards, wineries were getting into more and more extraneous businesses. First they sold only wine in their tasting rooms, but then they began adding T-shirts and hats with winery logos. After that came books about wine and wine paraphernalia such as corkscrews or coolers. Sterling Vineyards, which looked like a modern monastery complete with a bell tower, took visitors from the valley floor to the winery in an aerial tram. The *Napa Valley Register* newspaper called it "Napa Winery Disneyland." The term stuck and became the shorthand for critics to refer to anything new they didn't like.

By the late 1980s, residents who worried about the expanding line of business being conducted in wineries made another attempt to slow down change. Jim Hickey, the county planning director, set off a long and impassioned public debate by simply posing the question, "What's a winery?" Then from 1987 to 1990, the county debated which business activities could take place in a winery and which should not. Andy Beckstoffer, the largest grape grower in the valley though he didn't own a winery, played a major role in the debate over the restrictions. The Robert Mondavi family, with Michael now taking a more active role than his father, was among the leading opponents to new laws that would limit business. Grape growers and wineries split into hostile camps: the growers for the ordinance, the winemakers, with a few exceptions, against it. Pro- and anti-ordinance candidates ran for county supervisor in the 1988 county election.

In January 1990, the Board of Supervisors unanimously adopted Ordinance No. 947, which was nicknamed the Winery Definition Ordinance. It ruled that a winery means "an agricultural processing facility used for (1) the fermenting and processing of grape juice into wine, or (2) the refermenting of still wine into sparkling wine." A grandfather clause recognized as legal all winery activities that commenced operations prior to July 31, 1974. But a number of other uses by wineries established after 1974, including farm-labor housing, were not permitted without special permission. The ordinance also severely restricted wine tours and tastings as well as the marketing of wine at wineries. For Beckstoffer and other Napa grape growers, it included the clause that "75 percent of the grapes used to make still wine, or the still wine used by the winery to make sparkling wine, shall be grown within the County of Napa." Not long thereafter Jim Hickey, who had collected too many enemies in his crusade to limit growth, lost his job as county planning director.

Together the Agricultural Preserve and the Wine Definition Ordinance changed the way wine tourism developed in the Napa Valley, which is different from the eleven other wine regions that I visited in researching this book. In other areas, wineries lead tourism developments. Wineries in those countries often operate small hotels and restaurants. But in the Napa Valley, wineries can't undertake those activities. So hoteliers have built hotels, and restaurateurs have started restaurants, but Napa Valley wineries must stick to their knitting, selling only wine and a few souvenirs in their tasting rooms. Domaine Chandon is still the only winery in the valley with a public restaurant at its facility. When I explained this to Europeans, who consider the United States to be the home of unbridled capitalism, they were shocked and found this hard to understand.

The new ordinance, though, didn't stop Francis Ford Coppola, the movie producer, director, and screenwriter, from taking wine tourism to a new level. Coppola had first gotten to know the Napa Valley area in 1972, while making the movie *American Graffiti* in nearby Petaluma in Sonoma County. He started out looking for a modest winery where he could make wine in the basement just as his immigrant grandparents had done in his native Detroit. But thanks to the success of his movies *The Godfather* (1972) and *The Godfather II* (1974), Coppola was able to expand his horizons and began looking for something more spectacular. Coppola and his wife, Eleanor, in 1975 bought one of the treasures of the Napa Valley, the historic home built by Inglenook's Gustave Niebaum in Rutherford and 120 acres of surrounding vineyards, which were considered to be among the best in the valley. Niebaum wines had won gold medals at the 1889 Paris World's Fair. In 1995, Coppola also purchased Niebaum's winery, which was founded in 1879.

For the director and his wife, buying the Niebaum estate was like something out of the movies. As she described her first visit there, "We drove up the driveway and saw the lawns, the elegant house under the branches of a grand old valley oak tree, the swimming pool and gardens set in over a hundred acres of vineyards and surrounded by untouched natural landscape climbing up to a distant ridge line. It looked like a movie set! We were enthralled."

Coppola liked to remind people that Bacchus, the Roman god of wine, was also the god of the theater, and the movie director wanted to create not only good wine but also good theater. In so doing he brought huge crowds to his winery. With a director's eye and his Hollywood production manager advising him along the way, Coppola treated the property like a movie set. First he tore down an old cement barrel-storage building that blocked the view of the winery. "It offended my aesthetic sense that such a lovely château should have an ugly cement building in front of it," he told me. Then he took out a small fountain and put in a new and bigger one. The result was an open view of the ivy-covered winery from Route 29. His model for the grounds was the Luxembourg Garden in Paris, a lively, lovely place in the heart of the city filled with grass, statues, buildings, and above all elegance. Inside the winery, Coppola built a mammoth wooden staircase at a cost of $1 million that looked like the one at Tara in the movie *Gone With the Wind*. Also in the winery Coppola installed a museum of his movie memorabilia, including a Tucker sedan from his film of the same name about an automobile entrepreneur, Oscars won for the *Godfather* movies, and a potpourri of Hollywood relics. In the tasting room, there was the normal wine bar, but also a collection of wine and food products that could have filled a Williams-Sonoma store, which was his model. Visitors could buy espresso cups and kitchen utensils, not just a few hats or corkscrews. Of course, there was a tour of the winery that dwelt heavily on Niebaum's legacy. "I wanted more than just a place to sell T-shirts," Coppola said. "We gave people an experience."

When Coppola and his wife first arrived in Rutherford in 1978, they made great efforts to become popular with the locals, holding dinner parties and making donations to the right charities. One afternoon Robert Mondavi and Margrit Biever showed up unannounced to welcome them to the valley. While the Coppolas were well liked, some winery owners were horrified by what they saw. It was so commercial! So Hollywood! The renovated winery was soon dubbed "Francis's Folly," and the Coppolas began getting letters from neighbors expressing their disapproval. But that didn't stop them.

The public loved it. Crowds flocked to take Coppola's tours and taste his wines. They also bought plenty of wines and other goods. Visitors were even doing their Christmas shopping there, and soon the retail shop had $1 million a month in sales.

Coppola later moved much of the movie memorabilia to another winery he bought in Sonoma County, and in an attempt to reduce the crowds raised the price of the Napa Valley Tour to $25 at what is now called **Rubicon Estate**. He believes strongly that wine tourism and the personal experience at his wineries are crucial for his wine's success. "It's like meeting a politician and shaking his hand," he says. "You always feel later that you have a personal relationship with him. If you've been to a winery and walked through the vineyard, you feel it's yours and you order its wines."

By the early-1990s, Robert and Margrit Mondavi were spending more and more of their time traveling and promoting the company and projects that revolved around their shared passion for wine, food, and the arts. From their travels in the world of wine, they had been impressed by wine museums built by Baron Philippe de Rothschild in Bordeaux and Georges Duboeuf in Beaujolais. At the same time the couple was concerned that the prosperity wine tourism had brought to the valley had bypassed the city of Napa, where Margrit had lived for many years and where she still had strong ties, especially to its small art colony. The valley's main roads and thus most tourists skirted around the city on their way to the wineries up Route 29 or the Silverado Trail. Slowly the idea began taking shape of building an educational center for wine, food, and the arts, perhaps in the town of Napa. Town fathers trying to make the Napa River the center of the city's urban renewal staged a boat trip for the Mondavis in May 1993 on two barges. As the party traveled up the river, they were greeted first by a Native American carrying a salmon, who stood on the bank and shouted, "Welcome back to the river!" A little farther up, a family of Spanish settlers also called out, "Welcome back to the river!" Finally a person in a coonskin cap representing the town's founder, Nathan Coombs, yelled, "Welcome back to the river!" Two months later, Mondavi bought a 12-acre piece of property on the riverfront with plans for building a cultural center there.

Mondavi eventually put up $35 million to finance the endeavor that cost $70 million. He also attracted Julia Child, America's favorite chef, to support the project. She even agreed to let them call the center's main restaurant Julia's Kitchen, the only eatery in the world that used her name. Some people grumbled that the project was costing too much, but the town had great hopes when **Copia: The American Center for Wine, Food & the Arts** opened on November 18, 2001. Copia is the Roman goddess of abundance. Founders optimistically predicted 300,000 visitors a year would pay the $12.50 admission price to visit its extensive exhibits and participate in the food and wine programs. The staff included a Master of Wine, Peter Marks, who developed wine-education programs, plus museum exhibits of both creative arts and the history of American food and food packaging. There was also an edibles garden, with a full-time horticulturist, who supplied Julia's Kitchen with a steady supply of fresh herbs, vegetables, and other produce.

Copia, however, was plagued with problems from the beginning, some that were out of its control and some of its own making. The most serious one was that it opened just two months after the September 11, 2001, terrorist attacks, which was a major blow to tourism around the globe. After the initial enthusiasm of the grand opening that brought 10,000 people, crowds never approached the numbers that had been expected.

Critics complained that Copia lacked a clear focus. It didn't appear to have a mission statement or at least didn't follow one. The merging of wine, food, and the arts didn't seem to work. The paintings didn't go with the wine tastings. Some of the food history displays were static and dull. Visitors come to the valley mainly for the wines, but wine seemed to take a backseat to food and art at Copia. As a result, the center captured few local visitors or tourists.

In its first seven years Copia went through three management teams, with the last taking over in the spring of 2008. The last president was Garry McGuire Jr., who was formerly the chairman of the board of trustees. He planned on moving the organization to San Francisco and making other changes. But before those could be implemented, Copia filed for bankruptcy and in December 2008, went out of business.

Stand-alone wine museums, rather than ones that are part of a winery, do not appear to be a natural part of wine tourism. They are part of a field known as "edutainment" that combines education and entertainment. Sometimes it works; often it doesn't. Centers similar to Copia in Adelaide, Australia, and London have faced many of the same problems as Copia's.

Nonetheless, the Napa Valley remains the most popular wine tourism destination in the world. Wine enthusiasts travel there to taste the wines, see the vineyards, take a balloon ride, get married, have a memorable meal, and more. Most of them leave happy and immediately start planning their next wine vacation.

The basics of a Napa trip haven't changed much since the 1960s, when students and young professionals drove from San Francisco for a day of free tasting. There is now just more of everything. More wineries, for sure. Compared with the two dozen when Robert Mondavi built his new property on Route 29, there are now more than four hundred wineries in the Napa Valley. Route 29 and the Silverado Trail remain the most popular locations, but more and more wineries are up in the hills on either side of the valley. Thanks to the Wine Definition Ordinance, visitors to most of those facilities have to call in advance for an appointment, although that can usually be done on short notice.

What has changed dramatically since the 1960s are the prices. Napa Valley has become a luxury destination, and the still small village of Yountville (pop. 3,000) has become the epicenter of self-indulgent affluence. Long gone is the old seedy veneer. No other city of its size in the United States has so much food power concentrated in such a small area. Visitors can find world-class dining at The French Laundry, which has three Michelin stars, as well as Redd, Bistro Jeanty, and Bouchon, each of which has one star. The Étoile restaurant at the Domaine Chandon winery retains the quality that made it famous. And while it used to be hard to find a good place to stay overnight, Yountville is home to several top hotels, including Villagio Inn & Spa, Vintage Inn, and Napa Valley Lodge. Rooms at all three average more than $400 a night. Free tastings in the Napa Valley are rare these days. Heitz Cellar is one of the few to continue the tradition. Most others have moved on to tastings that can cost as much as $60 at wineries such as Cliff Lede Vineyards and Robert Sinskey Vineyards.

Outside Yountville there are many other wonderful places to eat and stay, but again prices are high at resorts such as **Auberge du Soleil** in Rutherford and **Meadowood** in St. Helena, which both have Michelin stars. For those who don't worry about the steep cost, Meadowood's master sommelier will provide a personal wine tour of the valley.

The paragon of expensive Napa is **Napa Valley Reserve**, a private club where rather than play golf, members make their own wine. It is the brainchild of Bill Harlan, a former real estate developer once best known around San Francisco for driving fast cars and dating beautiful women. Harlan is the longtime managing partner of the Meadowood resort and founder of **Harlan Estate**, a California Cabernet Sauvignon cult wine. France's Michel Rolland, the world's most famous flying winemaker, consults with both Harlan Estate and the Napa Valley Reserve.

Located right next to Meadowood, the club has its own vineyard, winery, gardens, and hospitality center. The more than four hundred members pay an initial fee of $165,000 to join, and then they can participate as much or as little as they want each year in the Reserve's wine production. Manager Philip Norfleet says the Reserve appeals to people who want some ownership of their wine without the hassle of actually operating a winery. He compares the wines the club produces to those of Harlan Estate, which are made nearby by the same winemaking team. Each member can buy annually for $75 a bottle between six and seventy-five cases of wine that carry his own label. During the year, the Reserve offers two wine education events a month on such topics as wine blending or designing a label. The highlight of the year is harvest on a Saturday morning in the fall, when members go into the vineyard and pick the grapes that will go into their wine.

While curious winery owners from around the world still travel to the Napa Valley just as Christian pilgrims travel to Lourdes in France or Muslims trek to Mecca in Saudi Arabia, I found many of them have come to think that Californians have taken wine tourism over the top. International visitors still steal ideas from Napa, but now they are also trying to avoid what they consider to be the excesses. Salvador Barros Vial, the manager of Viña Luis Felipe Edwards in Chile, told me, "I had some bad impressions when I was in Napa, especially at Mondavi. All I remember are three hundred Japanese and Ukrainian people drinking cheap wines and buying dreadful souvenirs." Argentina's Santiago Achaval, founder of the Achaval-Ferrer winery, concurred, "We're looking at the Napa experience, but trying to avoid the mistakes we think they are making when wine tourism turns into a very impersonal experience."

Two Napa wineries epitomize for me Napa's going over the top, where money is spent extravagantly, but in poor taste. Both look like transplants from Disneyland or Las Vegas, although the comparison might be unfair to those two entertainment centers.

The first is **Darioush Winery** on the Silverado Trail just north of the town of Napa, built by Darioush Khaledi, a construction executive who escaped his native Iran in 1976 just as the Shah's regime began to totter. Khaledi then made a fortune in Southern California grocery stores, which provided the money for the dream winery. The Darioush Winery is a replica of a royal palace in Persepolis, the ceremonial capital of the Persian Empire, with towering stone pillars in the front. It is as out of place in Napa as a log cabin might look in the middle of Iran. It's not necessarily ugly, but stands in glaring conflict with its surroundings. Souvenirs inside include Persian artifacts that often have absolutely nothing to do with Napa or wine. Darioush Winery is a monument to Khaledi's homeland and its culture, but an insult to the wine culture of the Napa Valley.

Across the valley on Route 29 and far to the north is the equally out-of-place **Castello di Amorosa Winery**. The Sattui family got into the wine business as V. Sattui Winery in the late 1800s in San Francisco but went bust during Prohibition. In 1972, after two years of kicking around wine in Europe and working as a guide at Beaulieu Vineyard, Daryl Sattui, who now calls himself Dario, restarted the business on Route 29 in St. Helena on a small plot of land that was zoned for commercial use. He turned it into a highly successful business that included a tasting room selling only Sattui wines and a delicatessen. Now one of the Napa Valley's best values, day-trippers can buy lunch and a bottle of wine, and then picnic on his grounds. Since V. Sattui sells all its wines at its shop or through its mailing list, its profit margins are the highest in the valley. And those profits allowed

Daryl to make a big splash. In 2007, he opened a 121,000-square-foot Italian *palazzo,* custom-built in Italy and shipped to the Napa Valley in pieces. Surrounding it is a 30-acre vineyard. Cost: $30 million. Much of the materials came from Napa quarries, but some were handcrafted in Italy. The *palazzo* includes six stone towers, a moat, a chapel, and even a torture chamber in the dungeon. Built mainly as a showpiece for tourists, some of the barrels and bottles on display are empty. Again, Castello di Amorosa might look fine in Tuscany, but stands out in jarring juxtaposition to its surroundings in the Napa Valley.

Despite the excesses at some wineries, the Napa Valley can still provide wonderful wine experiences. **Quintessa** in Rutherford, one of the most beautiful wineries in the valley, is owned by Agustín Huneeus. Its public face on the Silverado Trail is a sweeping crescent-shaped stone wall behind long rows of grapes. After making the obligatory reservation in advance, I enjoyed a tasting that included generous servings of two vintages of its Bordeaux-style Cabernet Sauvignon, the only wine it makes. Accompanying the wines were cheeses and olives. A well-trained and knowledgeable hostess sat at a small table with me and discussed the Quintessa vineyards, winemaking philosophy, and people. The price for a tasting is now $65, but it's worth it. The experience was a reminder that some wineries in the valley still do things with elegance and style.

Lisa Hopkins and Tim Anderson had a similar wonderful wine experience in the Napa Valley. They were living in San Francisco when they fell in love with wine and each other. Since they traveled to the Napa Valley many weekends to explore wine country, it seemed only natural for them to be married there. As soon as they were engaged in January 2007, they started planning a small, private wedding for October. They quickly found out, however, how difficult it would be to have their dream come true. They first looked at doing the wedding at V. Sattui, one of the rare wineries where it's possible. The price, though, started at $15,000 and would go up quickly from there. Stag's Leap Wine Cellars produced some of their favorite wines, so they then investigated doing part of the ceremony there, but learned it was impossible to have a wedding reception at the winery. It could only be called a private party, and there could be no signs of a wedding cake, flowers, or a wedding dress.

In the end, the couple went to the Harvest Inn, a small hotel in St. Helena that offers what it calls an Elopement Package for a maximum of six people, which included the cake, white-rose bouquet, photographer, and rooms for two nights. Behind the hotel is a Hall Winery vineyard, which provided a beautiful backdrop for the Friday afternoon wedding ceremony. The photographer made it look like they were married amid the vines.

After the ceremony, the wedding party went to The French Laundry for a celebratory dinner. Getting into the restaurant had been a real challenge. You can only make reservations exactly two months in advance, and so on August 19, at one minute before the appointed time of 10:00 a.m., Lisa and Tim plus two friends from the wedding party began demon dialing the reservation number. A half hour later, they finally got through and reserved a table for six.

Special wines were an integral part of the wedding, starting right after the ceremony with a 1986 Charles Krug Champagne. Then at dinner they had a bottle of 1988 Stag's Leap Wine Cellars SLV and one of 2003 Screaming Eagle. They had brought along a 1990 and a 1991 Caymus Cabernet Sauvignon Napa Valley Special Selection, but could not open the 1991 because the restaurant will not let customers bring wines that are on its wine list. The couple wanted to drink both together, so they saved them for the next evening and had the sommelier match wines by the glass to the food they were enjoying. The dinner for six, including wines, cost $4,000.

Saturday, the newlyweds hired a limousine and with the four other people in the wedding party toured their favorite wineries. That night they went to the Martini House in St. Helena, where they had cheeseburgers plus the two Caymus Special Selection wines. It was the end of an unforgettable wedding weekend built around wine and a happy start for Tim and Lisa's life together.

Despite some recent excesses, the Napa Valley remains a part of paradise for wine tourism. The diversity of its offerings is unmatched around the world. But be sure and pack lots of money before you leave home because its myriad enticing offerings can get expensive.

Diary of a Wine Tourist

May 29

A Moveable Feast

Up and down Route 29 and the Silverado Trail, the Napa Valley's two main north-south roads, tasting rooms stand cheek by jowl, and any day of the week, but especially on weekends, are filled with happy oenophiles. They are participating in a ritual immortalized by the classic wine movie *Sideways*. In one scene the main character loses it and starts drinking the contents of the bowl into which tasters spit wine they don't want to swallow. I once asked the person behind the counter at the **Grgich Hills Estate** winery whether anyone had ever done that. He laughed and said no, but added that a man had once tried to see if anything was written on the bottom of the spitting bowl and then accidentally poured the contents on himself.

Every person who has visited Napa has a favorite tasting room. It's a personal experience that depends on the people you are with and the staff behind the bar. If the winemaker happens to show up while you're there, that's an added benefit. Other times you may feel that you're getting the bum's rush from a server who doesn't know what he's talking about in answering your questions. The person simply splashes a hopelessly small amount of wine into your glass and moves on to the next sucker.

Whenever I travel to Northern California, I try to set aside a half-day to do the Napa Valley, going from winery to winery to see what's new or try a place I haven't been before. The alcohol consumption by the end of the day can be heavy, and some Napa visitors hire a limousine to drive them, so they can both taste and swallow the wines. Before I left my motel, I pledged to use the spitting bowls because if I swallowed all the wines I was going to taste, I'd be DWI before I was half-finished.

The Robert Mondavi Winery on Route 29 in the late 1960s turned tour and tasting into an art form, and it still does them with style and professionalism. So I decided to start my afternoon there. It is now owned by Constellation Brands, the largest wine company in the world, but still retains many of the features Mondavi started.

Mondavi has several tasting areas, and I like the To Kalon room, which is tucked off in the back and offers wines produced in such small quantities that they are available only at the winery. One of the best parts of any tasting is to experience wines that you can't get at home. The samples at To Kalon are a generous two ounces, at least twice as much as you usually get elsewhere. On this visit I tried three wines for $20: the 2005 Fume Blanc Block I, the 1999 Marjorie's Sunrise To Kalon, and the 2000 Sauvignon Blanc Botrytis. All were great.

Many wineries pour servings of only their standard wines; I went to two of those. I had previously tasted at **Whitehall Lane** on Route 29, where you get five wines for $12. The stop was okay, but nothing special. Then I drove over to the Silverado Trail to try **Pine Ridge**, which was a new tasting room for me. They offered four wines for $15. In the old days, wineries used to give visitors their tasting glass as a souvenir, but that is less and less common. Pine Ridge sold them for $10.

Next I went back to Route 29 and went to **Beaulieu Vineyard**, one of the valley's oldest wineries. Beaulieu follows the Mondavi pattern and offers different levels of tasting. Turning in off Route 29, the first thing you see is a sign pointing right to the Main Tasting Room and left to the Reserve Tasting Room. Walking into the Main Room, I received a glass with a splash of a complimentary wine, a Beaurosé. At the bar the tasting of five wines costs $15. The staff was both knowledgeable and casual. Across the way in the Reserve Room the scene was different: crowd smaller, lights dimmed, and staff serious. The price was $30 for a tasting of four wines topped by the Georges de Latour Private Reserve Cabernet Sauvignon. That was something special.

Opus One is a winery that requires a reservation for a tasting, which costs $35. I showed up there just before the appointed hour of 3:00 p.m.

The winery's exterior looks like a flying saucer that has landed in a field, and the interior resembles the sitting room of a fashionable French mansion. The guide talked a lot about Baron Philippe de Rothschild, who started the winery with Robert Mondavi in 1978. The barrel room was spectacular, and the tasting at the end of the tour was generous.

Rick Kushman, a writer for the *Sacramento Bee,* and his buddy Hank Beal, a wine buyer, set out to visit each of the 141 tasting rooms in the Napa Valley in a single season and graded them in their book *A Moveable Thirst.* As they wrote, "For wine guys, and pretty much anyone who doesn't live for theme parks, Napa is the real magic kingdom." My afternoon of tasting confirmed Kushman's conclusion.

CHAPTER THREE

Stellenbosch, South Africa

Portuguese, Dutch, and English explorers looking for a sailing passage from Europe to India in the late fifteenth century had reason to call the Horn of Africa that separates the Atlantic Ocean from the Indian Ocean the Cape of Good Hope. After the often-frightening trip down either coast of Africa, the gentle bays and lush green foliage on towering mountains were friendly looking places to Europeans. The most spectacular sight from ships off the Cape was a long majestic mountaintop whose peak was so flat that it looked like a giant with a magic sword had simply whacked off the top. Newcomers soon called it Table Mountain. Early settlers first thought they had rounded the horn when they entered a large body of water that turned out to be only a giant inlet, which they appropriately named False Bay. It was only later that they learned that the southern tip of Africa was actually about 90 miles farther to the southeast.

European travelers had a hard time getting used to the idea that the seasons were just the opposite of what they knew at home: the warmest months of the year at the Cape were January through March, while the coldest ones were June to August. The climate, though, was generally moderate all year long, and the spectacularly beautiful region reminded many travelers of Mediterranean Europe.

The landscape around Cape Town, the first city settlers founded, is just as staggering today. Hugh Johnson and Jancis Robinson, in the fifth edition of *The World Atlas of Wine,* wrote, "The most dramatically beautiful wine country in the world is surely South Africa's. Blue-shadowed stacks of Table Mountain sandstone and decomposed granite rise from vivid green pastures dotted with the brilliant white façades of 200-year-old Cape Dutch homesteads."

As explorers gave way to traders carrying cargo both east and west, False Bay and the nearby Table Bay became stopping off spots where they could take on fresh provisions and give the crew a little R&R. The Europeans encountered members of the Khoikhoi tribes, who fifteen hundred years earlier had begun migrating to the bottom of Africa from an area that today is northern Botswana. The Dutch called them Hottentots, after the Dutch word for stammer or stutter because that was how they seemed to speak. From the beginning, the newcomers and the locals didn't get along. Nonetheless, the Europeans kept returning to the Cape and developed a system of leaving letters and navigation tips under marked rocks to help later travelers.

The British made the first attempt to colonize the area in 1615, leaving ten criminals there who had been sentenced to the gallows. But they died without establishing a settlement. Then in 1652, three ships commanded by Jan van Riebeeck from the Dutch East India Company sailed into False Bay with ninety men and large supplies of seeds, agricultural equipment, and building materials. They established the first permanent European settlement in the shadow of Table Mountain. The purpose of the outpost was to provide fresh food for Dutch ships sailing to India and other destinations.

The Dutch settlers had little, if any, experience with viticulture since grape growing and winemaking were not part of agriculture at home. But three years after he landed, Van Riebeeck, the first governor of the Cape colony, planted the first vines, which had come from France, Germany, and Spain. He was anxious to make wine because the Dutch had noticed that the crews on Portuguese and Spanish ships had less incidence of scurvy, a disease caused by the lack of vitamin C that results in bleeding gums and liver spots. The Dutch thought the explanation might be that Portuguese and Spanish crews drank wine during their sea voyages. The first vines planted near the Liesbeek River in Cape Town failed to produce, but grapes did better at a second site. Finally on February 2, 1659, Van Riebeeck scribbled in his diary, "Today, praise be to God, wine was made for the first time from Cape grapes."

In 1657, Jan van Riebeeck made two decisions that reverberated through South Africa's history. First, he decided that the Dutch East India Company could get more agricultural output from settlers if he freed married men from their obligations as indentured employees and gave them land to farm. The independent settlers were called free burghers, and many soon set up large, productive agricultural operations. The same year he also instituted slavery for both domestic and farm work. Most of the slaves came on Dutch ships from the coastal area of eastern Africa and from Mozambique. Despite those two changes, the white population remained small, and a century after the first settlement there were still only eighteen hundred free male burghers, who owned more than eleven hundred slaves.

In 1679, Simon van der Stel, an enthusiastic, but still amateur, supporter of wine, replaced Jan van Riebeeck as governor. He established South Africa's second city, which he named Stellenbosch after himself. Winemakers in the Cape got lucky in the late 1680s, when French Protestants known as Huguenots arrived in South Africa to escape religious persecution at home. Some of them came from the winemaking region of Provence and established a settlement far inland in a region where lions still roamed, which became known in Dutch as Franschhoek (French corner). They brought their winemaking skills with them, and both the quantity and quality of South African wine increased dramatically. When he retired in 1699, Van der Stel developed South Africa's first major winery, **Constantia**, south of Cape Town. It remains one of South Africa's most famous wineries.

The next three centuries were periods of ups and downs for South Africa's wine business, which remained largely isolated from world wine markets and had to survive with only meager supplies of such products as oak barrels. Most of the wine was drunk locally, and little foreign wine was imported. With neither foreign competition nor comparisons, there was little impetus to improve the quality of South African wine.

The British seized control of South Africa in 1795 during the Napoléonic Wars in order to keep the vital spot on the sea route from Europe to India out of French hands, and a major migration of British farmers arrived in South Africa in the 1820s. Although Britain outlawed slavery in its entire empire in 1807, it didn't end in the Cape until 1834, and the official end of slavery meant little in the real life of the black population, which still lived in near bondage. Nonetheless, some 12,000 white South Africans of Dutch heritage protested both the English rule and new raids by African tribes by moving north in a displacement known as the Great Trek.

The new British connection led to an export boom for South Africa and a vast expansion of wine production. In the next half-century, South African vines increased from 13 million to 55 million, and output jumped from .5 million liters to 4.5 million liters annually. A few South African wines even became famous in Europe. The most popular of all was Vin de Constance, a sweet white wine made from Muscat de Frontignan grapes. Among its fans were the English writer Jane Austen and the German kaiser Frederick the Great. On his deathbed, Napoléon asked for a bottle of Vin de Constance to ease his way into the next life.

During this time, the center of South Africa's winelands, as the locals call them, shifted east from the small region south of Cape Town to the much larger area around Stellenbosch. There the vines grew in some of the oldest and richest soils in the world and enjoyed ocean breezes during long sunny days.

Thanks to the favorable growing conditions, South African winemakers soon had a huge overproduction of wine. In an attempt to save bankrupt grape growers and winemakers, the industry in 1918 established the Ko-operatiewe Wijnbouwers Vereniging van Zuid-Afrika Beperkt, which was known by its initials KWV. The cooperative introduced increasingly strict controls over all aspects of the alcohol business, regulating the types and quantity of grapes farmers could grow and the price they earned as well as rules for the production of still, sparkling, and fortified wine plus brandy. The level of government control was similar to that in the Soviet Union in the worst days of its centralized economy. The unintended consequence of the *dirigiste* regime was the destruction of South Africa's quality wines. Since farmers were now paid for the quantity, not the quality, of their product, they began growing mainly high-yielding and low-maintenance grapes such as Chenin Blanc and Cinsaut.

In addition to the poor quality of its wines, South African racial policies were isolating the country from the rest of the world. Starting in 1948, South Africa adopted strict rules of racial separation that took away civil rights that nonwhites had enjoyed for decades. Everyone was put into racial categories—whites, blacks, mulattoes, and Asian

Indians, and rules governed their lives in often maddening minutia. Descendents of the original Dutch settlers, known as Afrikaners, were the driving force behind the policy called apartheid.

A growing number of nations around the world boycotted South African products, including wine, to protest the country's racial policies. In addition, local winemakers had a hard time buying abroad such viticulture equipment as wooden barrels and tanks. In Amsterdam and elsewhere, apartheid opponents broke store windows and intimidated shopkeepers who dared to stock South African wines.

By the 1970s, though, not only was the country's black population rebelling against the racial policies but also the South African wine community was protesting the restrictions dictated by the KWV, which locally earned the nickname KGB. One of the people trying to pull the country's wine business into the modern world was an unlikely German refugee from Communist Poland.

Born and raised a German, Spatz Sperling was liberated by the Russians at the end of World War II, and the area where he lived became part of Poland when borders were redrawn. The late 1940s were starvation years in Poland, and Spatz went into farming just so he could be closer to the food that would keep him alive. Many days he would sneak into the state-run farms just before harvest and steal potatoes. Emigration offered an escape from starvation, and the Poles were just as happy to be rid of the ethnic German.

In 1951, twenty-one-year-old Spatz Sperling arrived in South Africa to live and work with his aunt and uncle, Hans Otto Hoheisen and his wife, Deli, who had a 494-acre farm on the Simonsberg Mountain outside Stellenbosch that produced a variety of products, including a little wine. The uncle had named his farm and later winery **Delheim** (Deli's home) in honor of his wife. The young Spatz knew nothing about making wine, but gradually picked up the basics from his uncle. During the 1960s, German wine experts regularly traveled to South Africa and taught locals how to improve their wines. Sperling was one of their best students since he could communicate easily with the teachers in their native language. He also has an extrovert's personality and his presence fills any room. At the same time, Sperling was fighting the bureaucrats at the KWV, who once threatened to arrest him because he had loaned some winemaking equipment to a neighbor, which was forbidden. The rebel Sperling told officials it was only one example of their many regulations that made no sense.

Through it all, though, the short but solidly built Sperling maintained a knee-slapping sense of humor that knew no bounds and was often directed at himself. He still loves to tell the story of how one of his most famous wines got its name. On a Sunday afternoon in 1961, a group of visiting Germans, he says, was "frolicking around the pool in all stages of undress and inebriation." In an attempt to impress his visitors, Sperling invited them down to his wine cellar to evaluate his "latest—and best—vintage." He was particularly anxious to show off Tank 13, which contained a new semisweet white wine. The wine was admittedly not good, considering it was one of his early attempts at winemaking. After a German woman tasted it, she barked back at him, "Spatz, this is really *dreck* (shit)!"

Undeterred by the criticism, Sperling continued improving the wine and finally began selling it. He decided to give it a name based on that original judgment, calling it Spatzendreck. His name Sperling means sparrow in German, and his nickname Spatz is the diminutive of Sperling. So the wine's name means "little sparrow's shit." He ordered up a sample label that showed a baby sparrow defecating into a wine barrel. Sperling still roars with laughter when he recounts that in 1979 Britain's *Decanter* magazine gave it an award for the "worst label of the year."

Franz Malan, the owner of the nearby Simonsig Estate, in 1971, came back from Europe inspired by the wine routes for tourists he had seen in France. Sperling, Malan, and Niel Joubert of the Spier winery decided that South Africa needed to introduce something like that. In those days, wineries could not sell single bottles of wine directly to customers. KWV laws regulated that wine could only be sold in cases of twelve bottles. Nonetheless, the three winemakers decided to establish a French-style wine route in Stellenbosch. When they asked road engineers if they could put some signs directing visitors to their individual wineries, the bureaucrats objected, arguing that they would be distracting to drivers.

With only marginal support from fellow winemakers, the three pressed on and started handing out maps showing directions to participating wine farms. First came students from nearby Stellenbosch University looking for something alcoholic and free. Their parents and friends soon followed. Business became so strong that Sperling put his gardener to work, welcoming and counting the cars that came through the farm gates. The high-tech method of counting consisted of giving the gardener two buckets, one filled with stones and one empty. When a car entered the winery, he took a rock from the bucket of stones and put it in the other one. Then at the end of the day they counted the rocks in the previously empty bucket and multiplied that by four, figuring that each car had four passengers, to see how many visitors the winery had that day.

The Stellenbosch wine route was an instant hit, and Sperling's Dutch-born wife, Vera, began looking for new ways to promote Delheim wines. They gave cellar tours and painted an old wagon that took people around the vineyard. Then she came up with the idea of selling cheese platters and eventually a light lunch of chicken liver pâté, homemade bread, cheese, and tomatoes. Soup was added in winter. Through constant pressure on local officials, Sperling and the others eventually got many of the restrictive rules governing wine sales overturned.

In 2002, American Express became the official sponsor of what became known as the Stellenbosch American Express Wine Routes. There are more than 135 wineries on the tour as well as four subroutes, and well-marked signs now direct visitors to one of South Africa's top tourist attractions.

While the route's three founders in the 1970s set South Africa on the road to wine tourism, the country still faced a serious problem attracting visitors or selling their wines abroad because of the country's racial policies. On some days, Delheim had 10,000 visitors, but except for an occasional German or other European they were all South Africans. Furthermore, tourists were scared away from the country by the racial violence that simmered just below the surface and threatened to explode at any moment into all-out warfare.

When I visited South Africa in early 2008 to research this book, it was my third trip to the country. The first one was in October 1986, when I was editor of the world section for *Time* magazine, and South Africa was one of the biggest stories on the international scene. It was a tense

time in the country's history. Everyone talked about black-on-black violence among rival African groups, and black-on-white or white-on-black
revenge killings. Some whites were arming themselves in expectation
of an upcoming civil war. Meanwhile, blacks were killing their black
opponents by necklacing, a gruesome execution that involved filling a
tire with gasoline, throwing it around a victim's chest, and then setting
the tire on fire. Winnie Mandela, the wife of Nelson Mandela, a longtime political prisoner, portended a dark future when she said, "With
our boxes of matches and our necklaces we shall liberate this country."

Apartheid is now history. In February 1990, Prime Minister F. W.
de Klerk released Nelson Mandela from prison after twenty-seven years
of confinement. The two men then maneuvered the transfer of political power from whites to blacks, an achievement South Africans call a
miracle and which in 1993 won them a joint Nobel Peace Prize. In May
1994, Mandela, a man whose charisma is universally appealing, became
the country's first president elected by universal suffrage. Today, huge
social issues remain as the country's black majority moves into positions
of political and economic power at all levels, and its institutions are
still evolving. The progress South Africans have already made toward a
multiracial society is historic. Yet it is still too early to be confident that
South Africa can establish a government that will provide all its people
with solid economic growth, a thriving democracy, and a public administration untainted by rampant corruption.

The immediate result of the power transfer was that South Africa
went from being an international pariah to being the in-place to visit
and it was suddenly chic in Europe and the United States to buy its
wines, especially Pinotage, South Africa's signature wine. South Africans, black and white, called it "Madiba Magic" after Mandela's nickname in Xhosa, his native language, which means "great leader."

Unfortunately, many of the new international wine consumers didn't
like what they tasted. The years of isolation had hidden the fact that
South African wines had fallen behind international standards. Pinotage, in particular, was often rough and astringent. The country's vineyards also had to deal with a major infestation of roll leaf virus, which
forced many wineries to replant entire vineyards. By the turn of the millennium the Madiba Magic had worn off, and the country's winemakers

had to reinvent themselves. "But we were lucky that a new generation was just coming along," says Jean Engelbrecht, the proprietor of the Rust en Vrede Estate. "They had traveled, and they also realized that we had to have a completely new approach to winemaking. The challenge for us was to make a style of wine that was acceptable in both North America and Europe because they have different palates. We had to find a middle way that was also authentic." Wine tourism also became a part of that reinvention of the South African wine business.

The heart of South African wine tourism is the region around Stellenbosch, and the best example is **Vergelegen**, an estate located in Somerset West, which is south of Stellenbosch. The 7,413-acre property is steeped in history and provides visitors a special view into the way the world's most privileged people used to live. In addition, Vergelegen produces outstanding wines that compete in quality with any in the world.

With two guttural g's, the name Vergelegen, which means "remotely situated" in Dutch, is difficult for the non-Dutch world to pronounce properly. Vergelegen was originally an army outpost, but Willem Adriaan van der Stel, the third governor of the Cape Colony, thought the wilderness location was too beautiful for the military, so he gave it to himself in 1700. He then spent extravagantly to build his personal nirvana with the money coming from his employer, the Dutch East India Company. With the help of ample slave labor, he constructed in only four years a compound complete with white Cape Dutch houses, a slave quarter, expansive gardens, and vineyards. At the entrance to the homestead Van der Stel planted five towering Chinese camphor trees that still stand. Vergelegen was Versailles in the African bush. An early visitor described it as "a country seat, large beyond measure, and of such broad dimensions, as if it is a whole town."

After the Cape's free burghers complained to Amsterdam about Van der Stel's extravagances, the Dutch East India Company recalled him in 1706 and sacked him along with several other officials. The property went into private hands in 1709, and was under different ownership for nearly three centuries. Vergelegen was no longer making wine in 1987, when Anglo American, a British company that has a long history in South African mining of both gold and diamonds, bought it. Managing Director Don Tooth explains that his company purchased Vergelegen to preserve it as part of the country's national heritage, saying with no exaggeration, "If someone came here and nowhere else in the Cape, he could experience all that Cape culture has to offer in this one place."

Anglo American invested extensively to restore the property and to reopen the winery. Vergelegen now includes dozens of thatch-roofed Cape Dutch buildings, seventeen gardens, three eating facilities, a wine-tasting room, and a winery whose design was inspired by Opus One in the Napa Valley as well as Bordeaux's Château Lafite Rothschild and Château Pichon Longueville Comtesse de Lalande.

Vergelegen offers tours three times a day that start in the tasting room and then continue at the winery located in the mountains high above the main buildings. The winery is ultramodern with stainless steel walkways that provide an excellent view of winemaking. From a patio in front of the winery is perhaps the most spectacular view in the entire world of wine tourism. Looming up to the sky are Helderberg Mountain, the Hottentots Holland mountain range, and Stellenbosch Mountain. In back, far in the distance but easily visible, is False Bay.

Vergelegen produces some 65,000 cases of wine per year and exports 50 percent of them, although the wines are still difficult to find in the United States. The winery is best known for its reds, which make up 60 percent of production. The top V brand is a blend of Cabernet Sauvignon, Merlot, and Cabernet Franc that sells in the United States for $150. The leading white, called simply Vergelegen White, is a blend of predominantly Sémillon and Sauvignon Blanc and sells for about $50.

Vergelegen hosts a variety of events at its property. Several times a year it brings in such big-name international artists as Celine Dion, Elton John, and Josh Groban for performances held on a lawn near one of the gardens. Tooth says they are limiting the number of concerts because they don't want those to overwhelm the history and the wine.

Buildings occupy only a small section of this huge property. Most of it is wilderness covered by what South Africans call fynbos, the natural vegetation in one of the world's richest habitats. The Cape's floral kingdom hosts more than 8,600 plant species, as compared with only some 1,500 for the whole British Isles. That plant life attracts many animals, including Steppe Buzzards, which migrate each year from Siberia. Unfortunately, settlers introduced a number of plants such as eucalyptus trees to the Cape that are now threatening native vegetation by using up an inordinate amount of water. Anglo American has invested $3 million on a ten-year project to restore the fynbos to its natural state. The company hired Gerard Wright, a leading environmentalist and once an outspoken critic of Anglo American's management of the Vergelegen wilderness, to direct the project. The goal is to eventually offer guided group tours of this unique natural wonder. Vergelegen's vast wilderness, though, can pose dangers. In February and March 2009, a massive brush fire swept over the property destroying 27 acres of prized experimental vines. Winemaker Andre van Rensburg called the fire a "borderline disaster."

Vergelegen is such an attraction that the estate is already worrying about how to manage all the tourists. It currently receives about 75,000 visitors annually, and it doesn't want the number to rise much above that. "We're very concerned about ruining the tourist experience for everyone," says Tooth. Vergelegen introduced a modest 10 rand ($1.00) admission fee to discourage the curious, and it does not accept bus tours. The restaurants serve lunch, but not dinner, as another way to keep traffic down.

♑ ♑ ♑

Charles Back at **Fairview Wines**, which is north of Stellenbosch in Paarl, offers a different kind of wine tourism experience than Vergelegen. Many of his fellow winemakers consider Back the godfather of South African wine tourism. As several wine people told me, he has always been a decade ahead of everyone else in finding new ways to welcome visitors.

Although Back's name may be unknown to Americans, his line of Goat wines is the best-selling South African brand in the United States. His herd includes Goats do Roam, Goat Door, Bored Doe, and more. On the back label of Goats do Roam is the apocryphal story of how some animals broke away from the goat tower on Back's property and got into the vineyard. There they ate the "the best and tastiest fruit," and "their choice serves as our inspiration for this wine." French wine

authorities took legal action to stop Back from using the similar sounding names, claiming that his puns were trademark violations against
Côtes du Rhône, Côte d'Or, and Bordeaux.

Customers and Back ignored the French and just keep chuckling.
More than 200,000 people annually visit the Fairview winery, which
has a goat tower in the front with a ramp for the animals to walk up and
down. Many visitors stop to have their picture taken with the famous
goats. People always smile at the goats, and the goats sometimes seem
to smile back.

As with all white South Africans, Back's family came from somewhere else, in their case Lithuania. His grandfather was the youngest of
seven or eight children, he doesn't know for sure how many, in a family
that owned a flour mill. He didn't see much of a future there with so
many siblings and began looking for alternatives. Periodic persecutions
of Jews were another reason for him to leave for South Africa, where he
arrived in 1902, working first as a butcher. The family bought the farm
that now houses Fairview in 1932.

Back's father took over the family farm and tried raising poultry,
sheep, cattle, asparagus, mushrooms, and more. He made cheese after
he found a Frenchman who claimed he knew how to produce it. That
was nearly a half-century ago, but Charles Back still remembers that it
was inedible. Nothing really hit big for Back's father, however, who was
often ahead of his time.

The Back farm also grew grapes, which the family sold to nearby
wineries. But in 1974, it began making wine, which it marketed under
the Fairview brand. Four years later, Charles graduated from the enology program at Stellenbosch University and became the winemaker.

Back doesn't try to look for business models in other countries. "I've
traveled to Australia and California and learned that we can compete
with them in wine tourism," he says. "Plus we have the advantage of
our great scenery." He says it took him twenty years of serious thought
to come up with a business philosophy that works for him, which he
sums up by saying, "This place must reflect this country, warts and all.
Blend slick and schlock in the right proportions, and be authentic to
what you are. Don't try to out-chic California or outsmart Australia.
Know who you are."

Things started coming together for Fairview and wine tourism in the late 1980s. Along with many other white South Africans at the time, Back thought of emigrating to get away from the country's racial problems and had a good offer to work in the London wine trade. "But I have a love for my land, and you can't take your land with you," he says.

After taking over the operation from his father, Back's first objective was to get the wines right. His grandfather had not bought great *terroir,* so Charles looked for more promising land and began making handshake deals to buy the best grapes he could find. He nearly doubled the size of his vineyards by buying land about a forty-minute drive from Fairview in Swartland, which he thought had the potential for producing Rhône-style wines. Next came another try at achieving his father's goal of making cheese. He hired a young cheese maker, Louis Lawrence, who soon began winning awards just in time for a cheese boom in South Africa. The cheese maker is still with Back, turning out nearly two dozen boutique products, and Fairview has become South Africa's largest specialty cheese producer.

Back turned a small 14-by-20-foot section of the Fairview stable into the winery's first tasting room. The space kept expanding and expanding and now occupies the entire first floor as the busy epicenter of Back's empire. At one end is a food shop that sells Fairview cheeses and olive oil. At the other end is the tasting bar. Off to the side is a new venture, where Back is trying out a more expensive, sit-down tasting of wines, cheeses, and olive oils. The regular tasting costs $1.50, while the sit-down one is $4. As in most tasting rooms, there are plenty of souvenirs for sale, but at Fairview that's done with the Back sense of fun. A black shirt with the picture of a goat that vaguely resembles Marlon Brando promotes the Italian-style wine The Goat Father. Charles Back has never heard a pun about goats he didn't like.

Fairview's now-famous goat tower helped bring in guests. "That made us a recognized place—'that place with the goat tower.'" The farm has eight hundred goats to provide milk for the cheese, but he keeps four or five nonproductive ones at the tower to amuse the tourists.

Back also built a small restaurant, which he named the Goat Shed. At first, it only offered free cheese samples, but now serves lunch and light foods in a casual setting with lots of noise that no one seems to mind. Most days it's packed with a predominantly young crowd.

Despite all his fun with goats, Back retains a commitment to his wine. "We are serious winemakers and always push the envelope to make better wines," he says. Back now has three lines that overlap in price and compete with each other. The Goat brands sell for $10 to $20, the Fairview wines range from $10 to $50, and a Spice Route line, which has its own winemaking facility and winemaker, sells for $15 to $40. Back may eventually spin off the Goat brand, which now represents half his sales, as a separate company lest it overwhelm his wine ventures. In the meantime, he's just having fun. And his customers seem to be enjoying it as much as he is. Just so he doesn't take himself too seriously, Back doesn't even have an office and manages his business by wandering around Fairview.

♆ ♆ ♆

Rust en Vrede, which in Dutch means "rest and peace," was founded in 1694 and is one of South Africa's oldest and most respected wineries. For his dinner in Oslo in 1993 to celebrate receiving the Nobel Peace Prize, Nelson Mandela served Rust en Vrede Estate, a Bordeaux blend. Jean Engelbrecht grew up on the winery's grounds, where his father was the proprietor, but the son never wanted to make wine. He felt he had a higher calling—flying. After graduating from Stellenbosch University, he moved to the United States and became a pilot for Conair, a Delta feeder airline. While living in Orlando, Engelbrecht often flew to Napa to check out the wine scene because he always figured that after his flying days ended he might go into wine marketing.

Two things in Napa really caught his attention. The first was The French Laundry. "The first time I went to The French Laundry in 1998 was a real eye-opener," he recalls. South African cuisine has only recently escaped from the English-inspired culinary dark ages where dinner meant simply "a meat and two veggies." Engelbrecht not only liked the Napa cuisine and the long wine list, but he was also impressed by the restaurant's atmosphere. "There was a lighter, informal style," he says. He's since been back many times, looking to see how he might bring to South Africa some of the things he found so appealing.

The other thing that impressed Engelbrecht was Silver Oak Cellars, one of the pioneers of the valley. He liked the fact that it made only one type of wine: its highly praised and highly priced Cabernet Sauvignons, one from Napa Valley and one from Alexander Valley. Rust en Vrede has a similar philosophy. It only makes red wines: Cabernet Sauvignon, Merlot, Shiraz, and a Bordeaux blend. Engelbrecht met often with the Silver Oak founders, investor Ray Duncan and winemaker Justin Meyer, and found he shared with them many of the same ideas about making high-quality, low-volume red wines.

In 1996, Engelbrecht left commercial aviation, though he still flies as a hobby, and returned to Rust en Vrede to succeed his father as proprietor. His first objective was to introduce some of the things he liked in the Napa Valley. "I just stole what the Californians did and brought it over here and made it fit with what we do." He soon signed a joint venture agreement with Silver Oak and started thinking about food possibilities. "The options food and wine offer are endless, and I enjoy that," he says.

Engelbrecht also began a close business relationship with international golf star Ernie Els. The two had been friends since their university days, and Jean introduced Ernie to his wife. One project was Ernie Els Wines, which produces limited quantities of high-end Bordeaux blends, Ernie's favorite wine. The modern winery opened its doors in December 2004 and quickly began garnering 90-point scores from critics. The two also teamed up on the Guardian Peak winery, which specializes in New World–style wines. What really set Guardian Peak apart, though, is its restaurant, which opened in December 2005. Accompanying each dish is a glass of wine the chef thinks pairs best with it. The customer can order another wine later, but first gets the recommended one. In the fall of 2008, Engelbrecht and Els also opened a wine bar in Stellenbosch called The Big Easy, Els's nickname. It serves light food, and they plan to take the concept internationally.

The partners have been slowly rolling out another wine tourism project, which will bring together South Africa's top three tourist attractions: animal safaris, wine, and golf. The premium, twelve-day package includes playing golf at several of the country's top courses, visiting the best wineries in the Stellenbosch area, and an animal safari to the Tswalu Kalahari Reserve in northern South Africa. So far, they have quietly done trial tours for Europeans and plan to soon open annual trips to others. Cost: $10,000 per person. Engelbrecht calls the Ernie Els Wine and Golf Safaris the "trip of a lifetime."

Finally in late 2007, Engelbrecht achieved his dream of building something like The French Laundry at Rust en Vrede. It's a small (forty-seat), premium restaurant serving international cuisine for dinner only and doesn't have a name because he didn't want it to have a separate identity from the winery. After searching the country, Engelbrecht hired David Higgs, a top South African chef who was working in restaurant management but wanted to get back to cooking, his real passion. The restaurant has an open kitchen, where Higgs provides a floor show directing the kitchen staff while guests watch. "I wanted the kitchen right in the middle of the restaurant to make it less formal," says Engelbrecht.

Scores of other wineries, big and small, are finding their own ways to attract visitors. Kevin Arnold at the **Waterford Estate**, who looks like a Ralph Lauren of the vines with a mane of swept-back gray hair, is one of many South African winemakers who have traveled the world and are now introducing new thinking to an old business. After being a winemaker first at Delheim and then at Rust en Vrede Estate, he and his financial backer, Jeremy Ord, opened Waterford Estate in Stellenbosch in April 2000.

In 1981, Arnold spent three months working for the Robert Mondavi Winery in the Napa Valley, which left a strong and permanent impression on him. "It took me almost twenty-five years to design and build my own winery, but when I did, I introduced things that I first learned from Robert Mondavi such as that a winery should be a unique place for tourists to visit," he says. The stone-rich Waterford Estate winery, which has an inner courtyard that looks like a cross between a piazza in an Italian village and a monastery cloister, is already getting more than 30,000 visitors a year.

Waterford Estate's wines are also winning high points in international competitions even though Arnold is still experimenting with blends of European grape varieties from Spain, France, and Italy in his search for what works best in his *terroir*. Arnold's flagship wine, The Jem, a blend of eight grape varieties, went on sale in late 2007 for more than $100 a bottle.

Arnold's special wine-and-chocolate pairings bring many visitors to his tasting room. On a flight back to South Africa from a sales trip to the United States in 2003, he read a story about chocolate in *Wine Spectator* that set off an idea. "I wanted to teach people something about tannins, and chocolates contain them as well as wine," he says. It took Arnold and his staff several months of trials before they came up with what he now calls the Waterford Wine and Chocolate Experience. Unwilling to accept any chocolate off the shelf, he found a Belgian chocolatier to custom-make three kinds to his specification. The first is designed to go with a Shiraz, and contains masala chai, a spice tea, to match the spicy wine. The second goes with a Cabernet Sauvignon and contains a little rock salt, which neutralizes the tannins. The third is paired with his sweet dessert wine, which is a blend of Chardonnay, Sauvignon Blanc, and Chenin Blanc botrytis grapes. The first two are dark chocolates and have 70 percent cacao. The third is milk chocolate. More than half of all Waterford visitors now enjoy the wine-and-chocolate tasting.

Arnold plans another venture into wine tourism by introducing Land Rover Cruiser tours of his vineyards in the foothills of Stellenbosch Mountain. He was anxious to get visitors out among the grapes looking at the vines and the soil, so he built platforms at strategic spots where people can enjoy the wines that came from the vines around them. The view down the valley and out toward Table Mountain and False Bay is stunning, and in the afternoon gentle ocean breezes wash over the vineyard and visitors.

Dick Enthoven at the **Spier Wine Estate**, located between Stellenbosch and the Cape Town International Airport, is combining arts and wine. He has put together one of the most comprehensive projects in wine tourism that involves a hotel, top restaurants, art exhibits, and concerts as well as wine. After a successful career in business, Enthoven entered politics in the 1970s as an advocate of change on race issues during the darkest days of apartheid. His reform proposals were controversial, and he ended up being a member of four different parties during the four years he served in Parliament. Despairing over the future of his country, Enthoven in 1987 moved to London and began a new life there. When the Mandela–De Klerk transfer of power took place in the early 1990s, however, he returned to South Africa to do his part to build a new racially integrated country.

The Spier winery was started in 1692, but had fallen on hard times and was badly in need of repair. Partly to save the historic buildings, which included the oldest wine cellar in the southern hemisphere dating back to 1764, Enthoven bought the property in 1993 and reopened it two years later. Using as his models two country-house operas that he had known in Britain—Garsington, and Glyndebourne—Enthoven added to the winery a series of creative art projects that now include an amphitheater, where concerts and operas are performed, as well as the Spier Contemporary art show, which was held in 2008 in a dozen giant ship containers. In 2005, Spier's African version of the opera *Carmen,* set in the black townships and sung in Xhosa, won the Golden Bear, the highest award, at the Berlin International Film Festival. The Spier complex also includes a hotel laid out much like a Mediterranean fishing village with wandering streets and low buildings. At Moyo, an African-themed restaurant, native music plays in tents while wandering artists paint the faces of customers. Moyo is one of the hottest tickets in South Africa. The best seats are in trees above the tents, but reservations for those must be made long in advance.

Spier produces 1.7 million cases of wine a year, which have won many awards. Enthoven once had great hopes for developing wine tourism, and at one point hired a former Mondavi hospitality executive to teach them how to do it. There developed some differences, though, between the winemakers and the tourism consultant, who wanted to have harvest festivals and tours of the vineyard. The consultant quietly left after two years and few achievements. Enthoven seems genuinely disappointed that more wine tourism hasn't worked out. Spier now has limited wine offerings beyond a standard tasting for $1.00. There are no winery visits because the winemaking facility is far from the tourist area.

Spier, though, is accomplishing one of Enthoven's original objectives: job creation for blacks. He believes strongly that for the long-term viability of South Africa, the white community has a duty to train workers in basic job skills and give them gainful employment. He's proud that his high season workforce tops some fifteen hundred people, many of them working in the hotel and restaurants. Enthoven has great hope that the artistic talent seen in the *Carmen* movie can be tapped and speaks admiringly about how the Africans "have art in their DNA." One of his latest plans is to establish a Center of African Heritage at Spier, a first for the continent. It would be a symbol of the peaceful racial reconciliation that many thought South Africa would never achieve but is now on the path to becoming a reality.

Because of its political isolation for many years and the fact that it is so far from the United States (more than twenty-four hours by air), South Africa remains little known to wine tourists. Moreover, the country is still discovering its viticulture potential and the world is still discovering its wines. They received a boost after it was learned that Barack Obama celebrated his 2008 election night victory with South Africa's Graham Beck NV sparkling wine. Its Pinotage is unique, and its Chenin Blanc may eventually be considered better than that of France's Loire Valley, where it originated. The Forrester FMC Chenin Blanc, which is hard to find and sells for $60 a bottle in the United States, has already been called one of the world's great white wines. South Africa has great wine potential and should be visited before the world beats down a path to its door.

Diary of a Wine Tourist

January 2

Bagging Both the Big Five and Fine Wine

South Africa has two major tourist attractions: some of the best animal parks in the world and many excellent wines. So far only a few people are bringing them together in a safari/wine experience. The most successful is **Singita Game Reserves**, which operates nine lodges in South Africa and Tanzania. When I knew I was going to South Africa to research this book, I asked a winemaker friend there if he had a favorite game lodge. He immediately said Singita, and I later learned that this is the top choice of many people for viewing Africa's wild kingdom.

In times past, adventurers such as Teddy Roosevelt or Ernest Hemingway went on African safaris with machismo in their veins and dreams of killing the Big Five: buffalo, elephant, leopard, lion, and rhinoceros. With dwindling herds, it is no longer acceptable to most people to actually shoot the animals, although some hunters still pay exorbitant amounts of money for bagging and bragging rights. In the early 1960s, the advent of 35 mm, single-lens reflex cameras such as the Pentax Spotmatic opened up a whole new world of amateur photography and started the African photo safari. People could shoot animals with their cameras instead of their guns, and the beasts lived on.

Singita Sabi Sand has a 162,500-acre animal reserve next to the huge Kruger National Park in the northern part of the country. It was founded in 1993 with one overriding idea: when people go on safari they don't necessarily want to leave their creature comforts behind. So guests sleep in thatch-roofed cottages that are air-conditioned, a previously unheard-of luxury. Singita lodges are small. The first one, Ebony, started with just five cottages designed for two people each; it now has twelve. Each is a separate building and has a private pool, two decks, a large sitting room, and a bathroom as big as some Manhattan apartments. The only visitors you're likely to see are the monkeys that play in nearby trees.

For three days and two nights I stayed at Singita's Ebony Lodge. Twice a day (at 5:30 a.m. and 4:00 p.m.) six guests per vehicle rode in open Land Rovers through the bush looking for animals. Sitting in the front seats were a ranger and his assistant, the tracker, who had an incredible ability to see an elephant or a lion in the wild where I only saw trees or brush. By the end of the second day, I had already bagged the Big Five with my Nikon. In one unforgettable experience we sat perfectly still in the truck, while a leopard slowly walked past us not 3 feet away. On another trip a small herd of elephants, including several babies, ambled around our vehicle.

The Singita experience, though, can also be a wine adventure for those who want to take advantage of it. The first night, the person briefing me about the lodge mentioned that behind the bar was the wine cellar. It was unlocked, and I could order any wine I wished either with a meal or to have sent to my room. There would be an extra charge only for French Champagne. As soon as I looked at the selection in the cellar, I realized that the lodge offered South Africa's best producers: Meerlust, Rustenberg, Ken Forrester, and others. I asked to have sent to my room a bottle of 2003 Mulderbosch Barrel Fermented Chardonnay. *Wine Spectator* gave it 90 points. It's a fruity wine that starts well and then keeps on giving. I enjoyed it for several days in the late afternoon, and it didn't seem to diminish after being opened.

François Rautenbach, the director of wine for all the Singita lodges, started working for the company in October 2000 as the executive chef, but two years later the owner asked him if he would establish a wine program. Up to that point, the resort had offered mainly a selection of international wines and only a few South African ones. But local wines were improving dramatically at the time, and so the owner decided to provide only South African wines to showcase that aspect of the country. The one exception was for French Champagne. "We currently carry two hundred wines from the best South African wineries," Rautenbach told me. He said no other private game reserve has anything like the Singita wine offerings.

A sommelier is on staff at each lodge, always ready to make recommendations for wines to pair with lunch or dinner. At both meals I ventured into new experiences and was even tempted to ask for wine with breakfast. One day with lunch, I had a wonderful 2004 Ken Forrester FMC Chenin Blanc. In France this grape is usually found in the Loire Valley, and it is probably South Africa's best white wine variety. I had never tried the FMC before and was stunned by its rich intensity. At dinner one night, I had a 1999 Spice Route Flagship Pinotage. I was anxious to taste the country's national wine from one of its best producers and wasn't disappointed.

The first evening the sommelier offered to give me a wine tasting the next day at Boulders, another Singita lodge located only a short drive away. It has a bigger wine cellar and is better suited for such an event. So the next morning after looking for animals, I had an hour-long sampling. The sommelier and I enjoyed six wines, three white and three red. The whites were 2006 **L'Avenir** Chenin Blanc, 2004 **Springfield** Wild Yeast Chardonnay, and 2006 **Kanu** Sauvignon Blanc. The three varieties gave a good look at the spectrum of whites South Africa offers. I was most interested in the L'Avenir, a winery owned by the famous Chablis producer Michel Laroche. The wine comes from vines up to forty-two years old and is not aged in wood. It was fresh and delicious. Among the reds were 2000 Delheim Shiraz, 1998 **Simonsig** Frans Malan, and 2000 Rust en Vrede Estate. The Delheim was 100 percent Shiraz, while the Simonsig Frans Malan was a Pinotage blend, and the Rust en Vrede was a Cabernet Sauvignon blend. All of the reds were nicely aged, my favorite being the Rust en Vrede.

Singita allows you to take wines home with you, and I bought a bottle of 2000 Klein Constantia Vin de Constance, the wine Napoléon asked for on his deathbed. Behind every bottle there's a story.

CHAPTER FOUR

Mendoza, Argentina

All over the Spanish-speaking world, people tell the story of what happened in Argentina during the creation. As the tale goes, God gave a plethora of beautiful things to Argentina—a long and lovely coastline, a wonderful harbor in Buenos Aires, and the wild natural splendors of Patagonia. He then decided, though, that he had perhaps been too generous to the country, so he balanced off all the good things by giving it the Argentine people. Argentina is a country often breaking down. Through much of its history it has stumbled from one political and economic crisis to another and from one incompetent and often corrupt government to the next. Evita Perón told Argentina not to cry for her, but the world often cries for Argentina. The apogee of the country's political dysfunction occurred in December 2001, when four presidents came and went in a period of two weeks. Aerolineas Argentinas may be the worst airline in the world for service, and locals warn visitors not to take it unless they like endless delays, lost luggage, and random strikes. When they can, Argentineans fly Chilean airlines.

Wine has been a part of Argentine history ever since Spanish missionaries planted the first vineyards in the sixteenth century to supply wines for religious services. Winemakers soon learned the best place to grow vines was the high-altitude area near the town of Mendoza, where grapes were first planted in about 1570. Tucked almost in the shadow of the Andes, the world's longest mountain range, Mendoza is a semidesert oasis that resembles the southwestern United States between Palm Springs and Phoenix. While wine is made in other areas of Argentina, Mendoza accounts for nearly 70 percent of national production.

Mendoza, a city whose center has the charm of a small town, has ballooned into a less attractive metropolitan sprawl area of some one million people. The city's dominant feature is the Andes, whose white peaks stand nobly to the west against a rich azure sky (on most days). The best vineyards in Mendoza are located at altitudes between 3,000 feet and 5,000 feet and are often only a short distance from the foothills of the mountain chain. Andes peaks are snowcapped all year long, but the snow reaches down to the foothills during the winter months of June through August. The king of the Andes, as well as of the Americas, is Aconcagua, a peak that rises 22,841 feet above sea level. The derivation of the name is contested and comes from one of two Indian languages. One theory is that its origin is the Arauca word Aconca-Hue, which is the name for the Aconcagua River and means "comes from the other side." The second possibility is that it's from the Quechua language and means "sentinel of stone." Adventurers from around the world travel to Mendoza to climb the mountain only 70 miles away. Most foreigners in the city are there for either the wines or Aconcagua, and many enjoy both.

Mendoza is only habitable thanks to an excellent irrigation system that the Huarpes Indians built before the arrival of Europeans. It has been expanded and improved many times, but is still in use, capturing the water that flows down from the mountains and making it available in ample amounts to residents below. Water from the Andes still runs in open ditches in downtown Mendoza, and each morning shopkeepers and housewives use the plentiful water to wash down sidewalks.

Argentina's wine business experienced a wave of growth in the late nineteenth and early twentieth centuries when 1.5 million Italians and 1.4 million Spaniards migrated there, bringing with them grapes from their countries and a knowledge of winemaking. Production, though, was for domestic consumption, and the newcomers made little quality wine. Almost no Argentine wine was then being exported, even though the country was the world's fifth-largest producer.

Nicolás Catena, the founder of **Bodega Catena Zapata** and grandson of an Italian winemaker who arrived in Argentina in 1898, singlehandedly changed the reputation of Argentina's wines and has often been called the Robert Mondavi of his country. Catena, in the mid-1960s, took over control of his family's winery that made unpretentious bulk wine. He then had to live through another of the country's periodic political and economic crises that culminated in 1,000 percent annual inflation as well as the Falklands War of 1982 between Britain and Argentina. Shortly thereafter, Catena left his country to take a job as a visiting professor of agricultural economics at the University of California, Berkeley. Along with many other residents of the area, he often traveled north to enjoy the wines of the Napa Valley, which was then basking in the glory of the 1976 Paris Tasting, when two California wines topped their French counterparts in a blind tasting. Like winemakers in many other countries, Catena was inspired by what the Californians had done to bring their wines to a position where they could beat the French and concluded that perhaps he could do the same in Argentina. Among the people Catena met in California was Robert Mondavi.

After returning home in 1983, Catena, a serious man with piercing eyes that seem to drill through people, soon took his company in a totally new direction. He sold off the bulk-wine business, while keeping the fine-wine branch. His goal was nothing less than becoming a producer of world-quality wines. With an awareness of new winemaking technology that he had acquired in California, Catena started to plant vineyards at higher altitudes and closer to the Andes than had previously been done. His grandfather had started his first Malbec vineyard in 1902, and now the grandson decided that the grape was going to become his flagship wine. Malbec is a minor grape in France, used in small amounts in Bordeaux for blending, and is the dominant grape variety in Cahors wine. Catena created his own clonal selection of Mendozan Malbec and spent five years in the late 1980s and early 1990s on a line of superpremium Chardonnay, Cabernet Sauvignon, and Malbec wines that he named Catena Alta, which were produced with grapes from high-altitude vineyards. The first vintage was released in 1998. The wines began getting 90-plus scores from critics and changed the world's image of both Malbec and Argentina overnight.

Another thing Catena brought back from Napa was wine tourism, but he wanted to base it solidly in Latin American history. Building on his academic background and research experience, he undertook in the late 1990s a study of ancient cultures in the Americas. The Mayan civilization particularly intrigued him, and so he decided to build a new winery in its style for his company, which was now called Bodega Catena Zapata, the family names of both his father and mother. He' wanted it to be in the pyramid style of a Mayan temple located in Tikal, Guatemala. Catena opened it in April 2001.

There are now some twelve hundred wineries in Mendoza province, but fewer than a hundred are open to visitors. With its rust-colored rock construction, historic architecture, and manicured gardens, Catena Zapata is the most impressive. The winery asks visitors to make reservations a day in advance and is not open on weekends. It has a staff of fifteen tour guides and tries to limit groups to fifteen people. One of the added pluses is that visitors can enjoy a tasting of Catena Zapata's best wines for $25. Many high-end wineries offer only lower-level wines to tourists.

Another Argentinian went through a similar California experience in the 1980s, although he came from an accounting, rather than an enology, background. Santiago Achaval worked for an industrial firm in Córdoba, Argentina's second largest city, that was willing to send him to the United States to get a Master's of Business Administration degree if he promised to work for the firm for five years after his studies. So in 1987, Achaval headed off to the Stanford Business School, where, as he says, he "caught the Napa bug." When he returned to Argentina two years later and started working off his five-year agreement, Achaval realized that wine was what he wanted to do for the rest of his life. He talked about wine so incessantly at the office that one day his colleague Manuel Ferrer said that if Achaval ever started a winery he'd be interested in investing in it. "It took me about a minute and a half to accept the offer," Achaval recalls. They named the company **Achaval-Ferrer** in honor of the two founders and opened their winery in 1998. Ferrer told Achaval he knew an Italian winemaker named Roberto Cipresso, who was passionate about making wine with really old vines and might be able to help them find a good vineyard. Cipresso became a sweat-equity partner in the new winery, and soon the search was on for old vines.

On a Sunday night in the spring of 1999, Cipresso called Achaval at home in Córdoba. He started off the conversation by saying, "Santiago, we need to talk, and you need to trust me. Do you really trust me?" Cipresso went on to explain that he had found a Malbec vineyard named Finca Altamira that they had to buy. It was an old, low-yield property, getting probably only a quarter of the fruit per plant as a younger vineyard. The current owners weren't even going to harvest it that year because the output was so low. But Cipresso promised that the Malbec from this old vineyard would be great.

Achaval said he'd fly to Mendoza the next day to look at the property, but Cipresso said that would be too late. Someone else was interested, and they needed a decision right away. So sight unseen, Achaval told his Italian winemaker to buy the vineyard. They bought it on a Monday and harvested grapes on Thursday. Altamira was their initial single-vineyard Malbec, and British wine magazine *Decanter* later gave it the first five-star rating ever awarded to an Argentine wine. "The vineyard showed us we had the potential to make really great wines out of Mendoza with low-yielding properties," Achaval told me. "We consistently get less than a pound of grapes per plant, but the wine explodes with flavors, complexity, balance, and personality." Robert Parker's *Wine Advocate* reviewed ten Achaval-Ferrer wines between the 1999 and 2006 vintages, and gave them all scores of more than 90 points.

Santiago Achaval had plans for wine tourism at the new winery he built in Perdriel, Luján de Cuyo, but was unprepared for the avalanche of visitors that came his way starting in 2003. He didn't have anyone working in hospitality when phone calls started coming in from high-end hotels like the Park Hyatt Mendoza as well as from travel agents asking if their customers could take a tour. Finally in 2005, he hired someone who split her time between being a secretary and a tour guide. Before long the winery was getting six to eight groups per day with four to seven people each. "I knew tourism would be important, but I was surprised by how successful it would be here," he says.

Achaval-Ferrer now has three full-time people giving tours and tastings that can last up to two hours. Guides eschew complex technical discussions, although they can handle them if necessary. "People want anecdotes and funny stories," Achaval says. And they often want to buy wines. A group of eight tourists once bought $10,000 worth. Two of Achaval's favorite visitors came in October 2007, Americans who bought a bottle of his Cabernet Sauvignon and then left to go to lunch.

As they walked out the front door, though, they looked at the Andes peaks in front of them and decided they were never going to find a better view than that. So they went back into the winery and asked their guide if they could borrow a decanter and two glasses. They then spent the next hour drinking the wine and enjoying the spectacular scenery.

When I asked Achaval about his next projects in wine tourism, he replied that he would rather tell me what he's not going to do: "We're not going to do a restaurant." He explained that it's a completely different business and that every winery in Mendoza that's opened a restaurant is losing money on it. "We recommend restaurants; we won't open one," he says forcefully. He then added that he would soon start giving vineyard tours, which he sees as a natural extension of cellar tours.

Many foreign investors have been attracted to Mendoza because land suitable for vineyards is the least expensive of any quality wine region in the world. There is a high level of risk involved in doing business in Argentina because of periodic political and economic unrest, and timing is crucial lest an investor buy just before a devaluation, when the price of property in dollars or euros goes down. Among the famous international winemakers who have already invested there are France's Michel Rolland (**Clos de los Siete**), Jacques and François Lurton (**Bodega J & F Lurton**), and California's Paul Hobbs (**Viña Cobos**). A Dutch investment group owns the winery Bodegas Salentein.

Two recidivist American entrepreneurs have started the biggest and most interesting wine venture in Mendoza. Dave Garrett describes himself as an "Internet guy" who happened to land in Argentina because his girlfriend at the time had a passion for the tango. He started his first Internet business in 1993, creating an internal network for the U.S. Navy. He sold the company in 1998 and started a consulting firm. Following the crash of the tech world in 2000, he traveled around Latin America before landing in Buenos Aires because of his tango-loving girlfriend. While he was there with little to do, he took an introductory course called Wines in English, which taught him the basics about those of Argentina.

A good friend of fifteen years and business associate in the United States was Michael Evans, who long wandered amid the worlds of technology, presidential politics, and nonprofits. He started tech companies when not working on every Democratic presidential campaign from Bill Clinton's first in 1992 to John Kerry's in 2004. After Al Gore's defeat in 2000, he lived in California and became interested in wine. Following the Kerry campaign, Garrett suggested that Evans fly to Argentina and spend some time with him. He arrived speaking no Spanish and with plans for staying three weeks. Evans now speaks fluent Spanish and is still there.

While sitting around Buenos Aires, the two friends tossed around business ideas. Dave had seen an ad in a paper for an 80-acre property in Mendoza for $80,000, a price that got his attention. Land prices were then still inexpensive in dollars after the 2002 devaluation of the Argentine currency. So in early December 2004, the two friends traveled to Mendoza. The teacher of Dave's wine course told them to look up her friend Pablo Giménez whose family owned a winery. Garrett, Evans, and Giménez spent two days together, visiting ten wineries that opened their doors and their wines to the two gringos in a way they would never have done without the Argentine. At the first real estate agency they visited, the Americans learned the importance of having a local partner to help them get around in Argentine business. When the realtor pulled up listings of various properties for sale, Garrett and Evans noticed that he automatically doubled the price on the screen when he gave it to them, the dumb gringos.

Despite that experience, the two fell in love with Mendoza and its wines and went into overdrive thinking about businesses they might start. They also quickly decided to invite Pablo Giménez to join them as a partner. Using their experience and contacts in the world of venture capital, they reached out to family and friends looking for investors and tapped out their credit cards. Without much difficulty, they raised $200,000 in seed money.

At the same time, the three quickly honed in on two business ventures. The first was an easy, immediate one that would not require much capital; the second was more complicated, required more of an investment, and would demand longer commitment and outside financial backers.

The first was primarily aimed at American wine tourists. The three decided to set up a way for visiting Americans to avoid all the problems

Garrett and Evans would have had when they arrived in Mendoza—if Giménez had not been there to help them.

Mendoza at the time was not really ready for tourists. Armed guards often stood at winery gates and were less than friendly. Wineries, instead of being located near each other, as in the Napa Valley or parts of Bordeaux, were often miles apart. Making matters worse, there were almost no signs directing visitors to wineries. As a result of all this, it was impossible to enjoy a good Argentine wine experience during the few days a normal tourist has for a visit. "We wanted to solve the problems of a wine tourist in Mendoza," says Evans. "People fly five thousand or six thousand miles to get here, and they want to taste thirty to forty of the local wines in a short time. You couldn't do that easily."

For nearly a year Garrett and Evans split their time between working on their Spanish and getting to know the wineries of Mendoza. Applying the techniques they mastered in other business start-ups, they were obsessive about research.

In early January 2006, the three partners signed a lease on a run-down house just around the corner from the Park Hyatt Hotel with plans of turning it into a wine bar/education center where people coming to the city could learn about local wines and taste dozens of them by the glass. After a rapid renovation of the house, they opened the tasting room called **The Vines of Mendoza**. The facility has a full range of services, selling some ninety wines by the glass and fifty by the bottle. It also stages regular tastings and hosts weekly presentations by local winemakers.

At the same time, the partners worked on their second, more capital-intensive venture, which was to build a high-end hotel resort modeled after the Napa Valley's Auberge du Soleil. They visited more than seventy-six different pieces of land before locating a 20-acre property in the Uco Valley, about 70 miles south of Mendoza, that looked like the perfect location and was also the hot new wine area. It had been impossible to grow grapes in the Uco Valley until the Israelis developed technology for drip irrigation. Then the valley began attracting foreign investors. The three partners decided to follow the ancient wine maxim to buy land next to where great wine is already being made. The Vines of Mendoza gang drew up plans for a twelve-room bed-and-breakfast and began mailing their business plan to old friends. Respondents showed lots of interest; in fact, several asked if they could buy a small piece of land nearby where they might have a small vineyard.

A lightbulb suddenly went off, and the small B and B was put on the back burner. Why not start a vineyard where people could own a piece of land and make their own wine? Although Garrett and Evans were unaware of Bill Harlan's Napa Valley Reserve, their concept was similar except that in Argentina people would actually own land and could buy in for much less money. So instead of buying 20 acres, the partners bought or took options on 1,500 acres of prime Uco Valley property.

The Vines of Mendoza is now a mini wine conglomerate of three businesses, for which they have raised more than $3 million of funding. The first remains the wine bar/education center in downtown Mendoza. While not an important source of profits, it's the company's public face and makes both visitors and local winemakers aware of them.

The second business is **Private Vineyard Estates**. Located at 1,200 yards above sea level and less than 10 miles from the foothills of the Andes, much of the property is parched desert, more home to cactus than to grapes. They have already cleared 250 acres of land, installed an irrigation system, and planted vines. The first vintage will be in 2010. Investors can buy a minimum of 3 acres to a maximum of 10 acres, and nearly fifty people have put down money. They planted the first 23 acres in 2007, and in the next year another 27 acres. Fourteen grape varieties are in the ground, with Malbec accounting for just under half. Vineyard owners have control over what kind of grapes they grow and how much wine they produce. Given the crop yields managers are planning, owners could get about two thousand standard-sized bottles per acre. The Vines of Mendoza will manage the vineyards and sell surplus grapes if the owners don't want the entire amount in wine. The annual vineyard maintenance fee is a 25 percent surcharge over the actual costs, and is expected to be about $1,500 per acre per year.

The original vineyard land sold out quickly, and in July 2008 The Vines of Mendoza purchased an additional 670 acres contiguous to their first property. They have also hired Napa Valley consultants to help them build a winery.

Each owner has his own reason for making wine. One early vineyard buyer is a Chinese-American who is going to sell the wine in China. Some California vineyards plan to sell the wine in their tasting rooms, and restaurants want to make it their house wine. Most investors plan to keep the wine for their personal use.

A third business is the **Acequia Wine Club**, which exports Argentine wines from mainly small producers to customers abroad. This idea came from visiting Americans who wanted to buy more wine than they could carry home on airplanes or buy hard-to-get Argentine wines in the United States. There are two levels of membership based on the number of bottles shipped quarterly. Through the club, The Vines of Mendoza staff is learning how to ship wines internationally, especially to fifty American states that all have different regulations. That will be important when owners of Private Vineyard Estates begin sending wines home.

Dave Garrett has since left active management of The Vines of Mendoza, but remains an investor in the company.

Spaniard José Manuel Ortega Gil-Fournier, a businessman of the world, was also attracted to Argentina by the investment potential. Although born in Spain, he went to high school in Mobile, Alabama, before going on to Notre Dame University for a year and then to the Wharton School at the University of Pennsylvania. After graduating in 1990, he went to work for the Wall Street investment banking and securities firm Goldman Sachs in London, where he participated in many billion-dollar deals. Since he wisely didn't trust the stock market in the dot-com days of the 1990s, Ortega invested instead in wines, buying up mainly quality Spanish ones selling at depressed prices. He was later head of the private equity practice of Spain's Banco Santander, which frequently brought him to Argentina. Anxious to start his own wine business, Ortega, in December 1999, cashed in most of the frequent-flyer miles he had collected during a decade as an international banker and took himself, a viticulturist, an enologist, and two family members to Argentina to investigate buying or starting a winery. In May 2000, he bought his first property, 650 acres in the Uco Valley, only about 10 miles from the Private Vineyard Estates.

Ortega struggled to find a name for his new company that wasn't already used. He quickly decided not to call it Ortega because in the United States that was the name of a taco shell company. Spaniards have two family names, the first from their father and the second from their mother. His are Ortega and Gil-Fournier. He liked the second part of his mother's name, Fournier, because it sounded French, which he thought would be helpful in the wine business. So he took the first letter from his father's name and the second part of his mother's name to come up with **O. Fournier**. Some people mistakenly try to make him Irish by spelling it O'Fournier.

Given his background, it was not surprising that Ortega had an ambitious, well-thought-out plan for his wine business. His goal from the beginning was to become a producer of high-end wines in several countries, so he could spread the risk of a weather disaster, like hail or drought in one country wiping out production for a year. Owning wineries in different parts of the world could also let his winemaking team do two harvests a year, one in the northern hemisphere and one in the southern. Today Ortega owns wineries in Argentina, Spain, and Chile and is looking to buy more property in Portugal's Douro Valley and Spain's Rioja region.

Argentina was his first investment, and got his full attention. His immediate priority, largely for wine tourism reasons, was the design of his winery. Ortega selected a Mendoza architect and told him there were only two rules: first, the winemaker has the final word. There would be no debate between form and function; the winery had to fit the needs of the winemaker. And two, the winery should make an aesthetic statement. The architect followed both rules. The O. Fournier winery is modern and efficient, but also has a distinctive design that makes it look like the spaceship in the movie *Close Encounters of the Third Kind*. Sitting out in the middle of the high desert only 9 miles from the foothills of the Andes, the winery could easily have looked out of place, but the striking design works.

Ortega was on both sides of Argentina's 2001–2002 economic crisis.

In the early stages when inflation was soaring, he had to carry around bags full of the bloated currency's large banknotes to pay his workers. But later after a massive devaluation, he was able to build his winery in U.S. dollars that cost 70 percent less than they would have six months earlier.

Food and wine in Mendoza are a difficult combination. There are some good restaurants such as the 1884 Francis Mallman, but not much elegant cuisine. The local idea of a good meal in Argentina is a slab of the country's excellent beef that might be the size of a deflated football. The delicate sauces and artistic presentation so common in European cooking are rare. Ortega is trying to change that at his winery, which houses Mendoza's most sophisticated restaurant. It is run by his wife, Nadia Haron, an outstanding self-taught cook, and sous-chef Maria de los Angeles Collovatti. Ortega thinks the restaurant has great potential, in part because of the paucity of other tourist attractions. "You don't have much choice here," he says. "You either go to the mountains or to the wineries. There are no beaches or twelfth-century monasteries to visit, so food is relatively more important."

The O. Fournier restaurant is open daily for both lunch and dinner, by reservation only, and guests have to stick to fixed menus built around the best local foods available that day. They get a choice of three main courses, one of which is always vegetarian. With its large windows looking out at the Andes, the dining room has a spectacular view. On a nice day—and most days are nice—guests can sit outside on a deck overlooking an irrigation pond and the mountains. Michel Rolland, who as a Frenchman has high standards when it comes to food, dines regularly at O. Fournier when he's in town checking up on his nearby vineyard. Rolland even stores some of his own wines there to go with his meals.

O. Fournier wines regularly get 90 points from critics, and tourists are starting to come. Ortega's only wish is that he had a few winery neighbors that could create the critical mass needed to attract big groups. He currently offers lodging in seven rooms at three guesthouses, but has a business plan on the shelf for a five-star hotel and has already bought the property for it. "I'm waiting for the right timing," he says. "The theme will be food, and the architecture will be as spectacular as the winery." He tried to get eight other wineries to cooperate with him in building a nine-hole golf course, but couldn't put a deal together. Nonetheless that remains his goal. "If you want to be a destination site in tourism, you need a golf course and an airstrip for private planes," he says.

Several places in Mendoza are combining boutique wineries, restaurants, and lodging with lots of services but high prices. The one attracting the most attention is the **Cavas Wine Lodge**, located in the heart of a 35-acre vineyard down a bumpy road 20 miles south of downtown Mendoza. The husband-and-wife team Martín Rigal and Cecilia Diaz Chuit started it in 2005. He has an advanced degree in marketing from the University of California, Berkeley, while she once worked for such top hotel operations as Hyatt, Relais & Châteaux, and the Luxury Collection by Starwood. The lodge has fourteen stand-alone adobe bungalows, a small restaurant with a long wine list, and a spa that provides Malbec-seed body wraps. All the units have a terrace with a view of the Andes. Cavas has become a favorite for honeymooners and Hollywood stars, who both demand privacy.

Finca y Bodega Carlos Pulenta in Vistalba, also south of the city of Mendoza, has created an even more exclusive facility that has only two guest rooms. Visitors are treated as guests of the winery and get lots of pampering. The restaurant La Bourgogne has a French chef who manages other locations in South America and also offers cooking courses.

Bodegas Salentein, a still young winery located 60 miles south of Mendoza city, has eight rooms plus a dining room located in a lodge that overlooks Pinot Noir and Merlot vineyards. Salentein offers a range of outdoor activities from cycling to horseback riding. The modernistic facility is efficient, though a little cold.

In May 2008, a New York City–based investment company called the InvestProperty Group announced a 1,838-acre project near San Rafael, 150 miles south of Mendoza city. It's slated to take five years to build, but if it indeed makes it off the ground it could have a major impact on the area. The resort's plans include a luxury hotel, two eighteen-hole golf courses, two hundred luxury homes with vineyards, and a polo field. It will be built around **Algodon Wine Estates**, a boutique winery.

The mass tourism site in Mendoza is the **Familia Zuccardi Winery** in Maipú, on the outskirts of Mendoza city. The family has been in

Argentina since the late nineteenth century. Winery founder Alberto Zuccardi started out in the irrigation business, developing a new technology that opened more desert areas to vines. He planted his first vineyard in 1963 as a way of proving his system worked. His son, José Alberto Zuccardi, has become the winery's driving force, and they now produce some 1.2 million cases annually.

Zuccardi substantially increased its wine tourism two years ago, hiring a specialized staff and creating many new programs. An annual tasting in November, its biggest event of the year, draws 4,000 people, and the winery attracts about 50,000 visitors annually. On most days, though, it feels overcrowded. The retail store is packed so chock-a-block with merchandise that it resembles a Middle Eastern bazaar. Not just one T-shirt is enough; Zuccardi has a plethora of them in various styles, shapes, and colors. It offers a two-and-a-half-hour bike tour of the vineyards that includes stops at four spots, each planted with a different grape variety. Other programs give people hands-on experiences in the vineyards picking grapes and pruning vines; participants get a T-shirt at the end. Zuccardi also has cooking courses, a garden for picnics, and a sit-down restaurant that seats eighty, where visitors can watch the chef working outdoors over an open fire. On weekends there is afternoon tea. Zuccardi recently launched a line of olive oils. Hovering over all this much like the Mad Hatter of *Alice in Wonderland* is José Alberto Zuccardi. He's here, he's there, he's everywhere in the restaurant, in the shop, in the reception area. It's mass marketing, though, rather than a personal wine experience.

Some of Argentina's wines reach the highest international levels, but wine tourism there is still underdeveloped and struggling. As a result, Mendoza for the near term is likely to remain a destination for adventurous bargain hunters.

DIARY OF A WINE TOURIST

JANUARY 17

AN *ASADO* IN THE DESERT

In Texas they call it a barbecue; in South Africa it's a *braai*; in Argentina the name is an *asado*. In all those places the event is a social ritual where family members, business acquaintances, and strangers get together for an outdoor meal and some camaraderie, with each country adding its own unique local color.

Early in the afternoon some twenty people gathered in the Uco Valley, an hour-and-a-half drive south of Mendoza, for an *asado*. The event, hosted by The Vines of Mendoza, was to take place at its Private Vineyard Estates.

At about two in the afternoon, our cars began appearing on a well-worn paved road across the street from a sign for Finca Chacayes, a vineyard started by François and André Lurton from Bordeaux. Only some five miles away, Michel Rolland has his Clos de los Siete vineyards.

Eventually, a caravan began winding its way down a bumpy, makeshift road that had been whacked out of the desert to provide access to the The Vines of Mendoza property. Waiting for the group were Dave Garrett and Michael Evans, two of the three founders of Private Vineyard Estates. The third, Pablo Giménez, was on vacation. The two quickly began talking about their venture, pointing out the vineyards that had already been planted as well as the computer-controlled, drip-irrigation system that keeps the plants alive in the harsh desert environment. Perhaps the most excited people were Graham and Caroline Alexander, a British couple living in Morristown, New Jersey, who had recently bought, sight-unseen, an 8-acre vineyard. Francisco Evangelista, the project's viticulturist, explained that he was irrigating the plants three times a week and giving them small amounts of phosphorous and nitrogen fertilizer to get them started, but would cut that out shortly since he wants to grow the vines as naturally as possible in the ancient desert soil.

After a few minutes of a soft sales pitch under the hot sun, people piled into trucks and began making their way up and down rocky gullies to the place where the *asado* would be held. At one spot, visitors stopped to examine the ground where an earthmover had scooped up a hunk of dirt to reveal the subsoil of a future vineyard. The rock-strewn mixture of some 25 percent loam and 75 percent sand had a little clay and compact layers of earth, which meant the land would have good drainage. To a layman's eye, though, it looked like a swatch of earth that only a viticulturist could love and reminded me of John Locke's description of the soil he saw in 1677 in the vineyard at Château Haut-Brion in Bordeaux, which he thought was "scarce fit to bear anything."

When the group finally reached the *ramada,* a tentlike structure made of tall wooden poles and covered with a canopy of branches, a crew of three Argentines was already preparing the meal on an outdoor cement stove. One chef, wearing a baseball cap, turned huge hunks of beef and pork on the grill with a long fork, while his two assistants, a man in his twenties wearing a broad-rimmed, brown gaucho hat, and a young boy wearing a similar hat made of straw, looked on. Off to the side were a half dozen saddled horses.

Under the *ramada* was a long table with wooden plates laid out along each side. Since this was an *asado* in a vineyard-to-be, it was only appropriate that a wine bar had already been set up at one end of the table. It contained a variety of Argentine wines ranging from such whites as Torrontés and Sauvignon Blanc to reds dominated, naturally, by Argentina's prized Malbec. The wine was served in elegant large glasses more suited for a formal dinner party than an *asado* in the desert. Dave Garrett was a diligent, but busy, host assuring that no one's glass went empty for long.

Off to the side of the tent an Argentine gently strummed a guitar and sang softly, as the crowd made new friends or exchanged warm *abrazos* with old ones. The group included a young American couple from New York City, nervous because the wife was pregnant, as well as a Dutchman who had been working in Argentina for several years.

One of the guests was Santiago Achaval, the cofounder of the Achaval-Ferrer winery, who had signed on to be the consulting winemaker for the project in exchange for 8 acres of vineyard, where he had planted Syrah grapes in hopes of adding that variety to his already established portfolio of Malbecs and Bordeaux blends.

After about a half hour of mingling, everyone sat down for the meal. I took the last free seat. Then the cooks began making their way up and down the table offering guests pieces of beef and pork from piled-high platters. First came the rib pieces and then the filets. Nothing fancy, no sauces. Just delicious pieces of Argentine meat. Accompanying it were large bowls of salads, one mixed and one simply sliced tomatoes, and plates of potatoes and onions that had also been grilled on the barbecue.

As the guests ate, the wines continued to flow, but now were all reds. After three passes of meat and vegetables, the prized wine of the day was opened. It was a magnum of 2002 Achaval-Ferrer Quimera, a blend of Malbec, Cabernet Sauvignon, and Merlot. After glasses were filled, Santiago Achaval explained that the wine was still a little young, but interesting nonetheless. I thought it was outstanding, with an intensity of fruit that complemented the rich meat. The supercilious Dutchman seemed to be trying to show off by complaining that the wine was a little tannic. Santiago graciously agreed and explained that magnums age more slowly than regular-size bottles of wine and that would disappear with a little more bottle aging. After his wine had been acclaimed, Achaval showed himself to be a man of many talents by picking up the guitar and playing a few songs.

A little later, host Dave Garrett offered everyone the chance to go back across the desert to their cars on horseback or in trucks. The Alexanders were anxious to see their vineyard, but decided to get there by different means. Graham joined a group of five who slowly rode off on horses toward the mountains now turning purple in the late afternoon sun, while Caroline went by truck. Less than a half hour later, the couple met up again at their vineyard. There was nothing yet to distinguish their rows of Malbec and Torrontés grapes from the others, but the couple knew they were theirs. Graham had told me earlier that this had been his "mad-money" investment, and he was obviously proud of it. As the Alexanders posed for a picture amid the two-month-old vines, they looked as happy as a bride and groom on their wedding day. The first vintage of their wine will be in 2010.

CHAPTER FIVE

Colchagua Valley, Chile

All countries are prisoners of their geography, left only to play the hand nature dealt them. Perhaps no country experiences this more so than Chile. Santiago, Chile, is less than an hour's flight from Mendoza, Argentina. But despite their common Spanish heritage, the two countries could hardly be more diverse. Argentina has spread itself across much of a continent, while Chile is a nation in the shape of a giraffe's neck: elegant and lovely, but you can't help wondering how it works. Chile is packed into an area that on average is only about 100 miles wide, but 2,600 miles long. In order to go overland from large sections of Chile to the country's southern tip, travelers have to go through Argentina.

Chile's isolation is integral to the country's history and helped form its national character. Most of the population, as well as the wine areas, are boxed in on all sides. On the west there is the cold Southern Pacific Ocean. On the east stand the mighty Andes. To the north is the Atacama Desert, the second driest spot on earth, fifty times drier than California's Death Valley, and to the south is Antarctica. That isolation has had some benefits. For example, phylloxera, which devastated vineyards in Europe during the late nineteenth century, never reached Chile, although it affected other parts of South America.

Chile's wine country lies in fourteen regions, which are mostly valleys in the center of the country from the Elqui Valley in the north to the Malleco Valley in the south. New wine areas, though, are still being discovered. The valleys are high, luminous, and cool in the north; fertile, warm, and sunny in the central part of the country; and cool and influenced by the Pacific Ocean and foggy mornings in coastal areas. As a result, Chile has a plethora of microclimates, and each region produces a wine slightly different from that made in the neighboring area. Historically, the Maipo Valley near Santiago was the heart of Chile's wine country, and its vineyards in the warm shadows of the Andes produce full-bodied, red wines. This is the home to **Concha y Toro**, the country's largest wine producer.

Starting in the 1850s, Chile enjoyed an economic boom thanks to nitrate and copper mining. Wealthy Chileans, who made fortunes in mining, enjoyed the good life, and part of that meant going to France to buy the best wine technology, equipment, and vines to replace the low-quality wines the Spanish conquistadores had given the country in the sixteenth century.

Chilean wine, though, was rarely exported because it didn't have to be, thanks to high domestic consumption. As a result, the industry stagnated during the late nineteenth and most of the twentieth centuries. In the 1930s, Chile had its version of Prohibition, when the government attempted to fight alcoholism by putting restrictions on new vineyard plantings, which set back the country's wineries. By the middle of the twentieth century, Chile had become the wine-producing country history had forgotten. The only people who drank Chilean wine were Chileans, and wineries had no incentive to improve it.

Concha y Toro was a sleepy maker of inexpensive, low-quality wines until the late 1950s, when a group of young entrepreneurs led by Agustín Huneeus took over the company and focused on exporting inexpensive wines called Chilean Riesling or Chilean Burgundy, even though they were made with few, if any, Riesling or Pinot Noir grapes. The wines were similar to the basic whites and reds that California's Gallo and Paul Masson produced at the time. Given Chile's low wages and ideal growing conditions, Concha y Toro was able to sell its wines at rock-bottom prices and soon captured an important U.S. market share. Many other Chilean producers later followed Concha y Toro's lead, but that cheapwine strategy eventually hurt all Chilean wineries when they tried to improve both their wines and their image.

During the 1960s and 1970s, the Chilean wine industry, along with the rest of the country's economy, was virtually destroyed by a long period of economic mismanagement. Left-leaning governments in the 1960s started nationalizing land holdings in the name of agrarian reform, a development that dramatically increased after the 1970 election of the Socialist Salvador Allende. During his three-year minority government, the country slipped into economic and social chaos. General Augusto Pinochet's 1973 coup d'état toppled Allende, but the military during its first decade in power ruled the country by brutal political repression and iron-fisted economic controls. Some of the country's leading wine people left the country. Agustín Huneeus, for example, quit Concha y Toro to run the wine operations for Seagram, the Canadian hard-liquor company, and eventually drifted into winemaking in California.

Then in the early 1980s, the generals turned economic policymaking over to a group of young economists who became known as the Chicago Boys because they followed the free-market and export-oriented policies advocated by the University of Chicago's Milton Friedman. The Chicago Boys recognized that their country had a great opportunity in wine exports, but the wine business in those days was still dominated by a few large producers such as Concha y Toro, Santa Rita, San Pedro, and Santa Carolina, which were more interested in the quantity of production rather than its quality.

The ascendance of the Chicago Boys, though, coincided with the arrival of a new generation of wine producers who put quality first. The forerunner of the group was Spain's Miguel Torres, who was already improving the wines his family made in Catalonia. He had first become aware of the wine potential in Chile from that country's Alejandro Parot, when both of them studied enology in Dijon, France. Torres in late 1978 made his first exploratory visit to Chile, and the following January bought a rundown winery in Curicó that a bank was about to take over. Torres spent heavily on new technology that most Chilean wineries had never seen and introduced new enology techniques, proving that better wines could be made in Chile.

Torres's initiatives were not lost on Chilean winery owners, and by the late 1980s a renaissance was under way. The leader of the movement was Alfonso Chadwick Errázuriz, a national polo star, who in 1982 took charge of the family winery **Viña Errázuriz**. It had been one of the leading quality producers in the nineteenth century, but had fallen into decline during the 1960s and 1970s. The company's main property is the Don Maximiano Estate in the Aconcagua Valley some 100 miles north of Santiago, which Don Maximiano Errázuriz, a mining tycoon of Basque background, established in 1870. The Chadwicks, an English family whose heritage goes back to the Domesday Book of William the Conqueror, married into the Errázuriz clan in 1909. Only a year after taking over Errázuriz, Alfonso asked his son Eduardo, who was then twenty-three and had just finished his engineering studies, to join the business as managing director. Along with all other Chilean wineries, Errázuriz was badly outdated with antiquated equipment and Italian pergola-style vineyards, where the grapes grew high off the ground, which made harvesting easy but didn't produce the best wine.

Father and son soon set off on a trip to France to catch up on developments in wine from such experts as the famed Émile Peynaud at the University of Bordeaux. Alfonso carried along with him a well-thumbed copy of Peynaud's classic treatise on winemaking *Le goût du vin*. Eduardo stayed on in Bordeaux and took courses in enology and visited other French wine regions. He returned from his studies and travels determined to drive the company into the forefront of international wine with new equipment and new enology practices. In 1993, at the death of his father, Eduardo took over the family business.

Exports and global competition were Eduardo Chadwick's guiding stars as he expanded his company's vineyards and sales. Errázuriz today exports 97 percent of its production. He also did two joint ventures with Robert Mondavi, both in 1995. The first, modeled after the one Mondavi already had with Baron Philippe de Rothschild that resulted in Opus One, was to create a premium red Bordeaux blend. Mondavi and Chadwick planted Bordeaux varieties in a self-contained hillside vineyard estate in the Aconcagua Valley. They called the wine Seña. The second was a more popularly priced line of wines called Caliterra produced in the Colchagua Valley, where Mondavi replaced Agustín Huneeus as the partner. In 2004, at the time Constellation Brands bought the Robert Mondavi Winery, Chadwick bought out Mondavi's share in both joint ventures. Eduardo also looked closely at Britain, his largest market. In 2002, and as part of the family's emotional healing after the tragic death of his young son Juan Eduardo, Eduardo moved his wife and four daughters to Oxford, where he started the Master of

Wine course and directed a major British sales offensive. The family lived in Oxford for two years before returning to Chile.

Despite the international success of his wines, Chadwick remained unhappy that they were not achieving world recognition. He now produces four ultra-premium wines: Don Maximiano, a Bordeaux blend; Kai, a Carmenère; La Cumbre, a Shiraz; and Viñedo Chadwick, a Cabernet Sauvignon. In an attempt to obtain the stature he thought they deserved, Chadwick organized a wine tasting in Berlin at the Ritz-Carlton Hotel in January 2004. With the help of Britain's Steven Spurrier, who staged the original Paris Tasting between French and California wines that put the Napa Valley on the map, Chadwick staged a blind tasting of sixteen wines—six Chilean, six French, and four Italian. All were from the 2000 and 2001 vintages. The wines were all top quality: Château Lafite, Château Latour, and Château Margaux from France; Sassicaia and Solaia from Italy; and his own three top Bordeaux-style wines. The thirty-six judges included European wine journalists as well as wine buyers and sommeliers.

Spurrier was sitting next to Chadwick during the tasting and later recounted the Chilean's reaction when the results were revealed: "When they announced that his wines had placed fourth, his relief was obvious. He wasn't even paying attention when they gave out the first and second places. When the first was announced and it was his, he could not believe it." In Berlin the 2000 Viñedo Chadwick came in first, the 2001 Seña second, a 2000 Château Lafite third, while the 2000 Château Margaux and a 2000 Seña tied for fourth. The event was little noted by the American wine press, but was big news in Europe and was soon dubbed the Berlin Tasting, although it did not have the historical impact of the original Paris Tasting.

The Berlin Tasting with some variations was later repeated in Brazil, Tokyo, Toronto, Copenhagen, Seoul, and Beijing with consistently excellent results for Chadwick. A Chilean wine did not win each time, but his wines always rated well. Chadwick was starting, albeit slowly, to raise the *renommé* of Chilean wines.

Chadwick's original home base was the traditional Maipo Valley south of Santiago, but in recent years he has been planting more and more vineyards in the Aconcagua Valley, where the Don Maximiano

Estate is located. Other winemakers are also searching out new areas. Pablo Morandé, who for twenty years was the winemaker for Concha y Toro and in 1996 founded **Viña Morandé**, did the preliminary work that recognized the potential of the Casablanca Valley, which is located halfway between Santiago and the port city of Valparaíso. The advent of drip irrigation made grape growing possible in the area for the first time, and it turned out to be an ideal place for such cool-climate wines as Chardonnay, Pinot Noir, and Sauvignon Blanc. Viña Morandé now makes a half million cases a year.

Casablanca has also developed into a good location for wine tourism because of its proximity to Santiago. Several wineries followed Morandé and set up in Casablanca, which is only a forty-five-minute drive from downtown Santiago on a major highway and is an easy stop for people escaping the city on weekends and vacations for the cooler, cleaner coastal areas around Valparaíso. That city has become a favorite port of call for cruise ships from the United States, and their operators now bring busloads of tourists to Casablanca wineries for lunch and wine tastings. The second most visited winery in Chile after Concha y Toro on the outskirts of Santiago is **Veramonte**, a Casablanca winery owned by Agustín Huneeus after his work at Concha y Toro and in American wine ventures.

While the Maipo Valley has more and older wineries and the Casablanca Valley benefits from its proximity to Santiago, the Colchagua Valley has become Chile's main wine tourism center. The person behind that development is Carlos Cardoen of **Viña Santa Cruz**, one of the world's most controversial businessmen.

Cardoen's grandfather, who hailed from the Belgian village of Izegem, was a metallurgy engineer who went to Chile in 1914 to deliver some railroad equipment; but when World War I broke out, the German army invaded his country and took over his company. Since he was no longer employed and couldn't go home, he became a Chilean citizen. Carlos was born in the small town of Santa Cruz in the Colchagua Valley, where his own father was also an engineer. The grandson followed family tradition, doing undergraduate work in metallurgy before pursuing graduate studies in the United States on a scholarship at the University of Utah, where he received a Ph.D. in engineering. After finishing his degree, Carlos in 1977 started a small company making mine explosives for his country's copper and iron industries and seemed to be headed for a routine business career.

As with so many things in Chile, General Pinochet's 1973 coup changed all that. In response, the United States in 1976 slapped a weapons embargo on the country. The Chilean army was worried about the impact of that embargo on national defense because of a border dispute with Argentina, and decided to build up its own armaments industry. In 1978, the military asked Cardoen to get into the production of army hardware, and within a few years, Industrias Cardoen was one of the country's biggest defense contractors, selling armored vehicles, bombs, and infantry weapons primarily to the Chilean government. At its peak, it employed one thousand workers and had five factories in Chile.

When the Iran-Iraq War broke out in 1980, Cardoen traveled to Baghdad to see if he could drum up some business. No officials would see him, but he left behind some of his brochures. The ploy worked because the Iraqis were interested in one particular piece of Cardoen matériel: cluster bombs, which were a prime weapon to use against Iran's tactic of sending waves of soldiers against Iraqi forces. The strategy left thousands of Iranians dead on the battlefield, but Tehran still captured some precious ground. Cardoen's cluster bombs set off 240 bomblets that killed soldiers with bloody efficiency over more than 50,000 square yards.

According to a U.S. government official, Cardoen between 1984 and 1988 sold $200 million worth of cluster bombs to Iraq. Others maintain he pedaled $400 million worth of cluster bombs to various countries. There's a picture of a smiling Cardoen and Saddam Hussein taken at this time, and the Chilean was later quoted as saying, "Honestly, he seemed to me a fairly balanced man, very well informed and with a great elegance and dignity. He gave off the impression that he was not a man who acted without full information."

The United States was technically neutral in the Iran-Iraq War, but the Reagan Administration was covertly pro-Iraq because it felt an Iran victory would upset the balance of power in the region and make Iran an even greater problem for the United States after the end of the long American hostage crisis. So Washington began a program to make sure Saddam Hussein could get the sophisticated arms needed to fight more effectively.

Carlos Cardoen did not get out of the armaments business after the Iran-Iraq War ended in 1988, but as time went by he seemed more interested in wine deals than arms deals. He told me it was in 1988 that he started trying to build up wine tourism in the Colchagua Valley. He obviously has enough money to maintain a pleasant lifestyle. He flies his personal helicopter each day between one of his two homes, one at the beach and one in Santiago, and his winery in the Colchagua Valley. He said he is interested in his country's history and wants to build up the economy of his hometown. "I have a passion to change dreams into three-dimensional objects. We have been efficient in improving life, but we forget that we came here to be happy. That is my aim—to be happy." Cardoen may be sounding a little more philosophical these days because of a recent bout with colon cancer.

Cardoen says he was always interested in history and over the years picked up things when he saw that they were going to be thrown out. Old machines particularly interest him. By his count, he had collected some fifteen thousand objects by the late 1980s and decided to make those the backbone of a museum in his hometown, the sleepy Santa Cruz (pop. 20,000). The Colchagua Museum, which is now housed in the town's main square, is the largest private collection of pre-Columbian, colonial, and modern Chilean artifacts.

At about the same time, he also got into wine. "Chile doesn't have the ancestors or the monuments of other countries such as Mexico or Peru. What we have to show is our tradition and our natural beauty," he told me. "We had to polish whatever we had and present it in an excellent way that would bring visitors here. Wine is an important part of that."

After talking in the late 1980s about Chile's wine potential with Spain's Miguel Torres and with executives at Concha y Toro, Cardoen started investing in wine ventures with an emphasis on the Colchagua

Valley. The local *Ruta del Vino* (Wine Route) was already in existence, but he pushed the concept further by hiring a full-time director and establishing an office in downtown Santa Cruz, where visitors could get information and arrange tours.

Next came a local hotel, since it is impossible to have wine tourism if people don't have a place to stay. "Santa Cruz was just a little town with no hotel, no nothing," he recalls. When he showed his father plans for a forty-room colonial adobe-style hotel with all the amenities found at international hotels, the father counseled him, "Son, why don't you start with ten rooms?" But Carlos went ahead with the grander plan and has since expanded it. The hotel is located in the town's main square, right across the street from the museum. When I visited Santa Cruz, work was underway for a new casino being built near the hotel, another magnet to attract tourists.

The **Colchagua Wine Train** is also a Cardoen project. Among the things he had collected was a coal-fired railroad steam engine, built in Britain in 1913. Local train routes had all been abandoned, but Cardoen began lobbying to start a wine train between San Fernando and Santa Cruz, on tracks no longer in use. One of the people he was pestering was presidential candidate Ricardo Lagos. At a victory reception in 2000, the president-elect told Cardoen, "Now that I'm president, I bet you'll keep bugging me about your train." After major work on the railroad cars and track, the *Tren del Vino* trips started in April 2004.

In 2003, Cardoen opened the doors of his Viña Santa Cruz winery in the town of Lolol, about 10 miles outside Santa Cruz. At many Chilean wineries there are armed guards on duty, and visitors sometimes feel like they're breaking into a prison. Viña Santa Cruz winery, though, has a welcoming Spanish mission-style main entrance. The 2,471-acre property has only 494 acres currently in production, and most of the grapes are sold off to other wineries because the winery now is only making about 30,000 bottles annually of Cabernet Sauvignon, Carmenère, Syrah, Malbec, and Petit Verdot. Winemaker José Miguel Sotomayor explained to me that the winery is still ramping up business and learning what its vineyards can produce. The wines are pretty standard fare. Viña Santa Cruz is not currently exporting any wines, but plans eventually to do so.

Carlos Cardoen and I spent almost half a day talking and touring his winery properties and having lunch. During that time he never refused to answer a question. After a formal interview in a conference room, we went for a winery tour, which started with a ride on a Swiss-made cable car that took us from the valley floor to an exhibition area at the top of a nearby mountain. The common denominator of the displays is that everything interests Cardoen. The most extensive part is devoted to Chile's three cultures: indigenous Indian, colonial, and Easter Island. Also on the mountaintop is an observatory, complete with a resident astronomer, and a small space museum that includes meteorites and an old Soviet space helmet. Before taking the cable car back down the mountain, Cardoen showed me with great pride his llama hut. With a light blue sweater draped over his shoulders and petting a llama, he was not exactly Hollywood's version of a merchant of death.

Elsewhere on his property Cardoen is building guesthouses. Modeled on the style of a Native Indian village, they will include ten to twelve buildings with three units each. Each building will have its own hot tub made out of a wine cask.

Over lunch I asked Cardoen about the charges that he had armed Saddam Hussein. Obviously replying with practiced answers to questions posed to him many times before, he explained that he "made explosives for Iraq and exported them as long as Saddam was a good guy." He admitted further that he sold weapons to Iraq during the Iran War, but "none after Saddam invaded Kuwait." In a final statement in his own defense, Cardoen said matter-of-factly, "I only did what the Americans were doing at the time."

♉ ♉ ♉

While Viña Santa Cruz is still getting its wines up to international standards, several other Colchagua wineries are already there. One of the best is **Viña Montes**. In the late 1980s, Aurelio Montes and Douglas Murray were both working for Viña San Pedro, Chile's second largest wine producer. Montes was production manager, and Murray export manager. The company was having serious financial problems, and the two didn't think management was going in the right direction by making bulk wines. International market research convinced Montes and Murray that people around the globe were drinking less, but better, wine; and so sales of low-quality wines would be declining. The two men thought that the future for a Chilean winery was to concentrate on producing quality wine for the export market. So in 1987, they left San Pedro and with two other partners started Montes, using mainly bought grapes and producing the wine in rented facilities. Their initial investment capital was just $62,000.

Aurelio Montes was particularly impressed by grapes he bought that came from the hilly section of Colchagua known as Apalta. He thought its mountainsides, where the slopes are as steep as 49°, would be an ideal place to plant a vineyard. That kind of thinking went against four hundred years of Chilean tradition of planting vines on valley floors. Nonetheless, the owners of the young winery bought land in Apalta and planted it with such Bordeaux varieties as Cabernet Sauvignon, Merlot, Petit Verdot, Cabernet Franc, and Carmenère. Aurelio Montes also planted Syrah, a Rhône Valley grape not then grown in Chile. The winery soon became famous for a wide range of quality wines, from inexpensive ones sold under the Montes Limited Selection or Classic Series labels to the premium Montes Alpha, and the iconic Montes Alpha M, a Bordeaux blend with 80 percent Cabernet Sauvignon; Purple Angel, which has 92 percent Carmenère; and Folly, a 100 percent Syrah.

After making its wine at other people's facilities for years, Montes in 2000 decided to build its own winery at Apalta. The company excavated the area so that much of the winery is underground. It was also designed in accordance with the Chinese practice of feng shui, which provides a balance of energies to a place and is believed to give success to those living there. Water, important in feng shui, flows through the winery starting at the entrance. The Montes barrel room must be the only one in the world where Gregorian chants are used to help the wines age. When I played back my taped interview with Douglas Murray, I could hear the melodic chanting in the background. The Montes winery has become one of the most popular stops on the Colchagua *Ruta del Vino*, receiving some 10,000 visitors each year.

Several French wine families have recently become interested in the

Colchagua region. French winemakers, who venture abroad with some hesitation, have long felt comfortable in Chile because of the country's involvement with France going back to the nineteenth century. The first French grapes were planted in Colchagua in 1850.

In November 1988, Domaines Barons de Rothschild, the wing of the family headed by Eric de Rothschild, owner of Château Lafite Rothschild, bought a 50 percent share of **Viña Los Vascos**, a winery that had been owned for more than two centuries by the Echenique and Eyzaguirre families. Rothschild eventually got a majority share when the original partners sold their shares. It has upgraded the facilities, expanded production, and put a French stamp on the winemaking style. The winery, though, has never made a serious attempt to attract visitors.

Another big French name investing in Colchagua was Marnier-Lapostolle, the family that owns both Grand Marnier liqueur and Château de Sancerre in the Loire Valley. Alexandra Marnier-Lapostolle, starting in the late 1980s, directed a search to diversify the family holdings, first looking in Europe at Spain, Portugal, and Italy but without finding the right property. Then Bordeaux wine consultant Michel Rolland, whom she had hired to help her, suggested Chile. She liked what she saw both in price and quality in the Colchagua Valley, and Marnier-Lapostolle in 1994 bought controlling interest in Viña Manquehue, whose wines were sold mainly in the Chilean market. The new owners changed the winery's name to **Casa Lapostolle** and made an initial investment of $20 million to update and expand it. Rolland still consults on the winemaking. In 2003, the family bought out its Chilean partners and now owns the entire winery. Lapostolle makes wines at a variety of prices from its Cuvée Alexandre line in the $10–$20 range to Clos Apalta, its prestige blend of mainly Carmenère, at about $90. Apalta was the *Wine Spectator*'s 2008 Wine of the Year.

In 2006, Lapostolle opened a stunning ultramodern winery close to Montes that is attracting lots of visitors. Five of the seven levels of the winery are located underground, and there is a beautiful tasting area in the room where wine in barrels gets its second year of aging. Outside the storage room architects left exposed rock that weeps moisture and gives an unusual picture of the conditions in which the vines grow.

Also on the winery property are four guest cottages named after the four grapes that go into the winery's flagship wine Clos Apalta: Carmenère, Cabernet Sauvignon, Merlot, and Petit Verdot. Primarily designed as the place for Alexandra to stay during her five or so trips per year to Chile, the guesthouses are now open to the public. She had a major hand in designing and furnishing them, and they are the most spectacular accommodations found in the world of wine. From the bar stocked with 150-year-old Grand Marnier to the cuisine made in a French style with a local touch, everything is top of the line. Alexandra normally stays in the Carmenère guesthouse. Guests are invited to have a predinner drink and then eat with family members who are present. Alexandra's husband, Cyril de Bournet, is a frequent visitor. The attractions beyond food and wine include horseback riding, a hike to a nearby Inca ruin, and a massage at the spa. Wine, though, remains the main attraction that brings guests to Casa Lapostolle.

Several smaller wineries in Colchagua have also built accommodations that can host a few guests. They all provide an intimate wine experience that often gives the opportunity to meet and perhaps have a meal with either the winemaker or the owner. None are as spectacular as Casa Lapostolle, but they are usually well equipped and offer an inside view of Chilean culture. Most serve meals that have a definite Chilean flavor.

Viña Casa Silva near San Fernando is an old winery that at the end of 2004 turned a family farmhouse into a seven-room hotel. It also has a restaurant that serves many fine local dishes, especially fish. Everything about the place makes you feel you are living in nineteenth-century Chile. This region is particularly proud of its cowboy or *huaso* tradition, and Casa Silva has a large facility for horses for both rodeos and polo. From September to April, there are weekly rodeos, and its polo team competes nationally. The winery is now into the fifth generation of ownership, but until the 1990s it produced only bulk wine. Now it is investing both time and money to improve quality with a goal of building exports.

Viña Bisquertt on the outskirts of Santa Cruz, which sells most of its wines under the Casa La Joya label, recently built a small guesthouse that is surrounded by magnificent gardens. Bisquertt has perhaps the most beautiful tasting room in Chile, exuding elegance thanks to a heavy use of wood. The winery also has an extensive collection of old carriages that have been restored to their former glory.

Colchagua only recently rolled out the red carpet to wine tourism. Just a decade ago, the region had few international hotels or good restaurants. It now has the facilities to go with the big and bold red wines that first made it famous. More and more fans of its wines are likely to be making a pilgrimage soon to the vineyards of Apalta.

DIARY OF A WINE TOURIST

JANUARY 26

A TRIP ON THE *TREN DEL VINO*

The crowds started arriving at the railroad station in San Fernando, Chile, shortly after ten on a Saturday morning. They came in cars, minivans, and buses. People were there to take Colchagua's *Tren del Vino* on the ninety-minute trip from San Fernando to Santa Cruz. Soon the crowd of people speaking French, German, and English as well as Spanish was gawking at the train's engine, which was billowing black smoke into the air. Children happily hopped into the engineer's seat and smiled as their parents snapped pictures. A group wearing green John Deere baseball caps was part of a corporate outing. The locomotive had lined up behind it three cars appropriately named after the valley's three principal grape varieties—Carmenère, Merlot, and Cabernet Sauvignon. In the back of the engine car, two young men, their faces already black with coal dust, were shoveling the black rocks to feed the little engine that could. The cost of the trip, including wines plus a platter of grapes, raisins, local cheeses, and empanadas or stuffed pastries that would be served after departure: $50.

Right on time, the train chugged, chugged, chugged its way slowly out of the station, with its whistle screaming in a joyful celebration of local pride. Only minutes after departure, the train's sommelier, Juan Carlos Hernandez, dressed smartly in a white shirt, burgundy tie and matching burgundy vest, began passing through the dining car with a selection of wines to go with the local foods already on the table. All the wines served on the train come from the Colchagua Valley. For this trip Viu Manent supplied most of them. The first wine was a crisp 2006 Sauvignon Blanc, one of the few white wines produced in this normally red-wine region. Soon after came a 2006 Carmenère Reserve, also from Viu Manent.

While the wines were being served, César Diaz, who has been working on the Wine Train since it began service in April 2004, gave a short talk over the loudspeaker in both English and Spanish about the valley's wineries and wines. Then Diaz began working the train, going from table to table of the dining car chatting up the visitors as the carriages gently rocked from side to side. Out the train's open windows travelers could see vineyards and orchards flashing past even though the train was probably not going more than 30 miles an hour. It passed vineyards with table grapes growing in the traditional style on pergolas about 5 feet above the ground.

After Diaz finished speaking, Ismael Carrasco, nicknamed Pelé, who had the body to play Santa Claus at Christmas, strummed a guitar and sang with *mucho gusto*. Fewer than half the people in the car understood the Spanish lyrics, but no one seemed to care. Pelé's enthusiasm carried the day.

The third wine, which came about an hour after departure, was a 2006 Viu Manent Malbec, which was accompanied by a plate of meat-filled empanadas. César Diaz sat down at my table and asked Juan Carlos Hernandez to pour him a glass of Malbec. Both proud Chileans told me Chile makes better Malbec than Argentina, even though their neighbors on the other side of the Andes are better known for it. While we sampled the Malbec, César gave me more information about the train and its history. The passenger cars were manufactured in Germany in 1923, but have been refurbished and painted burgundy. There was a staff of thirty aboard. Each Saturday about 150 people ride the train. Travelers are both tourists and local people, who get discounted tickets so they can also enjoy this trip into their rich history.

César was still at the table talking about the train like a proud papa discussing his children, when the fourth wine was poured: a 2006 Casa La Joya Cabernet Sauvignon Reserve made by the Viña Bisquertt winery. All the Colchagua wines served on the train, even this young Cabernet, had surprisingly soft tannins, which made them easy drinking. The wines were also confirmation of the old adage that wine tastes best when consumed where it's made. Sommelier Hernandez wasn't stingy with the wines, but he wasn't pouring too quickly either as the train rolled on toward Santa Cruz. People were jovial, yet no one appeared tipsy even after sampling four wines in an hour and a half.

Only five minutes behind schedule, the train pulled up in front of the simple yellow Santa Cruz railway station. There on the platform to greet the happy travelers was a local musical troop in traditional costume. One young man dressed in black played an accordion, while two men and a woman clapped sharply in unison. Off to the side, also in colorful dress with lots of reds and blues, were three young people, two boys and a girl perhaps eleven years old. As soon as the travelers piled out of the train, the trio went to work, stamping their feet to the music and dancing gracefully. The show stealer was a boy of perhaps five dressed like a *huaso,* the traditional Chilean cowboy, with a large, broad-brimmed, black felt hat. Performing the flirtatious *cueca,* which involves flicking a handkerchief at his partner in a flowered blue dress, the young boy soon had the crowd cheering. One of the women tourists rushed out to dance with him, and everyone else in the crowd wished they had the courage to join in, but were too shy. They simply smiled and clapped.

CHAPTER SIX

Margaret River, Australia

Located at the extreme southwestern end of Australia, closer to Singapore than to Melbourne, Margaret River was for centuries an almost abandoned piece of paradise. It has beautiful pristine beaches as well as dark, dense forests of karri and jarrah trees, and a moderate climate that's not too hot, not too cold, but just right. The region stretches some 75 miles from the lighthouse at Cape Naturaliste in the north to the lighthouse at Cape Leeuwin in the south and is about 15 miles wide. The town of Margaret River is the most prominent one in the area that's made up of two shires or counties, and a river named Margaret flows through it and empties into the Indian Ocean.

Until recently, Margaret River was more popular with magpies than human beings. After World War I, a grateful Britain thanked the Aussies who had fought in deadly Flanders fields by offering them 100 acres of land in Western Australia, promoting Margaret River as a biblical "land of milk and honey." Along with the land, emigrants also got an ax, a wooden shed with a dirt floor, and a cow. Unfortunately, most of them knew little about farming and soon lost the land, the ax, and the cow.

Enough settlers, though, arrived to start a timber boom by cutting down ancient trees, but deforestation ended that after a short time. Perth, the capital of Western Australia, was 170 miles north, too far away to be much of a market for farmers, who scratched out a living growing "stone fruit," the generic name for peaches, plums, and apricots that have pits Britons and Australians call stones. A few farmers grazed herds of cows, but for a long time they could not ship whole milk to Perth and had to produce low-priced butterfat. As late as the 1950s, the Australian government was still trying to entice people to emigrate there with the same "milk and honey" pitch. Advertisements also promised that teachers would come to isolated settlers in the bush and teach foreigners English. About the only local amusement in those days, though, was driving along a gravel path named Caves Road and shooting kangaroos or "'roos," as the Aussies called them.

The first outsiders to discover the isolated place in the 1950s were surfers in search of the perfect wave. Surfing was best at the point where the Margaret River reaches the ocean, and surfers could sometimes catch a wave that seemed to carry them forever. Waves were both powerful and consistent because of the thousands of miles of uninterrupted ocean between Africa and Australia, and rides could sometimes last for 2 miles. Boys unable to buy surfboards happily hopped on bicycles and pedaled out to sparsely occupied beaches to try their luck at body surfing. When they got the money to buy a board, the sport became all-consuming.

In the mid-1950s, a few doctors bought vacation homes in Margaret River. Dr. Bill Pannell, who lived in Perth, and Dr. Tom Cullity, a cardiologist in Perth, bought land for a weekend retreat from the pressures of their demanding practices. Kevin Cullen, who studied medicine in Melbourne and his wife, Diana, whom everyone called Di, had lived in Tasmania before becoming a pediatrician and a general practitioner in Busselton, a town at the northern end of the region. In 1956, Cullen bought 100 acres of land at the beach for £100 (US $280), and built what the family called his "fishing shack" on a small lot near the beach. In his spare time, Cullen was a jazz pianist. He and Pannell later shared a medical practice.

The three doctors all enjoyed a regular glass of wine, usually a Bordeaux-style red, which they called claret in the British vernacular. They also all became interested in making wine. In doing so, they were continuing an old and treasured Australian tradition, going back to Christopher Rawson Penfold, a doctor who advocated the medicinal use of wines and in 1844 started Penfolds, Australia's most famous winery.

In the spring of 1965, Cullen approached John S. Gladstones, a Ph.D. lecturer in agronomy at the University of Western Australia, and asked if he recommended growing lupines on some pastureland the doctor owned north of Margaret River town. Gladstones was the country's foremost expert on the protein-rich grain of Mediterranean origin and was familiar with the area because he used to spend summers with his parents and grandparents in Augusta, on the southern tip of Margaret River, not far from the Cape Leeuwin lighthouse and near where the Southern and Indian oceans meet. Gladstones told Cullen he had written a paper, which was currently at the printer, on the great potential for growing grapes in exactly that same area where he wanted to grow lupines. "I visited Kevin and Di and advised them to forget lupines and plant vines instead," Gladstones recalls.

Two years earlier, Gladstones developed the thesis that the area around the village of Margaret River was similar to that of Bordeaux. Both Bordeaux and Margaret River had maritime-influenced weather as well as similar levels of rainfall at about 43 inches per year. In some ways, Margaret River was actually a better place than Bordeaux for growing grapes. It has almost no rainfall during harvest, unlike Bordeaux, where vintners worry about fall rains damaging their crops. Margaret River is also slightly warmer and sunnier, ripening fruit a little faster and better than Bordeaux. Gladstones had always remembered that one of the special summer pleasures in his youth was eating stone fruit, which had a wonderfully intense taste. He instinctively believed wine grapes would also do well there. An abbreviated version of Gladstones's research appeared in the December 1965 issue of the *Journal of the Australian Institute of Agricultural Science,* under the title "The Climate and Soils of South-Western Australia in Relation to Vine Growing." The full version was published in April 1966. In the papers, Gladstones spelled out his conclusions in the precise language of a scientist complete with supporting documents and statistical tables. His works also included detailed information on the exact types of soils that should be scouted out as ideal for vineyards. The two papers were basically road maps for anyone wishing to make wine in Margaret River.

In both papers Gladstones acknowledged that he had learned about the relationship between temperature and grape cultivation from Dr. Harold Olmo, a professor at the University of California, Davis, the leading American wine research institute. Olmo had spent eight months in 1955 at the University of Western Australia working on viticulture problems in the Swan Valley, 15 miles east of Perth. His campus office was across the hall from the lab where young Dr. Gladstones worked, and the two men talked about a variety of wine topics. Olmo told him about the groundbreaking work Davis professors Albert J. Winkler and Maynard Amerine had published in 1944, which identified potentially good wine regions in California on the basis of the number of days the average temperature exceeded 50°F. Before leaving Australia, Olmo wrote a paper using that methodology to predict that a more favorable area for vines than the Swan Valley that he had studied, where grapes often became overripe, was a cooler southern region around Mt. Barker and Rocky Gully.

Gladstones took Olmo's work one step further and speculated that the Margaret River region might be even better than the two sites the American had spotlighted. In his December 1965 paper Gladstones wrote, "For light dry table wines, very good conditions appear to exist in the cooler, southern part of the state, especially around Mt. Barker and Rocky Gully, and perhaps even more, in the area north and north-east of Margaret River." As soon as his studies were published, Gladstones sent copies to the Cullens and then later to Drs. Cullity and Pannell.

The three doctors jumped on Gladstones's work, and Kevin Cullen organized an evening meeting on July 21, 1966, at Busselton's Esplanade Hotel, where Gladstones explained his conclusions to a crowd of about a hundred people. A week before that, as a way to drum up attendees, the local paper published a letter from him outlining his thesis, and news of the meeting was later picked up by the *Western Australian Countryman* magazine. The reaction, though, from the Western Australian Department of Agriculture, whose minister was a teetotaler and wanted nothing to do with winemaking, was decidedly cool. The agency put out a skeptical press release with the headline: "Southwest Wine Growing 'Not Practical.'"

That, however, didn't stop the doctors, who were soon searching the area looking for soils similar to those Gladstones recommended, so they could plant vineyards. He spoke with all three, directing them to look for fields where marri trees, a type of eucalyptus then called red gum, grew. Gladstones thought a small area called Wilyabrup near Caves Road looked like an ideal place for growing Cabernet Sauvignon. All three doctors eventually planted Cabernet vineyards in the

Wilyabrup region and had excellent results. Bill Jamieson, the state viticulturist, also assisted the doctors, spending much time with them in defiance of his department's views. In the cooperative spirit of the day, Dr. Cullen helped Dr. Cullity find 8 acres that looked promising, which he bought for $75 an acre and then later added an additional 10 acres nearby.

Australia's stiff agriculture quarantine regulations made it difficult to import grape varieties, and the first experiments included only Cabernet Sauvignon and Riesling vines. In 1966, Dr. Cullity, with encouragement from the Cullens, did a small experimental planting, but because of disease problems it was abandoned.

The next spring, Cullity planted a new vineyard at the winery he called **Vasse Felix**. This was the first successful vineyard and winery in the region and set the scene for all that was to follow. Cullity planted 4 acres of Riesling, 2 acres of Cabernet Sauvignon, and several rows each of Malbec and Shiraz. The doctor, though, soon took out the Riesling and planted more Cabernet. He also trained a falcon to keep other birds from eating his grapes when they were ripe with sugar near harvest, a major problem that Margaret River winemakers still face. One day the falcon took to wing and was never seen again, except on the Vasse Felix wine label. Dr. Pannell in 1969 did the second commercial planting and called his property **Moss Wood Wines.**

The Cullens were more cautious at **Cullen Wines**. They wanted to see how other winemakers in other areas practiced their craft and spent a year in California, where Kevin also got a chance to hear jazz pianist Earl Hines. Back in Margaret River in 1971, the Cullens planted vines on 18 acres of their cattle and sheep farm. The first plants included Cabernet Sauvignon, Riesling, and Gewürztraminer. Di Cullen took over winemaking and became a leading advocate of Merlot, preferring a Cabernet Sauvignon and Merlot blend to the popular 100 percent Cabernet.

Wines from the three doctors soon grabbed national attention by winning medals at regional wine shows that put them up against the best wines from all over the country. The 1972 Vasse Felix Riesling won gold and silver medals at the Perth Royal Show. Moss Wood Cabernet Sauvignon earned three gold and two silver medals at the 1976 Perth

Show. Di Cullen also won a trophy for her 1977 Riesling at the Canberra Wine Show.

The Hohnen family of farmers broke the doctors' monopoly on winemaking in Margaret River when they started planting vineyards in the early 1970s west of the city, naming the property **Cape Mentelle**. The family's second son, David, studied winemaking at Fresno State College in California, and then worked a short stint at Clos du Val winery in the Napa Valley and at Taltarni Vineyards in eastern Australia before returning home to take over winemaking at Cape Mentelle. Hohnen's wines quickly added to Margaret River's reputation. In both 1983 and 1984, he won Australia's most prestigious wine award, the Jimmy Watson Trophy, given each year to the nation's best one-year-old red wine. The string of medals at regional shows and the Jimmy Watson awards proved that Margaret River, although one of Australia's smallest wine regions, could turn out some of the country's best wine. Today Margaret River produces only about 3 percent of Australian wine, but some 20 percent of premium wine.

♉ ♉ ♉

While the doctors and the Hohnens brought wine to Margaret River, it was Denis Horgan, a man who thinks big and dreams even bigger, who spearheaded the development of wine tourism. He started by building the fifth winery in Margaret River, **Leeuwin Estate**. The Horgan family in the mid-nineteenth century escaped the potato-famine in County Cork, Ireland, by emigrating to Australia. Denis's great-grandfather was the first practicing attorney in Perth, and in the 1880s became a member of one of the first parliaments for Western Australia. Denis, the oldest of four brothers, left school after his father died and got a job as an office boy in an accounting firm while studying at night to become an accountant. By his mid-twenties, Denis had started his own accounting practice in Perth, but he soon realized that the big money was not in charging billable hours, but in putting together mergers and acquisitions, a field in which he soon prospered.

One day in the late 1960s, Horgan got a call from a friend who said a Perth plumbing company was up for sale because the owner had cancer and was trying to get his financial affairs in order before he died. The friend knew Denis had long liked to surf in Margaret River. The plumbing business also owned 500 acres there that were used for cattle grazing. The owner had bought the land from five settlers who hadn't made a go of farming. Was Denis interested in a plumbing business that had a Margaret River farm tossed into the deal? Horgan and his wife, Trish, made a quick trip south to see the property, and she immediately fell in love with the region. Horgan seized the opportunity, and then sold the plumbing business for what he had paid for the whole company. So in essence, he got the farm for nothing.

Four years later, in 1972, Horgan hadn't done much with the property, which only had a shack on it where a foreman lived. But one day he got another call from a lawyer friend, who said that a winemaker from the Napa Valley named Robert Mondavi was in Perth and was interested in buying the Margaret River property. Horgan told the friend to ask Mondavi to come by and see him. While waiting for the American to arrive, Horgan sent his secretary to the State Library to do some quick research on this unknown visitor. She returned with information that Mondavi was a big California wine producer. Although the Australians didn't know it, he had undoubtedly heard from professors at the University of California, Davis, about the studies based on their research methods that showed Margaret River had great wine potential, which by then had already been proven at the Vasse Felix, Moss Wood, and Cullen wineries. Horgan explained that the property wasn't for sale, but the two men agreed to a consulting arrangement whereby Mondavi would be Horgan's mentor, while vineyards were planted and a winery was built. Over the next few years, both Mondavi and his winemaking son, Tim, made frequent trips to Margaret River to advise on the project. Horgan, who was only twenty-nine years old when he acquired the property, knew nothing about wine. In fact, he was not a regular wine drinker. Along with most Australians at the time, his alcoholic drink of choice was beer.

Horgan named his holding **Leeuwin Estate**, after the cape located at the bottom of Margaret River, and planted his first grapes in 1974. Indigent surfers looking for spare change put in many of the first vines.

Unfortunately, they planted many of them upside down with the roots sticking out of the ground, so viticulturist Stan Heritage had to replant many of them correctly. The winery produced a small experimental vintage in 1979, and its first commercial one the following year. The Leeuwin Chardonnay showed early on that it would someday be ranked among the world's best. The 1980 Chardonnay won a gold at the Sydney Wine Show, and Britain's *Decanter* magazine cast the international spotlight on Leeuwin by giving its highest recommendation to the 1981. The secret of Leeuwin's Chardonnay is a 10-acre plot known as Block 20, which was planted in 1976 and is one of the most famous wine *terroirs* in Australia. It was laid out on a gentle, undulating slope where a red gum forest had once grown, the soil John Gladstones had recommended. The yields are a modest 2 tons per acre. Many people over the years have urged Horgan to market Block 20 as a single vineyard wine, but he keeps it as the backbone of his top-of-the-line Art Series Chardonnay, which now sells for about $100 a bottle.

Horgan knew from the beginning that he faced a major challenge getting visitors to come to Margaret River: "We were the most isolated place in the world, and so in order to get people here we had to do something." Using the slogan "The Art of Fine Wine," he set out to combine world-class wine with world-class art. The first step was the Art Series of Leeuwin's best wines, which were inaugurated in 1980 and carried original pieces of art by Australian artists on the labels. He got the idea while attending a dinner at Château Mouton Rothschild, which has original art on its First Growth red Bordeaux. Renowned landscape artist Robert Juniper did the first Leeuwin painting, and Horgan has by now commissioned nearly 150 works for his labels and has a rotating show of the art at the winery.

Food came next in 1983 with a winery restaurant that overlooks an expansive manicured lawn. All other Margaret River restaurants at wineries serve only lunch, but Leeuwin broke tradition by also offering dinner on Saturday nights. It's usually packed.

Paintings and food, though, were not enough. Horgan wanted to do something special that would bring the world's attention to his remote winery. So in 1983, he sent letters to the Perth symphony orchestra, opera, and ballet companies asking them all if they would like to perform in his beautiful location. One recipient didn't bother to answer him; a second said it didn't "play in the bush"; the third said it might come down and have a practice session sometime. A year later, though, the director of the Festival of Perth asked Horgan to help underwrite the cost of bringing the London Philharmonic Orchestra to Western Australia. Even though the winery was still losing money and would continue in the red for its first thirteen years, Horgan decided to "take a great punt" or gamble and agreed to underwrite the London group if it would also come to Margaret River and do an outdoor concert at Leeuwin. The festival director went down to look at the location, approved it, and a week later London agreed.

Everyone in both Perth and Margaret River, however, thought Horgan was absolutely mad. A world-class orchestra playing in a bush town that then had a population of about 4,000 and almost no hotels! Horgan recalls that "one good mate" tried strenuously to talk him out of the concert brainstorm. People thought the event would be a flop and would destroy all the work that had been done to build up Margaret River. The friend pleaded, saying there would only be twenty people in the audience and that the orchestra members would substantially outnumber the public.

Horgan admits today he honestly had no idea how many people would show up for the concert when he jetted off to London shortly after the announcement to work out details with orchestra managers. "When I got back, though, we already had reservations for nearly five thousand people," he says proudly. The only advertisement ever made for it was one announcing that they were sold out. Eventually 5,500 people signed up for tickets, and 500 had to be turned away because the facility at that time could only hold 5,000.

The Leeuwin summer performances have become one of the hottest tickets in Australia, attracting 12,000 people for Saturday- and Sunday-night performances. Corporations fly executives and guests in from as far away as Singapore, Japan, China, and the United States. Logistics then, and still today, are a major issue, and the winery takes over both accommodations and transportation not only from the town of Margaret River but also from as far away as Bunbury, 68 miles to the north. For the first five years, top executive visitors stayed in 140 tents set up on the Leeuwin grounds. In those days Horgan still surfed, and the morning after a concert when he went down to the beach he would see concert guests sleeping in their Bentley and Mercedes limousines.

Trish Horgan is now in charge of booking the world's biggest names from both classical and popular music. The fourth year of the concert was Australia's bicentennial and the country was awash with special events. That summer the Festival of Perth booked Sir Georg Solti to direct a performance of its orchestra and didn't want to have anything to do with Leeuwin, so Trish booked Ray Charles and set the date as the same night as the Solti concert. The Festival had a difficult time filling its seats, and even Solti's wife was down in Margaret River listening to Ray Charles. The message was clear: don't mess with the Horgans when it comes to holding a concert. The winery now stages three to five concerts a year, but the showpiece event remains the summer one.

While gradually buying more and more property around the winery as it became available, Leeuwin went from the original 500 acres to the present 1,650 acres, of which 370 acres are planted in vines. Horgan has plans on the drawing board for what might go into the part of the property not suitable for vines. He has already built an airstrip, which was originally constructed for Australia's Royal Flying Doctor Service, but is also handy for private planes since there is no commercial air connection to Margaret River. Horgan also has a design for an eighteen-hole golf course, with nine holes down near a stream and nine on the ridges. In addition, he's looking to build a five-star hotel with initially only about forty rooms.

One of the things holding back new investments like the Leeuwin projects is the difficulty getting manpower to staff a golf course or hotel. Thanks in large part to strong Chinese and Indian demand for its raw materials, Western Australia is enjoying a mineral boom, which is sucking up all the available workers. As a result, businesses are going slow on expansion or tourist projects.

The original five Margaret River wineries are still regarded as the best in the region. Some are now under new ownership, but others are still with the founding families. Most would be considered boutique wineries by world standards, producing relatively small amounts of wine that sell for top prices. Dr. Tom Cullity owned Vasse Felix for seventeen years and then sold it to his winemaker, who just three years later in 1987 sold it to Robert Holmes à Court, a South African corporate raider and owner of vast natural resource holdings who became Australia's first billionaire. He died in 1990 and his widow and four children inherited the winery. The family has an internationally acclaimed art collection, part of which is on display at the winery and has become a major part of its ventures into wine tourism along with a top restaurant. Vasse Felix produces about 150,000 cases annually, which are sold mainly in Australia and Britain. Less than 1 percent of its output reaches the United States. The winery is best known for its outstanding Cabernet Sauvignon.

Founder Dr. Bill Pannell in 1984 sold Moss Wood, which is only a short distance north on Caves Road from Vasse Felix, to his chief winemaker, Keith Mugford, who has been expanding his acreage and now makes a broad range of wines, including a Pinot Noir, a rare product in Margaret River. The winery keeps a low profile, and visits are only available by appointment. Moss Wood's flagship is still Cabernet Sauvignon, which often gets 90-point ratings from Parker.

Cullen Wines is located right next to Vasse Felix on Caves Road and retains its original low-key atmosphere under the direction of winemaker Vanya Cullen, the youngest child of Kevin and Di. Vanya wants to make great wine, but has no interest in building a giant winery. It produces only about 18,000 cases a year, and some 80 percent is sold domestically. Cullen continues to excel with the Bordeaux varieties, especially its Cabernet Sauvignon/Merlot blend, which is now called Diane Madeline and is included in the Langston classification of Australia's best wines. Diane Madeline comes from vines of the original 1971 planting of Kevin and Di Cullen.

Cape Mentelle is no longer owned by the Hohnen family, but is still making excellent wines and offering a good tasting-room experience. Since 2003, the French luxury conglomerate LVMH, has owned it. The French company also owns New Zealand's icon producer Cloudy Bay, another winery David Hohnen started. Cape Mentelle makes a full line of wines. One of its most unusual offerings for Australia is Zinfandel, a grape David learned to love during his time studying in California.

Leeuwin Estate remains in the family, with Denis and Tricia and their four children all actively involved in the winery. It now has three ranges of wines. The Art Series wines, which are designed to be aged, remain the top of the line. The Chardonnay is the most prestigious of all. The Prelude Vineyard line, on the other hand, is made from more readily expressive fruit and meant for earlier consumption. The Leeuwin Sibling wines are for daily drinking.

♇ ♇ ♇

After the first five pioneers, the Margaret River region soon developed into a major wine and tourism center. Western Australia's economic boom helped turn Margaret River into Perth's playground, where people go for both short and long vacations either to enjoy good wine and good food or to sample the area's many other natural attractions, which range from trekking through karri forests and surfing to exploring caves and playing golf. There are now more than 120 Margaret River wine labels, and about ninety wineries are open for visitors. Two major roads run the length of the Margaret River region, and most of the wineries are located either on or close to one of them. People in a hurry usually take Bussell Highway, which runs right through the town of Margaret River. Those not as pressed for time are likely to drive Caves Road, which is no longer a shooting gallery for locals looking to kill 'roos. Even at the height of the busy Australian summer there's unlikely to be much traffic on either road, and jaywalkers still wander through traffic on Bussell Highway in the middle of the city of Margaret River. Caves Road is by far the more scenic road and offers easy access to natural caves and to lovely, lonely beaches.

Most of the wineries, especially those open to tourists, have tried to develop something special to set them apart from the crowd. **Voyager Estate**, which is located right next to Leeuwin Estate, is perhaps the most distinctly different, if for no other reason than a huge Australian flag that flies over its main entrance, which is supported by the third-largest flagpole in the country. The other thing that makes Voyager stand apart is its Cape Dutch architecture. For a variety of reasons,

Australia and South Africa share much in common, and many South Africans moved there during the apartheid era. Voyager draws on that connection.

The person now behind the winery is Michael Wright, one of Australia's richest men whose ancestor Frederick Thomas Wright landed in Victoria from Scotland in 1854 and began investing in natural resources. The family later moved to Western Australia and was a major player in wheat, wool, and mines, before moving into other ventures including publishing and transportation. Wright bought Freycinet Estate in 1991 from its founder, changed the name, greatly expanded both the vineyards and wine production, and put the Cape Dutch touch on the property. He tells friends he bought the winery to get back into agriculture in a way where he could control the value added to the final product. He jokes that he can't influence the profit on a loaf of bread just because he grows the wheat.

Wright is one of the rare teetotaling winery owners. It's not that he can't control his wine consumption; it simply makes him nauseous. A few years back and at his doctor's recommendation, Wright seriously tried to like wine but failed. If you own a winery, though, you can make the product fit your tastes. So Voyager now produces a sparkling nonalcoholic grape juice for him. Wright's daughter, Alex, runs the property as the general manager and has not inherited her father's intolerance for wine.

Voyager is considered one of Australia's finest "cellar doors," as the Australians and New Zealanders call their wine-tasting facilities, because of its architecture and grounds. The winery gets more than 150,000 visitors a year and as many as 1,500 on a busy day. While the whitewashed Cape Dutch buildings are lovely with their ornate gables in the style of Amsterdam, the even bigger attraction is the walled-off gardens that spread in all directions. A visit to Voyager is a day of wine and roses. The property boasts more than one thousand rose bushes that are spectacular in late spring and early summer. The winery has a staff of seven gardeners to tend to flowers. Roses also adorn the Voyager label.

Another major attraction is an elegantly designed and slightly formal dining room, where lunch and afternoon tea are served. The restaurant has won several top national awards for both the quality of its food and the care of its service.

Michael Wright in 1995 discovered that ownership of the trademark for the Dutch East India Company had lapsed, so he bought it to underscore his country's and his winery's connection to both Holland and South Africa. In 1606, the small Dutch East Indian ship *Duyfken* discovered Australia, more than 150 years before the British claimed the territory. The Dutch made the first European landing on Australia at Cape York on the country's west coast. Voyager's gift shop now sells a line of food products and wines that carry the trading company's logo, the stylized letters VOC for the ancient company's initials in Dutch.

Despite all the emphasis on roses and history, Voyager has not forgotten its wines. The winery produces some 40,000 cases a year, and as one might expect from the next-door neighbor to Leeuwin Estate, the quality is high. One of Voyager's most popular wines at the cellar door is Chenin Blanc, but its Chardonnay and Cabernet Sauvignon also get high marks from such local wine critics as James Halliday as well as from wine magazines such as *Decanter*. Australia's best Chardonnays come from the golden triangle made up of the Leeuwin, Voyager, and Cape Mentelle vineyards.

Another Margaret River winery with a South African connection made a big hit by combining the area's seafood with the winemaker's favorite wine. In the early 1980s, Albert and Bridget Haak emigrated from South Africa to Australia. Albert was a viticulturist and brought with him a knowledge and love of Chenin Blanc. He then set out to find the best place to plant a vineyard and found a 166-acre area in northern Margaret River not far from Geographe Bay, a beautiful spot tucked away amid low undulating hills. With help from investors, the couple in 1985 started **Amberley Estate**. Amberley's first vintage was released in 1990, and it became a quick success largely because of the winery's location just off Caves Road. In those days Amberley was one of the first wineries that visitors driving down from Perth came upon after three hours on the road. Tired travelers were anxious to stop for something to eat, and Amberley was one of only a handful of restaurants in the area. Soon it was the most visited winery in Margaret River.

Amberley's Chenin Blanc has a touch of sweetness and went well with the Asian and seafood dishes the winery served. It was also an easy product for newcomers to wine to enjoy. Amberley was soon selling 65,000 cases of Chenin Blanc per year, half its total production.

Gary Cornes, a chef who had previously worked at Sheraton hotels and once had his own restaurant, joined the kitchen in 1991 and began changing the simple menu into one for elegant cuisine by pairing local products, especially seafood, with Amberley wines. "Food became a very important part of the business," he recalls. "We were doing three hundred lunches a day and still turning people away." The most popular dishes were Geographe Bay Filo and Icky Sticky Licky Toffee Pudding. Both dishes have been on the menu for years, and customers have valiantly fought back attempts by new chefs to drop them.

Longtime winemaker Eddie Price was passionate about his Sémillon, although it was not a big seller. In an attempt to make it more popular he came up with the idea of the Amberley Sémillon and Seafood Weekend that would showcase both. The first was held in 1995, and the weekend has become one of the most popular events in Margaret River, getting about one thousand people on Saturday and slightly fewer on Sunday. The event, held the first weekend in February, starts at lunch and ends when the last people leave about 6:00 p.m.

Amberley in recent years has been involved in two mergers. First, Vincor, a Canadian firm, took it over in 2004, and then two years later Constellation Brands, the giant American wine company, bought Vincor. All of the winery's production was consolidated at a larger facility, but the restaurant and tasting room stayed in place and remain popular with wine tourists.

Margaret River wine still had a strange attraction for doctors after the three pioneers, and two more doctors opened another winery in the early 1970s. Dr. John Lagan and his wife, Dr. Eithne Sheridan Lagan, emigrated from Ireland in 1968 just as The Troubles were getting worse but mainly because of difficulties they had practicing medicine with his father. Margaret River at the time was trying to get a doctor to move to the area, and on the day they arrived the previous doctor was cremated. With a declining population and no cultural facilities beyond a public library, Margaret River was not then a happening place, and Eithne says she cried the whole first year they were there.

Eventually, though, the area's medical community and its wine fraternity welcomed the couple. Kevin Cullen invited John to work with him at his practice in Busselton, and one day Tom Cullity urged them to buy some land and plant a vineyard. So in 1971, the Lagans bought 200 acres of land for $50 an acre. The following year, while his wife was back in Ireland, John Lagan bought another 200 acres for $65 an acre. In 1975, they registered their winery, calling it **Chateau Xanadu**, though the "Chateau" was later dropped. The name came from the opening lines of Samuel Taylor Coleridge's poem "Kubla Khan" that reminded John of Margaret River. In 1977, the Lagans planted their first vines and soon earned a reputation for quality wine.

The Lagans sold the property to investors who had plans to turn it into a giant producer, and in April 2001, Xanadu began trading as a public company on the Australian Stock Exchange. The expansion plans, though, ended in failure, and the stock fell to pennies a share. In August 2005, Doug Rathbone, who made his fortune with a chemical company, bought Xanadu with promises to get the company back to its wine basics. The Rathbone family already owned three Australian wineries and seemed to know what it was doing.

One of the main focuses of the new owners was to concentrate on wine tourism at the Xanadu restaurant. Their record, so far, is excellent. Xanadu received the 2007 award for the best wine tourism facility in Western Australia. It has also received a Gold Plate award as the best restaurant within a winery. The restaurant is casual in style, and the food is classical. The best item on the menu is the Taste of the Dragon plate that offers a tapas-style selection of chef Iain Robertson's best productions of the day.

One of the most talked about new wineries in Margaret River is **Laurance of Margaret River**, which opened in late 2006. Its most famous, or infamous, feature is the 15-yard-high electric blue pole in front of the winery that is topped by a 3-meter female figure finished with 24-carat gold that appears to be making a swan dive into the pond below. The sculpture is officially named *Free as a Bird*, but locals call it *Chick on a Stick*.

Laurance is the work of Dianne Laurance, wife of Peter Laurance, who in the 1970s built the Perth-based Pivot Group into a major developer of shopping centers, theme parks, and office buildings. The couple had been vacationing in Margaret River and looking for a place to buy for several years; finally in 2001 they found the perfect location on Caves Road and purchased 100 acres. As someone associated with Sea-World and Warner Bros. Movie World parks, Peter was anxious to find a location that would draw big crowds. Being right on one of the two main tourist roads of Margaret River was ideal from his point of view. After that, though, the project belonged to his wife, Dianne, who has been active in the Leading Women Entrepreneurs of the World organization as well as her husband's company. She designed the *Chick* and had a sculptor execute the artwork. Dianne also recruited her two sons, Brendon and Danny Carr, who had been working as commercial divers, to take over daily management of the property.

To date, Laurance's wines are sold only at the cellar door, so walk-in traffic is more important for them than for other wineries. The winery has two lines of wines, the less expensive Aussie Jeans Rock line, selling for about $14, and the upper end Laurance of Margaret River wines, which go into specially made bottles Dianne designed, that are about $21. Between the two, the winery is selling about 25,000 cases annually.

Laurance gets about one thousand visitors a week in the summer season, and many order food and wine platters that offer samples of three wines and cost $5. General manager Brendon Carr explains that a lot of thought went into the offering. First, they wanted to take the wine education experience from the serving area so as not to scare people. "When I was getting started in wine, I was intimidated at places where some expert stood behind the bar and rattled off things like, 'This wine is long on the back palate,'" he says. Laurance hands a visitor a yellow card with a three- or four-sentence description of each wine that he can read on his own, while sitting down at a table. The winery charges for the tasting, Brendon Carr says, so people "won't feel obliged to buy a bottle of wine just because they had a tasting." The crowds enticed onto the property by the *Chick on a Stick* seem to like the approach.

Another of the appeals is Dianne's rose garden. Spread around 25 acres of lawns and gardens are one thousand rose bushes. A rose is also part of the company logo, and Dianne's favorite wine is rosé. The winery's big seller at Mother's Day is the package of a robe, a rose, and a bottle of rosé. The staff includes three gardeners to take care of the roses as well as the family's three-hole golf course, which is adjacent to the winery.

Across Caves Road from Laurance is **Saracen Estates**, another business trying to pull in travelers off the road. This $10-million facility brings together Australia's two most popular alcoholic beverages: wine and beer. Saracen Estates sells wine, and the Duckstein Brewery sells beer. The slogan: "The Best of Both Worlds." The Saracen wines are made off-site and are only stored there, while Duckstein beer is made at the location.

Founders Michele and Anna Saraceni emigrated from Italy to Australia at the end of World War II, and their son, Luke, is now owner of Saracen Property, a real estate company that has some $1 billion in assets. Statues of ancient Saracen warriors greet guests at the entrance of the winery. Luke and his wife, Maree, in 1996 first planted vines in the Wilyabrup Valley of Margaret River and later hooked up with Duckstein for the combined project.

Facing out over a lake and toward the road, Saracen has both a wine-tasting room and a wine education center; but it also houses a German beer garden plus a restaurant that seats eighty people. There are also giant screen televisions to show sports events.

Laurance of Margaret River and Saracen Estates are the inevitable mass tourism developments that came after the elite operations of the wine region's founders. Margaret River today attracts hundreds of thousands of tourists annually and is no longer the "most isolated place in the world," as Denis Horgan once described it. For those willing to make the long trip, the payoffs in both scenery and wines are spectacular.

Diary of a Wine Tourist

February 16

Black Tie in the Bush

Whenever winery owners around the world talk about staging an event that will not only draw big crowds but also boost the prestige of their wines, they inevitably mention "doing something like the Leeuwin Concert." Each year on a Saturday and Sunday night in February, Leeuwin holds a concert that coincides with the release of the latest vintage of its flagship Art Series Chardonnay. Other wineries may try to emulate the Leeuwin event that attracts 12,000 people, but no one has ever matched it.

The first concert in 1984 featured the London Philharmonic Orchestra, and since then an eclectic collection of artists from both the classical and popular music world have performed, including Dame Kiri Te Kanawa, Ray Charles, the Royal Danish Orchestra, and Sting.

I timed my research trip to Australia for this book in order to attend a concert that showcased opera singers Yvonne Kenny and David Hobson with the more than eighty-musician-strong West Australian Symphony Orchestra. They performed a program divided almost evenly between arias from such operas as Gounod's *Faust* and Verdi's *La Traviata* and Broadways songs from musicals, including *The Music Man* and *My Fair Lady.*

Saturday night is corporate night, and about a third of the men are in tuxedos, hence the concert's nickname "Black Tie in the Bush." The Sunday-night affair is more casual. I carried my tux 11,000 miles across the Pacific to be properly dressed for the Saturday concert.

The event started with an alfresco reception where a first course of crayfish was served along with glasses of Leeuwin Art Series Riesling. Many people in the audience knew one another, as at any event where a country's power elite gathers. In the background, the Kalamunda Youth Swing Band played unobtrusively.

After an hour of mingling and networking, waiters asked guests to bring their glasses with them and to move to the concert location on a grassy field in front of the winery's restaurant. As people walked into the area, they were offered their choice of a bottle of either Leeuwin Classic Dry White wine or Leeuwin Cabernet Merlot blend. It was convenient that both of the wines were in screwcap bottles, which made opening them and pouring wine a lot easier than if they were sealed with a cork.

Getting into the low beach chairs on the grass was a challenge, especially when you have a bottle of wine in one hand and a glass in the other. No one in the audience, though, seemed to mind, and the program started on time at 7:30 p.m. Just before the orchestra began playing the opening number, the overture to *Marriage of Figaro,* conductor Guy Noble announced to applause that the 2005 Leeuwin Art Series Chardonnay, the winery's icon wine, was being released at the concert. People in the audience then proudly held up their bottle to celebrate.

The setting for the concert was like something out of a fairy tale. The acoustics were excellent, and music from the orchestra pit gently washed over the crowd. Two giant monitors provided close-up pictures of the performers. A little rain the night before had made a rehearsal difficult, but the weather cooperated on opening night. Only a few wispy clouds passed in front of the bright half-moon that was visible even in daylight during the first half of the program. I was seated with my bottle of Classic Dry White between the CEO of an Australian company that builds hydroelectric facilities around the world, who had flown in from Melbourne for the event, and a young Perth couple who had won tickets to the concert in the lottery Leeuwin sponsored.

As the orchestra made its way from classical to Broadway music, the crowd listened attentively and cheered with gusto at the end of each piece. The towering karri trees behind the orchestra seemed to wave majestically to the rhythm of the music as spotlights flashed on them. The half-moon hung in the sky for a long time above the trees as if it too wanted to hear the concert. A star slowly became obvious as dusk turned to darkness. Before one song, Yvonne Kenny called the evening "one of the great outdoor events in Australia," and the crowd roared.

Shortly before 10:00 p.m. and following two encores ending with Offenbach's "Can Can," the audience slowly got up out of their beach chairs and moved toward the exits. Some 1,700 people stayed for a postconcert dinner that required among other delicacies some 14,500 canapés, 900 lobsters, 4,000 prawns, and 2,600 oysters. Accompanying the food was an endless supply of Leeuwin Art Series Cabernet Sauvignon and the newly released Art Series Chardonnay. The Cabernet was good, but the Chardonnay was a knockout. Such big name companies as Qantas Airways, Deutsche Bank, and Coca-Cola co-sponsor the concert, and many of them had taken tables, where they entertained clients. Denis Horgan mingled in the crowd, accepting compliments from both friends and strangers for another successful concert.

After dinner, LA Gold, a rock group, played loud and long into the night. When we left the buses at the beginning of the evening, the Leeuwin representative asked everyone to please return to the buses by 12:30 a.m. so people could be taken back to their hotels. LA Gold was still playing strong until nearly that time, and it was after 1:00 a.m. before my bus left with happy, but finally tired, concertgoers. By then, almost all the black ties were hanging around the men's necks.

CHAPTER SEVEN

Central Otago, New Zealand

As soon as a visitor to Queenstown, the capital of New Zealand's vacationland, lands at the airport and steps out onto the aluminum stairway leading down to the tarmac, he immediately realizes that this is a special place. There seems to be something in the air that makes everything sharp and intense. It's like looking through a pair of binoculars when objects suddenly snap into focus. The mountains ahead are so close that you want to reach out and touch them; the colors of everything from flowers to bushes have an unexpected sharpness and deep color saturation. Residents are so accustomed to this phenomenon that they are hard pressed to explain the experience, saying it's simply the result of the country's "clean and green" ethos, the high levels of ultraviolet rays, and ocean breezes that constantly sweep across New Zealand. Whatever the cause, being in Queenstown and the surrounding Central Otago is like stepping onto the earth the day after creation.

At 45° south of the equator, Central Otago is in the lower part of New Zealand's South Island and is the southernmost place in the world where wine is made. It is also nearly the mirror reverse of Burgundy. Beaune, the capital of French Pinot Noir, is at 47° 16' longitude north, while Queenstown is at 45° 01' south.

At the same time, however, there is a vast difference in the population density between the northern and southern regions. More than 100 million people live between 44° and 46° north, while fewer than 400,000 reside in the same range in the south. The closest landfall to New Zealand is South America's Patagonia, and prevailing winds from the west and northwest keep Central Otago's atmosphere pristine.

The Maoris, Polynesian people who first settled New Zealand sometime before the thirteenth century, resided mainly along coastlines, venturing into Central Otago in search of greenstone or jade, which they used for tools and ornaments. The Maoris called the South Island the "land of greenstone water" because it was so easy to find them in the many inland streams.

Scottish settlers arrived in March 1848 with plans to raise sheep for wool in the area. The scrub brush then growing on the steep hillsides was filled with thorns, so the newcomers introduced bushes and other vegetation from home that made the land more suitable for grazing. Gold was discovered in Central Otago on May 20, 1861, a year after the first pioneer started a farm in the Queenstown area. The Australian Gabriel Read recorded his experience at a gully later named after him: "I shoveled away about two and a half feet of gravel, arrived at a beautiful soft slate and saw the gold shining like the stars in Orion on a dark frosty night."

Read set off a gold rush that brought in prospectors from around the world, who tore up the countryside looking for the precious metal. The Frenchman Jean Desire Feraud quickly made a small fortune, and in 1864 used some of his earnings to plant the first vineyard, Monte Christo near the village of Clyde, about 50 miles east of Queenstown. Two years later, Feraud built a winery and was soon winning medals at Australian wine fairs. Less than two decades later, though, he moved out of the area, first to Dunedin and then to Australia. The beer-drinking Scotsmen who lived in the area showed little interest in wine, and Feraud's winery was abandoned, although one of its stone huts still remains.

In 1895, the New Zealand government asked the viticulturist Romeo Bragato, an Austro-Hungarian by birth but Italian by education, to travel through the country and report on the winemaking potential. In the gold-rush village of Arrowtown, outside Queenstown, Bragato tried a glass of local wine, which he described as "made after the most primitive fashion" but still "need not be despised by anyone." Bragato was particularly impressed by the Cromwell Basin area about 35 miles east of Queenstown, calling the region "pre-eminently suitable to the cultivation of the vine, both of winemaking and table varieties." In his final report Bragato wrote, "The Central Otago district has in part a bright future before it in the matter of vine-growing." He told a meeting of the Dunedin Chamber of Commerce that the Burgundian grape Pinot Noir should do well there.

Bragato served as New Zealand's first government viticulturist from 1902 to 1909, but neither he nor the people of Central Otago seriously followed up on his recommendations. The region continued to concentrate on raising sheep on the rugged mountains and catering to a growing number of tourists who came to enjoy the sheer beauty of the area known as the Southern Alps. The entire Queenstown Lakes District, an area of 3,361 square miles, had a population as late as the mid-1990s of fewer than 15,000. But eventually inexpensive jet travel opened up Central Otago to tourists. First came the nature lovers who made Queenstown the jumping off point for trips to see the splendor of Milford and Doubtful Sound in Fiordland. Then came skiers attracted by the region's five skiing areas. Australians, in particular, were frequent winter visitors.

Queenstown also attracted people looking for exciting adventure experiences. Mountain climbing had long been popular, but thrills moved to a whole new level with the advent of the adrenaline-pumping sport of jet boating. Bill Hamilton, a Kiwi engineer in Christchurch who had once raced sports cars, developed a water-jet propulsion system that pushed boats across shallow water at high speeds. Hamilton's boats could race up rivers only a few inches deep at 50 miles per hour, easily maneuvering their way past jagged rocks, making hairpin turns, and sending giant rooster tails of water in their wake. One of Hamilton's favorite tricks was to race directly toward a dock and then at the last second veer off in a giant spray of water. Jet boats became a staple in James Bond movies and attracted thousands of wannabe 007s to Central Otago.

Two decades later, the region became the center of another new adventure for thrill seekers: bungy jumping. In the early 1980s, AJ Hackett and Henry van Asch were just another couple of New Zealand speed fanatics. Hackett grew up in the suburbs of Auckland, while Van Asch spent his youth on a dairy and sheep farm outside Christchurch. The two were attracted to anything that involved gravity-defying feats. One of those sports was skiing, and they competed for several years in Europe as members of the New Zealand speed-skiing team. Van Asch for a while held the New Zealand record for both speed skiing and mountain biking. The two met in 1985 through skiing and began talking about the ultimate gravity sport: jumping off cliffs or bridges with cords tied around their feet. British film producer David Attenborough first introduced the world to the jumps in the 1950s in films that showed divers on Pentecost Island in Vanuatu leaping from high platforms with vines tied to their ankles as part of their passage to manhood. In the 1970s, members of the Oxford Dangerous Sports Club began jumping from bridges using elastic ropes tied to their ankles. The first of the jumps took place on April Fools' Day 1979 at the 250-foot Clifton Suspension Bridge in Bristol, England. The jumpers were immediately arrested, but that didn't stop them from doing the same thing at the Golden Gate Bridge in San Francisco and other sites. Hackett made his first jump on Sunday morning November 23, 1986, off the Greenhithe Bridge in Auckland. The drop was 62.3 feet, and afterward he said he felt "completely stoked."

Hackett and Van Asch had the idea of not only jumping but also turning it into a business. "We figured if we charged $40 a jump and did 50 a day, we would be insanely rich. But if we did 15 a day, we'd be sunk," Hackett later wrote. He became the public persona of the company they founded, the daredevil who threw himself off bridges, while Van Asch also jumped but was the one in the background running the business on a daily basis. "We developed a brand around a name. AJ was the name, and I was the brand manager," Van Asch told me. Hackett and Van Asch took their plans to a Central Otago lawyer and proposed splitting the profits with him if he would come up with a release that would protect them from any legal claims in case of an accident. The lawyer quickly showed them the door.

Not easily deterred, the two pushed ahead and came up with a publicity stunt to garner them international attention and launch a new world sport. They had gotten to know and like France during their time skiing there, and AJ now had a French girlfriend. So he decided to jump off one of the world's most famous tourist attractions: the Eiffel Tower. Before the tower closed for the evening on June 25, 1987, Hackett and two friends carried camouflaged equipment up the Paris landmark and then hid there overnight. At dawn and with a camera rolling to record the feat, Hackett, wearing a tuxedo, dove off the tower's second level, 361 feet above the ground in a nearly perfect leap. The only thing that went wrong was that he was supposed to grab a bottle of Champagne when he got near the bottom from his girlfriend who was standing below. But they had slightly miscalculated the length of cord needed, and he couldn't reach the bottle. Police immediately arrested Hackett and took him off in a paddy wagon, but then released him ten minutes later.

Basking in a flood of international publicity, Hackett and Van Asch returned to Queenstown and continued working both to perfect the equipment for the sport and to get permission from local officials to start bungy jumping there. The abandoned 141-foot Kawarau Bridge just outside the city seemed like the perfect site. The Department of Conservation owned the bridge, and the two convinced bemused bureaucrats that they could restore the structure and more from the profits from jumping. They proposed giving the department 5 percent of revenues. It was a deal, and AJ Hackett Bungy opened for business on November 12, 1988. It was an immediate huge success, and before long they were "insanely rich." In the early days, and as another publicity stunt, Hackett and Van Asch offered any woman a free jump if she would do it topless. They had so many takers, though, that the offer had to be withdrawn. Before long the company began opening sites both in New Zealand and around the world. Hackett was particularly interested in their international operations. More than 30,000 people annually now jump off the Kawarau Bridge, while another 50,000 leap from two other bungy sites in Central Otago.

Jet boating and bungy jumping solidified Queenstown's claim as the adventure capital of the world. No other place comes even close. The town soon had a half-day adventure circuit called the Awesome Foursome. It included a helicopter ride over mountains around the city, a jet boat ride up the Kawarau River, a bungy jump off the bridge, and then a white-water raft ride. That produced enough adrenaline for a lifetime.

At the same time adventure tourism was rapidly expanding in Central Otago, a small band of pioneers was trying to see if it could make wine in the region. Working at first alone but eventually in close collaboration, they were an eclectic group of dreamers who had a lot in common. First, they were amateurs. All but one of them had no experience growing grapes or making wine. When they started, most had drunk a lot more beer than wine. None had much money. They did it all by themselves with only modest help from wine-education institutions, unlike other wine regions around the world where places such as the University of California, Davis and the University of Bordeaux train winemakers. With little understanding about what they were up against or how to solve their problems, they battled enemies as deadly as frost, which could wipe out a year's work in one cold evening, and as relentless as rabbits, who burrowed their way through vineyards like an eighth plague from the book of Revelation. The wine novices called themselves the Tight Five, borrowing a term from rugby, New Zealand's national sport, which signifies the five toughest players in a scrum.

Public officials actively discouraged their winemaking plans. In 1958, the Department of Agriculture had proclaimed that Central Otago was too cold for grape cultivation, stating flatly "the economics of grape growing" are "not very favourable." Queenstown's temperatures often fall to 32°F in winter, and severe frosts can still hit in early summer.

The experts, though, were ignoring the warmer climate outside the city in such places as the Gibbston Valley and the Cromwell Basin, which Bragato had earlier identified as having wine potential. Conditions there are much more favorable to viticulture, even though there is a large diurnal temperature range between hot days and cool nights. During the warm weather from January to March, temperatures can swing from a high of 95°F to a low of 40°F. There's an old and widely believed adage among winemakers worldwide that the best wine is made in challenging areas, and those swings account for the intense flavors of Central Otago wines. The newcomers had no idea which grapes might do well in their climate, but they began spending the little money they had on experiments to find out.

The earliest pioneer was Rolfe Mills, who came from a family that owned a wool and shoe business in Christchurch. While traveling through Portugal in 1958, he was struck by the similarities he saw between the steep Douro Valley, where the grapes that go into port grow, and Central Otago. If grapes could grow there, why not at home?

Mills was still thinking about that in 1973, when he inherited a piece of property his family owned on Lake Wanaka, 50 miles from Queenstown via the fast route and 60 miles on the scenic one. He later called it **Rippon Vineyard**. Only three years before, Mills, a widower with three teenage children, had married Lois Plimmer, twenty-four years his junior, and they then moved to the lake and set up a farm. His passion was wine; but he also raised Angora goats, which paid the family's bills in the early years.

In his attempts to see which grapes would survive or do best, Mills planted a hodgepodge of vines year after year during the 1970s. He soon learned that such Bordeaux varieties as Cabernet Sauvignon or Merlot performed poorly by the lake. Even as late as 1981, he still had thirteen different kinds of grapes growing on 5 acres.

Rolfe and Lois were still uncertain that they really wanted to make a life as winemakers, so in 1980, along with their three young children, aged ten, eight, and three, they headed off to southwestern France to learn more about winemaking. They rented a house for $20 a week in the village of Sigoules near the wine town of Bergerac, where mostly reds but also a few whites are produced. They lived there for nine months, and came home reinforced in their determination to stick with winemaking.

Many miles from Lake Wanaka in the outskirts of Queenstown, Ann Pinckney, a trained childcare nurse, was also experimenting with grapes. She started with a smattering of book knowledge and a little practical experience, the most of any of the pioneers. In 1974, she earned a horticulture degree from Lincoln University in Christchurch and later worked at or visited wineries in Australia, Germany, Italy, and France. She planted cuttings from eleven different grape varieties in her mother's garden in 1976 to see how they would do. Pinckney's experiments included mainly white wines: Chardonnay, Gewürztraminer, Müller-Thurgau, Chasselas, Muscat, and even the obscure Reichensteiner from Germany.

Two years later at a wine conference at Lincoln University, Pinckney met Rolfe Mills and was surprised to learn that someone else was looking at wines in Central Otago. Shortly afterward and through her medical work, she met Denise Brady, who was giving birth at the

Queenstown Maternity Hospital and whose husband, Alan, was also trying to grow grapes. Small world. Mills, Pinckney, and Brady began to exchange information and experiences, but things moved slowly because none of them had much money for experiments, and vine trials take time.

Alan Brady was born in Northern Ireland, where his father owned a weekly newspaper, and in 1959, moved to New Zealand to see some of the world before he settled down at his father's business. Brady worked for two New Zealand papers before switching over to television broadcasting, which made him into a well-known local figure. In 1976, he purchased a small piece of property with a stone building left from the gold-rush days. He had no idea of getting into wine and merely wanted a place to unwind from his intense work. Then at the end of 1977, Brady decided to chuck his career in television and get into growing something on his new land. For a while he considered cultivating gooseberries, but that plan was abandoned after he discovered there was already a world glut. Then a television assignment took him to the Rhine vineyards of Germany. Just as the Douro had reminded Mills of Central Otago, the Rhineland brought up the same vision for Brady. He returned home with the idea of planting at least part of his property with grapes and making wine for his own consumption.

In early 1978, Brady's wife was having another child, and so Alan and Denise again saw lots of Ann Pinckney and the talk often turned to wine. Pinckney encouraged Alan Brady to grow grapes and volunteered to help him. So he cleared a half-acre for a trial plot, and in 1981 Ann Pinckney provided him with cuttings of Müller-Thurgau, Gewürztraminer, Chasselas, and Riesling to plant. In 1984, he added Pinot Noir, Cabernet Sauvignon, Chardonnay, and Pinotage to his vineyard, which was rapidly becoming a Noah's ark of vines with a few plants of every variety. Along with Mills and Pinckney, Brady thought he had to try everything to see what would work in their soil, which had heavy layers and schist, and in their climate, where the danger of frost could never be totally forgotten. He soon named his property the **Gibbston Valley Winery**.

Some 40 miles away near the town of Alexandra and not far from Clyde, where the Frenchman Jean Desire Feraud had planted his vineyard in the mid-nineteenth century, two other newcomers to wine were also having a go at it. Verdun Burgess, a carpenter by trade, was as rough-hewn as the wood with which he worked. After a long sojourn in Australia, Burgess arrived in Alexandra in 1979 with a trailer full of tools, $300 in the bank, and a plan to go into business as a carpenter. He liked a piece of rocky hillside about 3.5 miles out of town, but local regulations required him to turn it into agricultural land if he bought it. His father had run a commercial market garden, so "I knew how to grow spuds," says Burgess. But he wanted to find the best crop he should grow there. One night in a pub, a patron suggested growing grapes and making wine. Burgess figures that at the time he might have drunk six bottles of wine in his life. But he was only thirty, and at that age anything is possible. Even a beer drinker could become a winemaker. About this time, Burgess met Sue Edwards, a teacher in the local adult-education program. Both had failed marriages behind them, and they soon became partners in life and in the vineyard. They were not foolhardy, however. Both kept their day jobs. In fact, Burgess was working three jobs: he was a journeyman carpenter; he was building a house for himself and Sue; and he was a fledgling grape grower. Sue did not leave her teaching job until 1997, when she retired.

Unlike Mills, Pinckney, and Brady, Burgess didn't plant everything. "I looked at the northern hemisphere to see what they were planting at about forty-five degrees north. That was Riesling, Gewürztraminer, Pinot Noir, and Chardonnay," he says. "Then I looked at what was getting medals at competitions. Gewürz was winning a lot, so I decided to plant that first. I had never heard of Gewürztraminer before, but it seemed like a good idea."

Burgess and Edwards called their property **Black Ridge Vineyard**, which is sometimes confused with California's Black Ridge Vineyard. They might have called it Rabbit Ridge because of the infestation of rabbits they faced. The animals were everywhere, burrowing into the vineyard and eating young vines before they could take root. Burgess tried shooting the rabbits, with limited success. He had only slightly more luck with placing explosives down rabbit holes. Finally he got some Burmese cats, a breed he liked, to go on rabbit patrol. That method was effective, and when I visited Black Ridge, cats were still on the lookout for rabbits.

Birds were another natural problem for Burgess, as they continue to be for all New Zealand winemakers. People told him to put netting over the plants as soon as the grapes began to ripen. Birds don't eat green grapes, but will devour sweet ones. He couldn't afford the netting, but he had no other option.

Still, there was so much to learn. One day a viticulturist happened to stop by the vineyard and casually told Burgess and Edwards that their vines had powdery mildew, a disease that can ruin a crop. The two looked at each other dumbfounded and then asked, "What's that?" The visitor explained the problem and how to solve it, and the couple took action. After she recounted the powdery mildew story to me, Sue still roared with laughter at their naïveté in the early years.

Only a couple of miles from Black Ridge lived Bill Grant, a some-time teacher and sometime mason, who along with Mills and Brady, got the idea of growing grapes in Central Otago while traveling through Europe. Many New Zealanders go off to Europe just after they finish school in a Kiwi rite of passage before getting on with their life at home. Grant and his wife, Jill, made the trip, returning in 1958 with their first child and just enough money for a deposit on 16 acres of land. The Grants had enjoyed the wine culture in Europe, so they planted a few grape cuttings in the vegetable garden, and later expanded the vines into a more serious research project with the help of a horticulturalist from the Agriculture Department. Grant got some other cuttings from another study that had been completed, but then he killed nearly all his vines by accidentally spraying them with the wrong product. Only two varieties survived: Müller-Thurgau and Chasselas.

All through their experiments, the five pioneers kept in close touch with each other. Nothing was secret; they shared everything, the good, the bad, and the ugly. Burgess openly admitted, for example, that his first three vintages turned to vinegar only a few months after bottling.

Gradually the pioneers began reaching some conclusions from all their studies. One variety stood out: Pinot Noir. Researchers at the Earnscleugh Experiment Orchard, in Alexandra, planted the first Pinot in 1973, and Ann Pinckney later did the first private planting. Word spread among the Tight Five that this appeared to be the grape with the most potential, so they began pulling out such vines as Cabernet

Sauvignon, which clearly would not ripen properly in the cool Central Otago climate, and planted more Pinot Noir.

It was one thing to grow grapes, but turning them into wine was another skill they had to learn. Verdun Burgess in 1985 harvested a small container of Gewürztraminer grapes and decided to try making them into wine, crushing the grapes with his feet and filtering the wine through a pair of silk knickers. He got only enough wine for twelve bottles, and that was vinegar nine months later.

That same year, Alan Brady asked a German working at a state wine research facility near Auckland to make the first wine for him. Brady harvested about 700 pounds of Müller-Thurgau, Gewürztraminer, and Pinot Gris grapes in plastic bags, put them into garbage cans, and then persuaded passengers flying from Queenstown to Auckland to carry them north. The next year, Brady tried to make the wine himself in an attempt that is best described as a learning experience. Finally in 1987, Brady hired Rob Hay, who had recently returned from Germany, where he had gone to study winemaking after picking up a degree in physiology in New Zealand, to make his wine. It was the first commercial vintage for Brady's Gibbston Valley Winery.

Rolfe Mills at Rippon Vineyard took the most systematic approach to producing wine. In 1986, he hired Tony Bish, who was taking a six-year correspondence course in enology from Charles Sturt University in Australia and had been kicking around New Zealand and Australian wineries. Rippon's first vintage of 250 bottles went on sale in 1988, and the following year it had its first commercial production of 2,000 bottles.

The Tight Five in those days hadn't yet built any wine production facilities. So in 1987, Rolfe Mills, Alan Brady, and Ann Pinckney all made small amounts of wine at Taramea Wines, a facility Ann had recently licensed. Her production of only 800 bottles quickly sold out. In the cooperative spirit of the Central Otago pioneers, Bish also made wine for Bill Grant, who was calling his new business William Hill Wines, and for Verdun Burgess, who had given up on making it himself.

Tony Bish stayed only three harvests at Rippon, and was replaced by Rudi Bauer, an Austrian who had wine training and experience in both Austria and Germany. He had come to New Zealand to work a harvest at Mission Estate in 1985 in Hawke's Bay on the country's North Island. But he fell in love with a local girl, and after working at wineries in California and Oregon in 1990 returned to New Zealand to become Rippon's winemaker. Bauer quickly put Central Otago on the world wine map. Working in close contact with the Tight Five, he took all their wines to a higher level, and all concentrated more and more on Pinot Noir.

In the early 1990s, New Zealand wine judges began recognizing Bauer's wines in national competitions. The first award was a gold medal for a 1990 Rippon Rosé at the annual Air New Zealand Wine Awards. Then the 1991 Rippon Pinot Noir was judged as the best Pinot at the 1992 Liquorland Royal Easter Wine Show and also as the best red wine at the New Zealand Air Show.

Rippon, however, wasn't alone in bringing home awards. Alan Brady's Gibbston Valley Winery won the gold medal for the best Pinot Noir at the 1995 Air New Zealand competition. Then Gibbston Valley's 2000 Pinot Noir Reserve garnered the top prize at the International Wine Challenge in London, the biggest wine show in the world. It was the first time a Burgundy wine had not won in that category, and the certificate had to be reprinted to call it the award for the best Burgundy/Pinot Noir. The winemaker was Grant Taylor, who developed a cult following during his thirteen years at Gibbston Valley. In 1998, Taylor left Brady to start Valli Vineyards.

In addition to making award-winning wine, Alan Brady had a vision for wine tourism at Gibbston Valley. He realized early on that his winery, located just 12 miles outside Queenstown, was ideally located to take advantage of all the skiers, bungy jumpers, jet boaters, and other visitors to the city. So he turned his location into a tourist destination. The most important step in that direction was building a wine cave, which opened in 1995. It was the only one in Central Otago and attracted thousands of visitors each year, including brides anxious to be married in such a romantic setting. He also built a restaurant, and buses began bringing groups for a tour of the cave and lunch. He added a cheese shop that was popular with wives whose husbands were sampling wines. Gibbston Valley then opened a large shop that sold corkscrews and wine books as well as New Zealand woolens and, of course, bottles of wine. Some 80,000 to 100,000 tourists now spend upward of $1 million annually in the Gibbston Valley store.

The original Tight Five played an important role in Central Otago's wine history, but their personal stories did not all end well. Brady, the visionary, saw the potential of both wine and wine tourism as well as the elements to make them succeed, but he lacked the capital and business experience to make it happen as he had hoped. Gibbston Valley was always undercapitalized, and over the years he had to bring in more and more outside investors in order to keep it going and growing. As he did that, his share of the company kept diminishing. In 1997, Mike Stone, an American who had worked for the financial firm Merrill Lynch before moving to New Zealand and becoming a citizen, took over as executive director, and Brady left to start the nearby **Mount Edward Winery**.

Ann Pinckney had unfortunately selected the wrong location for her vineyard, which repeatedly suffered serious frost problems. She eventually pulled out the vines and sold the Taramea production facility.

The other three wineries in the Tight Five are still in the hands of their founding families. Rolfe Mills died in 2000, but his clan now runs Rippon. Verdun Burgess and Sue Edwards still manage Black Ridge Vineyard. Bill Grant owns William Hill Winery and Vineyards and has nothing to do with William Hill Estate in the Napa Valley. None of the three New Zealand wineries, though, have made it big on the international wine scene, in part because of their relatively small production.

In the early 1990s, a second generation of Central Otago winemakers appeared, who were markedly different from the original five. They usually, but not always, had better professional credentials for winemaking and had often studied winemaking at academic institutions. They were well funded and better managed than those in the first generation. The majority of them located their wineries out in the warmer Cromwell Basin, where property prices were less expensive and more land was available. The second generation also planted more grapes on the hillsides of Central Otago and less on the valley floor. Since this group didn't have to repeat all the testing to see which grape varieties worked best, most immediately planted lots of Pinot Noir, which clearly had the greatest potential. Some experts think that Central Otago may be the best place in the world to make that wine, even better than Burgundy. British wine experts Hugh Johnson and Jancis Robinson have written, "Many believe that this is where the Pinot grail is to be found."

♀ ♀ ♀

The first winery of the second generation was **Chard Farm**, which was located right next to Gibbston Valley. Founder Rob Hay went out on his own in 1987 after making only one vintage for Alan Brady. Hay's brother Greg, who had recently graduated from college with a business degree, soon joined the venture. Chard Farm earned early kudos for its Finla Mor Pinot Noir and Judge & Jury Chardonnay. Unlike its neighbor Gibbston Valley, Chard Farm hasn't made a concerted effort to entice tourists to venture up a bumpy, sometime frightening road to its tasting room.

In 1990, Stewart Elms, a fifty-five-year-old sheep and cattle farmer, was the oldest student in the winemaking course at Lincoln University, and Blair Walter was the youngest at twenty. They were assigned to be wine chemistry lab partners, and later when Elms started his winery, he asked Walter to be his winemaker. A no-nonsense person, Elms selected the location for his vineyard on the basis of government overlays of properties that reported on temperature and soil types. One spot jumped out at him as the best: a site on Felton Road in the town of Bannockburn in the Cromwell Basin. Elms bought the property in 1991 and planted a north-facing vineyard to minimize the danger of frost. Walter made the first vintage of Pinot Noir under the **Felton Road** label in 1997. While the winery also makes Chardonnay and Riesling, it is best known for its Pinot Noir. Felton Road exports two-thirds of its wines, with the United States the third-largest market after Australia and Britain.

The British gave colorful, descriptive names to places in New Zealand such as Doubtful Sound, so named because Captain James Cook doubted he could get his ships out of that inlet once they had sailed in. Another is Mt. Difficulty, which is near Felton Road. Robin Dicey, a third-generation winemaker, left South Africa in 1977 because of rising racial tensions. He wanted to emigrate to an English-speaking wine country, and the first job offer came from New Zealand, so that's where he went to make wine for Corbans, a bulk producer. While taking a hovercraft boat trip on Lake Wanaka during a 1988 family ski vacation, he spotted the Rippon Vineyard and forced the boat's driver to stop and let him see it. Two years later, Dicey and two partners bought property on Mt. Difficulty and named the winery after it. He planted the first vineyard with 60 percent Pinot Noir. While the vines were maturing, his son Matt Dicey was finishing a graduate program in winemaking and working harvests in Oregon, South Africa, Burgundy, and Tuscany before coming back to his father's property. In 1998, the year he left Gibbston Valley, Alan Brady started the first vintage at Mt. Difficulty, and later Matt finished it. **Mt. Difficulty** is now one of Central Otago's largest wineries, producing 30,000 cases a year—two-thirds of it Pinot Noir. It has a small restaurant that offers a lovely view of the Cromwell Basin.

Carrick Wines, another second-generation winery, is located on the east side of Bannockburn. Owner Steve Green was an executive in local government in Nelson and Hawke's Bay, two other wine regions where he had lots of dealings with wineries that inspired him to get into the business. In 1993, Green was a manager for the Dunedin City Council, when he and his wife, Barbara, bought 62 acres of land in an area where nothing but brush had ever grown. Three years later, the couple moved to the property. Barbara managed the vineyard, while Steve kept a regular salary as the executive of the Central Otago District Council. The first two harvests, the Greens sold their grapes to Mt. Difficulty. The next two years they marketed the wine under the Carrick label, but produced it at the Gibbston Valley Winery. Finally in 2002, they built their own winery. From the beginning their focus was on Pinot Noir, which makes up 70 percent of production.

Wine tourism was an integral part of the Green business plan. Barbara insisted they couldn't start a winery without a good restaurant to go along with it. At the time, restaurants in the area served mainly mundane food, but she wanted quality cuisine designed to accompany their wines. The couple thought there were by then enough wineries in the Cromwell Basin to make their place a destination for wine fans willing to make the hour-long journey from Queenstown. The strategy worked, and Carrick is now a tourist target not only for its wines but also for its food, especially the game dinners in autumn.

By the end of the twentieth century and the beginning of the twenty-first, a third generation of wine people began coming to Central Otago, and they were different from either of the first two groups. They had generally made large fortunes elsewhere; most of them were investors rather than hands-on winemakers or managers; and they were primarily buying into the wine lifestyle.

While running his bungy-jump business, Henry van Asch enjoyed an insider's view of the growing wine scene in Central Otago. The young people making wine were also frequently jumping off the Kawarau Bridge. Greg Hay, who was running Chard Farm with his brother Rob, jumped almost daily. Late in the afternoons, Henry and his wine buddies would often swim in the river and then have a barbecue. During those sessions, Greg told Van Asch about the problem the new wineries were having getting enough good grapes. The business was growing so fast that the grape supply simply couldn't keep up. At the same time, the bungy business was also growing rapidly and leaving lots of profits for the owners. So as a result of his talks with Hay and others, in 1992, Henry van Asch planted a new vineyard with one-third Chardonnay and two-thirds Pinot Noir in the Gibbston Valley. He sold the grapes mainly to Chard Farm.

Over the years, AJ Hackett and Henry van Asch had developed differing views about where their business was going. Hackett was spending most of his time making high-publicity jumps at glamorous locations around the world and setting up new bungy sites for the company in France, Australia, and the United States, while Van Asch was interested in running the operations in Queenstown. Their personal styles also clashed. Henry was intense and focused on the bottom line. AJ was the relaxed mate who liked to kick back and have a beer with the staff. He was also spending much of his time in France, where he had a wife and young family.

Finally in 1997, after several years of tense relations, the two partners decided to split up their company. The final agreement gave AJ the foreign jump sites, while Henry got four New Zealand ones. The name of the company remained AJ Hackett Bungy since it was an international brand that the world knew because of that crazy guy who jumped off bridges. Relations between AJ and Henry have improved since the split and in 2007, Henry appeared on the New Zealand television show *This Is Your Life* that honored Hackett.

Looking forward to a life that could include more than just bungy jumping, Van Asch in 1997 used some of the grapes from his vineyard to make his first wine under the label HOC, which stood for Henry Out of Control. Van Asch now says the winemaker wasn't a good match and HOC only produced one vintage.

Two years later, however, he was ready to try again and this time he was more serious, working closely with Alan Brady and Grant Taylor. The second viticulture venture, **Van Asch Wines**, worked and now includes three labels and nine vineyards. Freefall is a line of inexpensive Pinot Noir, Chardonnay, and Sauvignon Blanc—wines for daily drinking that capitalize on the bungy connection and appeal to a young audience. Their slogan: "Adventure in Wine." The Van Asch line of more expensive wines includes Syrah, Pinot Noir, Pinot Gris, Riesling, and rosé. Finally, Henry markets eight organic wines, which his brother-in-law makes in Marlborough under the label Rock Ferry.

Delving further into wine tourism, Van Asch in 2005 opened The Winehouse & Kitchen, a wine-tasting room and restaurant directly adjacent to the Kawarau Bridge Bungy facility. It is only twenty minutes from downtown Queenstown and profits from the thousands of people visiting the jumping site to either watch or leap. The Winehouse & Kitchen gets about 1,600 visitors a month and offers a menu with items paired with Van Asch wines.

American Tom Tusher has also moved into Central Otago wine tourism in a big way. Tusher in 1972 was setting up operations for Levi Strauss, the blue jeans company, in Australia and New Zealand, when he traveled to Queenstown for the first time. While there, he visited a large property at Blanket Bay, 27 miles west of the city at the end of an unpaved road. It took him three and a half hours to make the trip in the summer, and he was told the route was impossible to traverse in the winter. Facing the north end of beautiful Lake Wakatipu with towering mountains behind it, the property was not only awesome but also for sale. Tusher's wife thought he was crazy to consider buying it, as did just about everyone else, but he did so anyway.

Tusher's business career took him to the top of Levi Strauss in San Francisco, and for the next twenty-five years he did nothing with his New Zealand property. But after retiring as president at age fifty-six in 1997, he decided to turn the lakeside investment into a small luxury hotel. He talked with several people in the hospitality field, including Bill Harlan and John Montgomery of Meadowood and Mark Harmon of Auberge du Soleil, both high-end Napa Valley resorts. They all discouraged him from doing it. Undeterred, Tusher pressed on and at the end of 1999 opened the **Blanket Bay Luxury Lodge**, which regularly ranks among the world's most exclusive resorts. British actor Sir Ian McKellen stayed there while filming the movie *Lord of the Rings* and later called it "one of the very special places on earth."

Comprised of nine rooms in the main building and four suites in two nearby chalets, the facility can accommodate twenty-six people at a time, at a daily price of $856 for a double room and $1,266 for a suite. A staff of forty-two is on hand to pamper guests and provide such activities as flying by helicopter to Milford Sound and landing on a nearby glacier, fly-fishing, hiking, horseback riding, jet boating, and more. Blanket Bay's chef and sous-chef have both won awards as the top chef of New Zealand.

While living in California, Tusher was on the board of Cakebread Cellars in the Napa Valley, so it's not surprising that he has also ventured into New Zealand wine. In the 1990s, Rob Hay of Chard Farm and John Darby bought Lake Hayes winery just outside the city. The vineyard produced only modest white wines and no Pinot Noir at all, so the owners began looking for better land and found a large, promising plot for a new vineyard some 45 miles east of town. By 2006, Hay was looking for an exit from Lake Hayes, so Tom Tusher and Darby became the major investors in the winery, which bought the 1,236-acre Amisfield sheep farm and renamed itself the **Amisfield Wine Com-**

pany. They planted a new vineyard in 1999, and the first Amisfield vintage was in 2002. The Lake Hayes vineyard now grows grapes that are largely used for making sparkling white wine. Amisfield opened its own production facility in 2006. All of the Amisfield wines are made from estate-grown grapes on a more than 150-acre vineyard at the new property. The winery currently produces some 25,000 cases of wine a year, but has a short-term goal of increasing that to 50,000. That would make it, by far, the largest winery in Central Otago.

The owners hired Fleur Caulton, who had previously owned her own restaurant in Queenstown, to start an upscale restaurant at the site of the Lake Hayes winery. She explains, "We realized we had a great asset in this property. It might not be the best place for growing grapes, but it is a wonderful location for wine tourism." The Amisfield Bistro opened in 2005, and the tasting room and restaurant now receive about two hundred visitors daily.

Both Amisfield wines and the bistro have enjoyed major success with critics. *Wine Spectator* placed the Amisfield Pinot Noir 2003 and 2005 vintages on its annual Top 100 list in 2005 and 2007. The New Zealand magazine *Cuisine* awarded the Bistro its winery restaurant of the year award in 2006 and 2007.

Central Otago receives fewer wine tourists than most regions profiled in this book, which is one of the reasons it does not have any large international hotel or motel chains. Instead, a new type of accommodation has evolved with particular appeal to wine enthusiasts: bed-and-breakfasts with a wine connection. All the facilities are small, and many are expensive. But they can be delightful.

Brian and Maureen Dennis run the **Mt Rosa Vineyard Estate** in the Gibbston Valley only twenty minutes outside Queenstown, which has three suites, each with its own entrance and beautiful views out over vineyards, valleys, and mountains. Brian has excellent connections with the local wine establishment and also has his own small vineyard just outside their front door. Breakfast and evening drinks are served in the large lodge room that provides beautiful views and a fireplace.

Cardrona Terrace Estate, in Wanaka, is not far from the historic Rippon Vineyard where Rolfe Mills started the area's wine boom. When founders Sharon and Kevin Alderson were getting started in the late

1990s, they asked Mills to give them some advice on which vines to plant. He told them to grow grapes for wines that they liked to drink "because you may end up drinking a lot of it." So the couple planted Pinot Noir and Riesling, which they grow right in front of their lodge.

Jon Davies used to be a top official at the New Zealand state tourism agency. Shortly before retiring, he and his wife, Lesley, bought 50 acres near Cromwell, where they built a new home on the valley floor that has spectacular mountain views and four guest rooms. It's called Aoturoa Luxury Villa. The Davieses offer a special dinner with the Pisa Range Estates in nearby Pisa Flats, which is owned by Warwick and Jenny Hawker. He was a New Zealand diplomat who served as ambassador to Iran among other places. They bought land in early 1995, but have only slowly brought the property into wine production. An evening at the Aoturoa lodge includes a winery tour and dinner of such local specialties as venison. Pisa Range wines are served.

Because Central Otago is still off the beaten path for most world travelers, visitors can enjoy many wonderful, intimate wine experiences along its quiet roads as well as a pristine climate that makes every day an experience in good living.

Diary of a Wine Tourist

February 27

Adventure at the Kawarau Bridge

Staffers at the AJ Hackett Bungy Jump on the Kawarau Bridge in Queenstown displayed laid-back Kiwi friendliness, but were perhaps also trying to make me relax by constantly calling me by my first name. One casually asked, "George, are you going to jump?"

I had been thinking about doing a bungy jump for several weeks, though I hadn't said a word about it to my family before leaving home. I had asked the cardiologist who was treating me for high blood pressure whether it was safe. After a little reflection and giving me a prescription for a new medication to control the problem, the doctor said that as long as I was taking the medication it would be okay.

So when the perky young woman behind the counter at the jump center repeated, "George, are you going to go for it?" I said sure and started going through the formalities. First I had to fill out a form giving my name, nationality, and required signature on the liability release. On the counter was a list of physical conditions that might cause a problem. I wasn't pregnant, but one of them was high blood pressure. I told them about that, but quickly added my doctor said it was okay. In that case, no problem. The perky lady asked me to take everything out of my pockets because "it will all fall out anyway." Then they weighed me, and a number was written with a red Magic Marker on my left hand: "79," meaning I weighed 79 kilos (174 pounds). That same number was also put on the slip of paper with my name. Then off we went to the Kawarau Bridge, 141 feet above a river with the same name.

I was introduced to Phil Clifton, who would be my jumpmaster and see me through it. He looked at the paper with my name and noted that I was going to be the thirteenth jumper of the day. "You're lucky, George," he quipped. He also explained he had been working there for thirteen years and had done "hundreds of jumps." Then Phil began suiting me up. First came a harness that went around my waist and between my legs. After that Phil folded a towel around my feet and between them. Finally came the clamps, one to hold the inch-thick bungy cord and the second emergency clamp on the harness.

Phil next asked me to move over to the jumping platform. My feet now were so tightly bound that I had to shuffle the short distance much like a death row prisoner inching his way to the executioner. Phil told me to put my feet a couple of inches over the edge and then to wave to the crowd below that had gathered to see the next person jump. I asked Phil if I should go off feet first or in a dive. He replied, "Go off in a beautiful swan dive, George." Then he added, "Don't look down. Look straight ahead at the bridge in front of you."

Staring intently at the bridge, I felt Phil pull back from me as he said, "I'm going to count down from five. Jump when I get to one."

"Five . . . four . . . three . . . two . . . one."

My arms went up, and off I jumped.

The green water below seemed to be rushing up toward me in a flash, but I felt no sense of panic or danger. I heard Phil yell from the bridge, "Beautiful, George. Good on you, mate." The adrenaline rush made everything extremely vivid. I felt intensively alive. A person being hanged knows it's over when the rope suddenly tightens and snaps his neck. A bungy jumper knows he's safe when he feels the cord hit bottom and then bounce up. Flashing through my mind as I felt the bounce was only one thought: "The bungy cord held!" Three more times I bounced, as a sense of calm swept over me. It was over.

Two young men in an inflatable boat then came out to pull me down. One of them held up a long white plastic tube and yelled at me to grab on to it. I missed it the first time, but caught it the second and was pulled down into the boat.

Both guys congratulated me, and one told me to look back up to the bridge and wave to the camera that was recording all of this. I waved, flashed a smile as wide as the bridge, and said to my mates in the boat, "And I didn't even die!"

The claim was not substantiated when several signs such as this were put up a half century ago, but no one would challenge them now.

The famous Stag's Leap outcropping on the eastern side of the Napa Valley. The vineyard is part of Stag's Leap Wine Cellars.

Aurelio Montes, the winemaker and one of the two main founders of Viña Montes in the vineyards in Apalta, Chile.

The vineyards and surrounding mountains of Vergelegen in Stellenbosch, South Africa, is one of the best sites in the world of wine tourism.

Charles Back in front of his goat tower at Fairview Wines, one of the most popular wineries in South Africa.

The controversial *Chick on a Stick* sculpture at the Laurance of Margaret River winery.

Carlos Cardoen, the controversial arms dealer turned winery owner. His Swiss-made ski lift takes visitors from the valley floor to a mountaintop, where there is a Chilean natural history museum.

The Finca Altamira vineyard, which is owned by Achaval-Ferrer. In the background are the Andes. The Malbec wines from this old vineyard get scores in the high 90s from Robert Parker.

Santiago Achaval, founder of the Achaval-Ferrer winery, the most highly honored in Mendoza, strums a guitar during an *asado*.

Chadwick La Escultura
Vineyard, Casablanca
Valley, Chile.

Denis Horgan,
founder of
Leeuwin Estate in
Margaret River.

In both Australia and New Zealand, winemakers must put netting over their vines near harvest time to protect them from birds. The Voyager Estate winery in Margaret River is pictured here.

The author makes a bungy jump off the Kawarau Bridge just outside Queenstown, New Zealand.

The Waitiri Creek winery in Central Otago has its tasting room in an abandoned church.

The Sharvazeebi family of winemakers in Georgia has watched over its operations for countless centuries and even the Soviets didn't dare shut them down.

Bodegas Ysios, the most famous of the many masterpieces of modern architecture inspired by the Frank Gehry–designed Guggenheim Bilbao museum. The Spanish architect Santiago Calatrava designed Ysios, which is located in the foothills of the Sierra de Cantabria Mountains, facing the ancient hilltop fortress city of Laguardia.

The Dinastía Vivanco winery in Rioja at harvest. The building on the right is the top of the winery; all of the rest of the structure is below ground. On the left is the family chapel.

The stately Château Pichon-Longueville Baron is in the village of Pauillac in Bordeaux.

Sister Thekla Baumgart runs the winery for the nuns at the Abbey of St. Hildegard above the town of Rüdesheim, Germany.

A boat makes its way down the Douro River toward Porto. The vineyards on the sides of the valley date back to Roman times.

Castello Banfi in Tuscany.

Donatella Cinelli Colombini (*left*), the founder of Italy's Movimento Turismo del Vino, and members of her all-female staff.

CHAPTER EIGHT

Rioja, Spain

During the Middle Ages, Rioja in northern Spain was the crossroads of civilizations. The cathedral of Santiago de Compostela in Galicia, a short distance west on the Atlantic Coast, was believed to be the burial site of St. James the Great, one of the original twelve apostles. Christians could earn complete forgiveness for their sins by making the pilgrimage to the cathedral along a route that became known as *El Camino de Santiago* (The Road to Santiago). The pious faithful walked the long trip from as far north as England and Germany down through France and then across the top of the Iberian Peninsula to Santiago. At the time, the more intellectually advanced Moors ruled most of Iberia, and they passed along their learning to less educated Europeans making the trip. A whole pilgrimage infrastructure grew up to support the travelers. Monasteries along the way became the Holiday Inns of their time, taking in pilgrims and giving them a meal, a glass of wine, and a place to sleep for a night before sending them on their way in the morning. Religious orders also established hospitals to take care of injured or ill pilgrims. At the Yuso monastery in the village of San Millán de la Cogolla, a monk in the thirteenth century carefully noted on parchment and in Latin that pilgrims there had received a meal and "a glass of good wine." In the margin, he wrote the same notation in the local dialect that would later become the Spanish language. Thus, history's first written record in Spanish was on the subject of wine. The people of Rioja still claim that their culture of food, wine, and hospitality goes back to the monks helping pilgrims on their way to Santiago de Compostela.

Rioja extends from the town of Alfaro in the east some 75 miles to Haro in the west, and at its broadest point is about 25 miles wide. A region of relatively small towns, the biggest nearby metropolitan area is the port city of Bilbao about 90 miles to the north. The Ebro River—Spain's most voluminous, although relatively small compared to rivers in other countries—flows through Rioja from west to east before emptying into the Mediterranean. The name Rioja comes from an Ebro tributary named the *Rio Oja,* or Oja River. The large Ebro delta is a rich agricultural area, producing bountiful crops of grains, fruits, and vegetables. Rioja, though, is best for growing wine grapes. The area gets its mild climate from two mountain ranges, the tree-lined Sierra de Cantabria in the north, which protects it from harsh Atlantic winds, and the snow-peaked Sierra de la Demanda to the south, which shields it from hot, dry winds blowing out of Africa and sweeping across the Iberian plains.

Grapes grow mainly in the broad valley between the two mountain ranges. Looking out at Rioja, a visitor sees a land of browns and reds, with vineyards covering the undulating countryside leading up to high mountains in the distance. Sticking up here and there across the valley floor like spikes on a board are ancient fortresses on hilltops such as the medieval town of Laguardia. Unlike in Colchagua or Napa Valley, few vineyards have been planted in hilly areas. Bush vines, individual plants with branches growing up and out in a chaotic fashion, were the standard way of cultivation until recently, when trellising was introduced by new wineries during the replanting of old vineyards. Another colorful sight in the vineyards is beehive-shaped stone huts, where workers store tools and escape from unexpected storms.

Rioja for centuries was a tempting target for wandering warriors. Celtic tribes lived there until the Romans drove them out about 200 BC. Romans introduced winemaking to Rioja, but the practice suffered under the Moors, who invaded at the beginning of the eighth century. Wine, though, made a comeback in medieval Europe, when new Christian kingdoms conquered the land and thanks to demand from *Camino de Santiago* travelers. While plentiful, the original Rioja wines were mainly rough reds that had little ambition for quality. Red wine still makes up 80 percent of total production, and 80 percent of that is Tempranillo, which according to British wine writer Jancis Robinson, monks brought from Burgundy on their way to Santiago de Compostela. The name comes from *temprano,* the Spanish word for early, because the fruit ripens before other red grapes. Small quantities of other reds such as Garnacha, Graciano, and Mazuelo are found in Rioja. The attitude of local winemakers toward them is evident from the aphorism that Graciano really stands for *"Gracias, no,"* or "No, thanks." Rioja white wines—Viura, Malvasia, and White Garnacha— are not aromatic, and only a few wineries can make good traditional white Riojas. Regulators in 2008 gave permission to grow Sauvignon Blanc, Chardonnay, and other international grapes. Early results indicate that they will do well in the area.

Rioja remained isolated from international wine routes until the nineteenth century, when viticulture problems in Bordeaux, such as the vine disease oidium or powdery mildew in the late 1840s, followed by phylloxera in the 1860s, led winemakers to look for new winegrowing regions nearby. The Pyrenees temporarily protected Rioja from the two infestations, so French winemakers started planting vineyards and producing wines there. The small railroad town of Haro developed into a major wine area because producers could ship wine easily to northern Europe. As a result of new French equipment and techniques, the quality of Rioja wines improved. Some of today's leading Riojan winemakers, such as R. López de Heredia Viña Tondonia and Herederos del Marqués de Riscal, were started in the middle of the nineteenth century.

The Spanish Civil War and then the long reign of Generalissimo Francisco Franco, however, isolated Rioja and its wines by making them politically unacceptable in many European markets. As a result, Rioja once again fell behind, with winemakers producing mainly tannic wines that spent years in old American oak barrels to soften their harshness. It was only the death of Franco in November 1975, and then Spain's entry into the European Union in 1986, that totally opened the door to Spanish wine exports and led to a new wave of innovation. After wine frauds in Austria and Germany in the 1980s damaged the reputation of producers in those two countries, Rioja tightened up on its regulations. All Riojan wine now has to be bottled in the region. Winemakers looking to export also began making lighter wines, often aging them in French oak. Rioja was awarded Spain's first designation in

1991 as a *Denominación de Origen Calificada* (Qualified Denomination of Origin). Strong foreign investment also helped bring Riojan wines up to international standards. Bodegas Marqués de Cáceres was a leader in producing a new-style Rioja that many wineries later followed.

Despite major changes in winemaking style and technique, Rioja remains an area of many small vineyards. The region has 148,000 acres under vine, but there are 19,000 grape growers working on nearly 114,000 plots. While the number of single vineyard wines is slowly increasing, most wineries still buy a large share of their grapes from other growers and then blend them together to make their wine.

In addition to being Spain's leading wine region, Rioja has also become famous in recent years as the home of some of the most beautiful wineries in the world. No other country begins to match it. This development was inspired by the Guggenheim Museum Bilbao, which opened in 1997. In the early 1990s, Bilbao was a dirty city that many residents thought was slowly dying. The port, the center of its economy and mainstay of local employment, was losing out in the competitive world of international cargo transportation. Violent Basque separatists gave the city a reputation for being a place of guys with guns similar to Chicago in the 1920s. Young people were leaving in hopes of finding better jobs and brighter futures elsewhere. Barcelona, its northeastern sister city, was then Spain's happening city and home to the 1992 summer Olympics.

From its base in New York City at an iconic building designed by Frank Lloyd Wright, the Guggenheim Foundation reached out and signed an agreement with the Basque Administration to construct a new museum in Bilbao. The Basques agreed to pay $100 million to build it, and Canadian architect Frank Gehry was selected to design it. As soon as the glass, titanium, and limestone structure was unveiled, it was immediately compared to Frank Lloyd Wright's Manhattan masterpiece. The museum calls itself "a magnificent example of the most groundbreaking architecture to have come out of the twentieth century."

Located along the Nervión River in the heart of Bilbao, the building and the museum of modern art that it houses became the centerpiece of the city's transformation into a dynamic leader in the art world. Designed to resemble a ship, the never-ending curves capture a visitor's imagination and then hold it in a titanium-and-steel grip. If ever a museum changed the history of a city, it was the Guggenheim Bilbao. Soon other architects were designing showpiece projects around the region. One of them was the new Bilbao Airport of white concrete and glass, designed by Spain's Santiago Calatrava. Nicknamed "The Dove" because it looked like a bird in flight, the airport became fully operational in 2000.

The Guggenheim immediately began attracting big crowds and also tourists who may have come for the art and then stayed on for a glass, or bottle, of Rioja. In addition, Gehry's work inspired winery owners to think about exteriors as well as interiors. Cathedrals in towns such as Burgos, Toledo, and Segovia were Spain's monuments in an earlier era, and wineries have become those of contemporary times.

The first, and still the most dramatic, new winery was **Bodegas Ysios**, named after the Egyptian goddess who ruled over the conversion of grapes into wine. Bodegas y Bebidas, then Spain's largest wine company with more than 160 brands, wanted a new winery to improve a reputation built on low-cost wine. The Banco Bilbao Vizcaya owned 40 percent of the company, and surprisingly it was the bankers who drove the decision to build a showpiece winery in the spirit of the Guggenheim and the Bilbao Airport. The theory was that it would improve the company's image and eventual resale value. Bodegas y Bebidas turned the job over to Santiago Calatrava, who designed what is perhaps the world's most beautiful winery. Work on it started in 1998. The winery is located in the foothills of the Sierra de Cantabria Mountains, facing the ancient hilltop fortress of Laguardia. The nearly 219-yard-long building with a front façade of rolling peaks and valleys echoes the mountains behind it. Bodegas Ysios makes heavy use of wood, aluminum, and water pools, and the final product seems more like a sculpture than a building.

While the building is spectacular outside, it is functional inside. Calatrava also designed the interior, putting curves everywhere to reinforce the image of barrels. The tasting room, which is the tall centerpiece of the structure, has huge windows looking out over a vineyard and directly at medieval Laguardia. The winery has become a favorite location for high-profile events such as receptions and fashion shows.

The corporate strategy of improving its image with a beautiful winery worked. Allied Domecq bought Bodegas y Bebidas in 2001, and was then itself taken over in 2005 by France's Pernod Ricard. Ysios produces only one wine, a Tempranillo Reserva. Some 80 percent of it is sold in Spain, and only a little makes it to the United States and Britain. Ysios wine generally gets good reviews, but the winery may always be better known for its architecture than for its wines. *Wine Spectator* called it a value wine at $30 a bottle and gave it 88 out of 100 points. Ysios has become a popular stop for wine tourists and sells 10 percent of its production at the winery. One of the highlights of the tour is the well-appointed room for club members, who have to pay two years in advance to buy a barrel (330 bottles) or half barrel (150 bottles), but then get their name on the label.

Marqués de Riscal is one of Rioja's oldest wineries, though not particularly noted for the quality of its wines. It generally scores in the 80-point range from *Wine Spectator* but sometimes as low as in the 70s. When the winery decided to open a hotel, it hired Frank Gehry to repeat his magic from Bilbao and turned management of the hotel over to the luxury Starwood Hotels & Resorts chain. As a way to seal the deal with the famous architect, Riscal offered Gehry a bottle of its wine from 1929, the year he was born. Gehry's design at Riscal was similar to that of the Guggenheim, with a roof that resembles a colorful collection of ribbons made of titanium. The combination of an old winery with a modernistic hotel sitting on top of it seems at first to be an unusual juxtaposition. But appreciated on its own, the forty-three-room hotel works. The Hotel Marqués de Riscal, the best in Rioja, has an outstanding restaurant whose chef-advisor is Francis Paniego of the nearby Echaurren Restaurant, the first in Rioja to get a Michelin star. The hotel also has a Caudalíe Vinothérapie Spa that uses the wine-therapy techniques for skin care first developed at Château Smith Haut Lafitte in Bordeaux.

López de Heredia in the village of Haro has done an excellent job of combining an old winery still making great wines with a modern architectural statement made by Iraq-born, Britain-based Zaha Hadid, who won the 2004 Pritzker Architecture Prize. She designed the winery's tasting pavilion, which is shaped like a flask. Originally built for the 2002 Alimentaria Barcelona food and beverage fair, the pavilion and the canopy sheltering it were dismantled and then reassembled at the winery. At the back of the ultramodern structure is a Belle Époque sales booth left over from the 1910 Brussels World's Fair.

Managing director María José López de Heredia represents the winery's fourth generation of family leadership. She has safeguarded its tradition of making quality wines with time-treasured methods that even include making their own barrels. Eric Asimov, the wine critic for the *New York Times* who normally holds his accolades tightly in check, once wrote that he is "obsessed with the wines of López de Heredia" and piled on praise not only for its reds but also its whites and even its rosés.

Tours at López de Heredia are among the best in Rioja and take visitors through an ancient winery where the mold-covered walls scream history. The tour wanders through a series of underground caves until the guide opens a door and visitors are almost magically outside, looking at wagons that used to carry grapes into the winery on railroad tracks. The most enjoyable part is visiting the area the Spanish call the wine cemetery, which wineries in other countries usually call the wine library, where old, unlabeled bottles rest, covered with a heavy coating of dust. Americans have been ordering bottles of old vintages for special events such as major birthdays or anniversaries. When María José López de Heredia gave me a tour, she explained that a New Yorker had once sent a letter complaining that the old bottles were dusty and wanted clean ones. María José replied with a polite note saying that most people liked the layer of dust to show the wine was aged. At the end of the tour, visitors sample several wines. López de Heredia hosts as many as two hundred people on a Saturday, but spreads them among eight tasting rooms, so the winery never seems crowded.

♉ ♉ ♉

Inspired primarily by Ysios, every winery in Rioja feels obligated to make a strong artistic statement with its temple of wine. Stunning architecture has quickly become a tradition. **Bodegas Baigorri**, the work of Basque architect Iñaki Aspiazu, stands atop a hill, with an entrance hall surrounded by 360 degrees of glass. That is the only part of the winery above ground. Below are six floors of gravity-flow production facilities built into the mountainside. At the bottom level looking out at the valley is a restaurant.

Bodegas Juan Alcorta's award-winning winery in Logroño, designed by the Spanish architect Ignacio Quemada, is ultramodern and simple in style with a rich rock exterior and wood interior. Its huge, underground aging cellar is spectacular.

The French architect Philippe Mazières designed the new **Viña Real** winery on the main road between Logroño, the capital of Rioja, and Laguardia. The centerpiece is a giant wine barrel made of concrete, wood, and stainless steel. The winery says its goal is to "combine the concepts of man, nobility, and modernity."

Haro, a town that is supposed to have more bars than any in Spain for its size (pop. 10,000), remains a center of Rioja wine production and has become a favorite destination for wine tourism. Anyone wanting to spend some time with the mayor knows he can always be found having tapas and a glass of wine before lunch in one of the town's many bars. On June 29 each year, the Haro "Battle of Wine" takes place, when people dressed in white throw wine at each other in a display of mayhem that ends with everyone stained red. Then there is a small and controlled running of the bulls to the bullring. No one remembers exactly who started this tradition, but rumor says it had something to do with an ancient land dispute.

Down the road in Haro from López de Heredia is **Bodegas Muga**, one of the innovators of wine tourism and a producer of prized Rioja wines. Muga is a relatively new winery, having been founded in 1932. It has been at its present location in a nineteenth-century town house near the railroad station only since 1962. The third generation of the Muga family now runs day-to-day operations.

Juan Muga admits that ten years ago, when Spaniards first started coming to the countryside for a weekend of wine tasting, his family's winery was not ready for tourists. Family members at first gave the tours, which he candidly says were unprofessional. But a trip to the Napa Valley gave them some ideas on how to do things better and soon the family was using its old town house and winery as the centerpiece for visits. Initially, Muga was not open on weekends, but it quickly realized that they were a peak tourist time and expanded its schedule. Muga now has daily tours in both Spanish and English, and often hosts two hundred people on weekends. The tasting room has the feel of an elegant English private club, with lots of antique oak furniture and an inviting fireplace. The tour takes an hour and a half, and ends with samples of two Muga wines.

One of the highlights of a visit is watching the three resident coopers make wine barrels. Muga takes pride in continuing to produce at least some of its own barrels at a time when most wineries have given up that skilled artisan work. As visitors see on the tour, there are no stainless steel tanks, since the winery uses only traditional oak.

Muga's wines regularly receive among the highest ratings in Rioja. In 2008, Robert Parker gave five Muga wines between 92 and 98 points. *Wine Spectator* had Muga wines in its Top 100 in both 2007 and 2008. Juan Muga explained to me that the winery makes different wines for different national palates. Torre Muga, a blend of 75 percent Tempranillo, 15 percent Mazuelo, and 10 percent Graciano, is tailored for the international market and foreign wine critics, who like more fruit. The 2004 got 96 points from Parker. The Prado Enea Gran Reserva, on the other hand, has 80 percent Tempranillo with the balance made up of Garnacha, Mazuelo, and Graciano. It is a more traditional Rioja wine for the local market.

A new Haro winery making a big splash internationally is **Bodegas Roda**, started by the family that holds the Coca-Cola franchise for Spain and twelve African countries. It was established in 1987, and produced its first vintage in 1991. The winemakers, though, were dissatisfied with it, so the staff opened all the bottles, poured out the contents, and sold it as bulk wine. Roda's breakout vintage was 1994. With six enologists on staff, it's not surprising that Roda is a research winery. One of the six, Gonzalo Lainez, told me, "We are trying to produce traditional wine in the vineyard and modern wine in the winery." He adds that they don't believe in "rock star winemakers" and manage by consensus. The winery still has a production of only 25,000 cases, and Lainez admits Roda is overstaffed. But he says the goal is that in fifty years the wine world will be talking about Penfolds

Grange, Domaine de la Romanée-Conti, and Roda all in the same breath.

Wine tourism is important for Roda, but it has to be a certain type of tourist. The winery is not interested in crowds. It wants people who already know its wines and are drinking them. "Wine tourism is important because it's all about loyalty, and success for me is when a person buys the second bottle," says Lainez.

For the right tourist, Roda will give an hour-and-a-half tour that starts with a trip in a Land Rover to the vineyard. "We know the best areas in our vineyards, but we need to learn more. Our sons and grand-sons will know where to grow the best vine." Lainez was the first wine-maker to tell me the secret of how an average tourist can get special treatment at an exclusive winery like Roda: get the winery's distributor to request a tour. In Roda's case, that's Kobrand. If a tourist comes via the distributor, the tour may stretch to three hours, and rarely includes more than six people.

Roda is almost as proud of its olive oil as it is of its wine. Many win-eries in Rioja sell olive oil, but few are as passionate about it as Roda. The owners originally had some land where olive trees grew and asked the winemakers if they could make olive oil. The six enologists had no experience with that product, but the chief enologist spent a year study-ing it and came up with a new production method that emphasized picking young olives quickly and then pressing them immediately. "We made a new-style olive oil and in effect rediscovered an ancient prod-uct," said Lainez. The Roda olive oil has been judged the best in Spain and among the top ten in the world.

Barón de Ley, another new winery, is just making its name for pro-ducing high-quality wines with modern methods at an ancient loca-tion. It was started in 1985 by a group of local investors who wanted to establish a winery based on the Bordeaux style of sourcing grapes from only vineyards the winery owned and controlled, rather than making a blend using grapes bought from several independent sources. Since many Rioja wineries already used Marqués in their names, the found-ers decided to give theirs the name Barón, although there was no baron in particular. De Ley means the law or someone you can trust, so the name can be translated as "Baron You Can Trust." Initially the owners planted 222 acres in the modern trellis style, but the winery now owns 791 acres.

This winery with the offbeat name has lots of history. Its main building was constructed in 1548 as a castle and was the scene of many battles between the kingdoms of Navarre and Castile. Later it was turned into a Benedictine monastery, which included a cellar where the monks made wine. The Benedictines lost the property in 1836, when the state seized religious lands. It then went into private hands, and at one point a Spanish general lost the castle and 2,471 acres around it in a card game to a French colonel, who turned around and sold it. The present owners restored the property that includes a gravel courtyard, chapel, and eleven monk cells that have been made into double bedrooms. They decided, however, not to open the facility to overnight guests, although its larger rooms are used for both official and private functions.

Barón de Ley focuses on producing wines aimed at not only the local market but also foreign ones, particularly in Europe. "New consumers are demanding wines with more structure, more power, and more fruit," says export manager Alex Tomé. The trellis system of planting allows grapes to ripen faster than they would get with bush planting. The winery produces only Reserva and Gran Reserva grade wines, and its top-of-the-line Finca Monasterio comes from hand-sorted grapes of the oldest vines. It is made with 80 percent Tempranillo and is unfiltered. It regularly gets 90-point scores from Robert Parker. Using a French term for a small winery with handcrafted procedures, Tomé calls it Barón de Ley's "garage wine," describing it as "very modern."

Given its location, buildings, wines, and target audience, Barón de Ley should be going after wine tourism in a big way. Tomé admits, "Our winery is designed to receive tourists." But currently it hosts only about 3,000 visitors a year, and 70 percent of those are wine professionals such as wine-store owners. Sales at the winery account for only 1 percent of revenues. The winery's approach has been to avoid hard promotion or heavy advertising. It's not actively discouraging visitors; it's simply not chasing them. That's too bad because Barón de Ley has a lot going for it.

One of Rioja's special places is the walled village of Laguardia. In an age when every corner of the world seems to be teeming with Americans bearing Japanese cameras and Japanese listening to American iPods, Laguardia is a throwback to an earlier era when a traveler could enjoy walking alone around a beautiful place. No cars are allowed within the city walls. The small wandering lanes don't seem to have changed since the town was fortified in the thirteenth century atop a hill of rock 2,100 feet above sea level. The tasting room at Bodegas Ysios has a stunning view of Laguardia, and the village is an equally good location to look down on the winery.

It's hard to believe that wineries and cellars were dug into the rock on which Laguardia was built, and some of them are still in operation today. The Posada Mayor de Migueloa, which dates back to the seventeenth century and has only eight double rooms, boasts a cellar located more than 25 feet underground where guests can have a single glass of wine or do a full tasting of Rioja's best.

Because large areas of Rioja are flat or gentle hills, this is an ideal area for cycling or walking vacations. The best time of year for both kinds of tourism is October during harvest. Butterfield & Robinson, the Canadian luxury tour company, offers a six-day bike trip of Rioja that takes in many of the top wineries and restaurants. Jenny Siddall, a British linguist who worked for other travel agencies before starting her own firm Walking with Wine, is based in Rioja and offers programs lasting three days or a week, plus tailor-made tours that usually spend lots of time in Haro and Laguardia. Siddall, who combines an outsider's perspective with an insider's love of the place, says that one of Rioja's charms is that it remains an untouched area where it can still be hard to find a postcard for sale.

♀ ♀ ♀

While researching this book, I visited dozens of wine museums and through the Internet have been able to experience many more vicariously. Without a doubt, the **Bodegas Dinastía Vivanco** Museum of Wine Culture is the best in the world.

Vivanco is another new winery making a big impact on Rioja. Two brothers, Santiago and Rafael Vivanco, now run it on a day-to-day basis. Their great-grandfather Pedro started the business in 1915, and at first made wine only for his family. In 1940, his son Santiago bought a small winery that had over the cellar door the inscription, "He who walks by and is thirsty, if the door is open, should enter and drink." But as with most wineries in Spain at that time, it hardly provided a living for the family. A third-generation son was also named Pedro, and it was under his direction that the business expanded greatly. After studying enology, he improved the quality of the wines and increased the family's land holdings from 49 acres in Rioja to the present 988 acres there and an additional 297 acres in nearby Navarra. Vivanco was a minority shareholder in Bodegas y Bebidas, and after Allied Domecq bought the company in 1999, Pedro took his profits from that sale and built a winery worthy of having the word "dynasty" in its name.

Pedro launched an ambitious new brand name, Dinastía Vivanco, with the goal of producing only top-quality wines. Then he developed plans for a major new complex that would include both a wine museum and a winery. There was never any question about where it was going to be located. In 1985, he had bought his first property in the village of Briones (pop. 1,000), located between Haro and Laguardia. Says Santiago Vivanco: "My father says he fell in love twice: once with my mother and once with Briones. He thinks you can make the world's best Tempranillo here."

Pedro's master plan included major roles for both his sons in the project. His younger son, Rafael, studied agricultural engineering in Pamplona, Spain, and then did two years of postgraduate work in enology at the University of Bordeaux. But the older son, Santiago, was already going in a different direction. He had entered the Jesuit order in 1991 and started his studies for becoming a Catholic priest, which can take up to fourteen years to complete. Santiago was well on his way to becoming a priest, having finished some of his philosophy and theology studies and discovered a love of history and art. The father, though, thought he might be able to lure his son back to the family business by having him run the planned museum. So in 1996 at the age of twenty-three, Santiago left the Jesuits and completed a law degree and also a Master's of Business Administration. The father then basically gave him a checkbook and told him to search the world looking for wine artifacts, saying, "Buy whatever you want, and build the museum you want."

The bedrock of the future museum was to be wine antiques that Pedro, an incorrigible collector of discarded wine equipment, had been storing in warehouses for years. His own father had told him he was crazy to buy the old stuff, but his mother had slipped him money to keep picking up such pieces as the first tractor used in Rioja. So with that old equipment as the core of a collection, Santiago began traveling the globe and visiting wine museums. He concentrated his search for antiquities on London and New York City, which had the most items for sale.

In the late summer of 1997, Pedro met with the Riojan architect Jesús Marino Pascual and spelled out his dream for the wine complex. First, there was going to be the great museum devoted to the history and culture of wine. Second, Pedro wanted to set up the Dinastía Vivanco Cultural Foundation, which would foster wine study and research. Finally, there would be a new state-of-the-art winery. Pascual was a natural choice as architect because he had earlier renovated the Wine Making Station in Haro, which was built in 1892. And since he was a local, Pedro was confident he would appreciate the importance of blending the medieval character of Briones with the new complex.

Pedro insisted from the beginning that the museum was not going to be about marketing Vivanco wine. "It was all about giving back to wine what wine gave my family," Santiago told me. "The museum is dedicated to the universal wine culture. It is not just our company, not just Rioja, not just Spain. It is about all wine." Today there is only one bottle of Vivanco wine in the entire museum, a 1998 Reserva near the end of the exhibits in an unobtrusive place that most visitors probably never even notice. Near the bottle is a quote from the Arab philosopher and poet Avicenna: "Everyone is happy, but no one is drunk."

The museum's permanent collection is divided into five sections. The first is dedicated to winemaking history and technology, with hundreds of pieces of ancient equipment and explanations of how winemaking developed over the ages. The second deals with wine storage and includes exhibits on barrel making, corks, and bottles. The third is about what happens in the cellar as the grape juice becomes wine and then is packaged and sent to the consumer.

The museum's fourth part is devoted to art and archeology. This is clearly Santiago's favorite section and what really sets Vivanco apart from other wine museums, containing a vast array of artifacts such as ancient Greek vases as well as medieval tapestries and modern paintings, including lithographs by Picasso, Miró, and Sorolla. Santiago told me he is proudest of two pieces he found: a Roman sarcophagus from the third century BC that has a carved image of Bacchus; and a painting by the Dutch artist Jan van Scorel, who in the sixteenth century personally introduced the Italian Renaissance to the Flemish school of art. The painting depicts the Holy Family with the infant Jesus grasping some grapes.

The last section of the collection is the fun part. When Santiago went out to buy whatever he wanted for the museum, Pedro told him to pick up every unique corkscrew he saw. Later Rafael joined in the hunt. Santiago eventually purchased 4,000, while Rafael added 2,000 more. And they are both still looking. The most interesting 3,000 corkscrews, which are made in all the ways the mind of man could imagine, are now on display. The corkscrew collection has become a popular part of the museum, as is a display of *tastevins,* the ceremonial cups sommeliers use for tasting wine.

King Juan Carlos inaugurated the museum in 2004. Consultants had warned Santiago not to expect it to attract a lot of visitors. They predicted the museum might have 20,000 to 30,000 visitors a year. The experts also advised that he set a high price of admission to help pay for it. Santiago disagreed and wanted to set the price low so it would draw big crowds, especially of young people and university students. The first year the Museum of Wine Culture received 108,000 visitors, and in 2007, it had 152,000. The museum is now the biggest tourist attraction in Rioja, hosting more visitors than the UNESCO World Heritage monasteries in nearby San Millán de la Cogolla.

The Vivanco Documentation Center now encompasses the world's largest private collections of wine artifacts, including 8,000 monographs, plus books on wine dating as far back as the fifteenth and sixteenth centuries. Vivanco digitized the documents, and in 2008 placed them all on the Internet, so scholars around the world could have access to them.

While the museum was going up, Pedro Vivanco and his winemaking son, Rafael, were working on the new winery, which opened in 2005 and is located between the museum and the vineyards. It was constructed mainly underground to provide natural cool conditions for winemaking and also so as not to block the view of the vineyards. The winery is outfitted with all the latest wine technology in line with Rafael's vision of producing fine wines that reflect the best of Rioja grape varieties grown in his family's vineyards. The most spectacular part is the wine-aging complex, located 17 feet underground and divided into two sections. One part houses French-oak vats for primary fermentation, and in the second are hundreds of small French barrels for malolactic fermentation. The barrel-aging room can also be seen from the fourth underground floor of the museum. In 2007, Rafael and his wife, Ana, held their wedding party in the aging cellar for some four hundred friends.

Vivanco is still building an international distribution system, but Rafael's wines are already starting to receive more and more attention, especially his three icon wines with the Colección Vivanco label. These wines reflect the cutting edge of Rioja today by combining both traditional and innovational viticulture and winemaking practices. The first is a 100 percent Garnacha, the second is a 100 percent Graciano, and the third, called 4 Varietales, is a blend of the four red grapes permitted in Rioja with 70 percent Tempranillo. Each grape variety is separately harvested, vinified, and aged in new French oak before blending and more bottle aging. One Spanish wine writer called the three wines the most exciting thing going on in the country today. All three wines received gold medals soon after the release of the first 2005 vintage.

Bodegas Ysios and the Bodegas Dinastía Vivanco Museum are only two examples of how Rioja has moved in just a few years from being a sleepy backwater of the wine world to being a major center of wine tourism. The future undoubtedly offers many more promising developments.

Diary of a Wine Tourist

April 4

Walking with the Elephants

Each day in cities around Spain, millions of people participate in the Elephant Walk, a celebration of local food and drink. The name comes from the slang term for being tipsy, which is the same word for an elephant's trunk, *trompa*. The ancient custom consists of going from bar to bar, enjoying a snack, a glass of local wine, and a chat with old or new friends. Even if you have eaten tapas elsewhere, there is nothing like enjoying them in a Spanish town. Wine in Rioja is traditionally red, which you order by simply asking for *un tinto* (a red), although these days the drink might also be a glass of white wine or even a beer. After a few tapas, people go on to lunch or dinner, or enough tapas can substitute for a meal. Tapas time at lunch starts after 1:00 and is usually finished by 3:00 p.m. In the evening it goes from about 8:30 to 10:30 p.m., but sometimes lasts longer, especially on weekends.

In the Rioja town of Haro, locals still tell stories about how in the olden days, the father of the family would enjoy ten or twelve tapas—and accompanying glasses of wine—before going home to lunch or dinner. Drinking today is down dramatically, and now people might have only three or four at lunch and then maybe the same number before dinner. I enjoyed tapas both in Haro and Logroño, the capital of Rioja.

The crowds in and around the tapas bars include a broad cross section of Spanish society. There are elderly couples with the men in gray suits and conservative ties, as well as teenagers in jeans. At lunch you're more likely to see men, though there are also some young career women. Night crowds are a more lively and interesting mix. There may also be entertainment. One night in Logroño, a saxophone player and a clarinetist played for change, and many more families were on the streets. My favorite sight was of a woman dancing with her young son, who was standing on a table. One family seemed to represent changing Spanish tastes. The father was drinking a *tinto,* his wife had a Coca-Cola, and their two adult children both drank beer.

The Elephant Walk always takes place in the old sections of the city, where dozens of bars are located side by side, and the merrymaking often spills out onto the sidewalks and streets. The main streets for tapas in Logroño are Calle San Juan, Calle Portales, and my favorite Calle Laurel. You don't have to know much Spanish to participate. Simply walk up to the bar and order a *tinto*. You're not there, however, just to drink. You also have to order something to eat.

My favorite bar in Logroño was Soriano. The neon sign outside showed a giant mushroom that told you everything you needed to know. In the back of the bar a cook busily prepared an appetizer made of mushrooms, bread, and shrimp. He gladly stopped and told me what he was doing. With a flourish, he finished by pouring a few drops of local olive oil on the top. Then he carefully handed the morsel to me on a toothpick. On the bar was an ample supply of napkins, which was convenient because the tapa was delicious, but messy. When you're finished, be sure to throw the napkin and toothpick on the floor. Everyone does, as you'll see if you just look down.

You can stay in one bar for hours nursing a glass of wine and getting caught up in conversations. But I enjoyed finishing my *tinto* and moving on to another place. The selection never ends. Casa Torres specialized in sausage, while Sebas had small pieces of potato omelet and stuffed red peppers. The Pata Negra had a dining room with a few tables, where you can get platters of local cheeses and sausages, but the real action took place in the bar. The most popular dish at Pata Negra was a hot ham and cheese sandwich. Don't leave Logroño without having one.

Wines served at the bars are generally young. A *trompa* is not a fine-wine experience. They are usually called *Joven* or *Crianza*. From

November until May or June, you will also find *Cosechero,* a Beaujo-lais Nouveau–style wine made by carbonic maceration. I thought the Spanish version fruitier than the French one and not as acidic. When I said that to Riojans, they invariably agreed it was indeed better, but said the French are better at marketing their wine. Enjoy the *Cosechero* in Rioja because it's never exported. In fact, enjoy the whole Elephant Walk.

CHAPTER NINE

Douro Valley, Portugal

The best place to appreciate the beauty of the Douro Valley is at the top of the mountains overlooking the Douro River. The trip from the bottom by bus, cab, or private car can take a half hour and is at times exhilarating as well as terrifying. There were few signs on the road, and no barriers to stop a vehicle that might make a bad turn and go off the road. Looking down, you realize that nothing would stop its fall until it came to rest on one of the many schist terraces that reach all the way to the river.

The view from on high, though, is worth the trip. The river at the bottom is as still as a sheet of plate glass. The only thing disturbing the water is the wake of occasional boats slowly making their way up or down the valley. The boats seem ethereal, quietly gliding their way through time and space. At your feet are vineyards arranged in terraces, with here and there an abandoned vineyard left over from the phylloxera epidemic a century and a half ago when farmers simply walked away from their ravaged land. Panoramas don't get any better than this.

While the Douro Valley is beautiful, it is also an inhospitable place to grow grapes. It is hard to imagine what inspired people to tame this savage land. The hillsides contain little soil and are mostly made up of schist and slate, often on 60° slopes reaching as high as 1,700 feet. In order to get vines to grow in those conditions generations ago, workers and their beasts of burden built horizontal terraces every 20 or 30 feet up the mountain. Carving those by hand three hundred years ago was a feat of engineering that rivals building the pyramids. Weather in the Douro Valley is also extreme. In winter, freezing cold cuts right through you, and snow covers the ground, while in August temperatures regularly reach 110°F. Cactus often grows near vineyards, a sign of low rainfall and heat. As a result of all that nature throws at Douro's inhabitants, this was long Portugal's poorest region.

The Rio Douro (Gold River) winds its way from its headwaters in Spain 576 miles through the Iberian Peninsula until it empties into the Atlantic Ocean just outside the city of Porto. For 70 miles the river is the border between Spain and Portugal. During much of its history the Douro was treacherous to navigate, but starting in the 1960s Portugal built a series of dams that basically turned the river into a string of lakes. Vines grow on the banks of the river for about 60 miles starting in the town of Régua and going to Barca d'Alva on the Spanish border. The heart of Douro wine country is Pinhão, a lovely little village that has a small train station with walls covered by blue-and-white Portuguese tiles or *azulejos* that show scenes of Port production.

The Romans in the first century BC planted the first grapes in the Douro Valley, but it was only in the seventeenth century that the region came into its own thanks to the on-again, off-again wars between England and France. London heavily taxed and sometimes even banned importing French wines, thus encouraging English merchants to look elsewhere for supplies. The natural place was Portugal, which has been a British ally since 1373. At a monastery in the Douro, two sons of a Liverpool wine merchant discovered in 1678 monks adding brandy to local wine before fermentation ended, which stopped grape juice from turning into wine and made the drink sweet. Later, merchants looking for a way to stabilize wine so it wouldn't spoil during the ocean voyage from Portugal to England also added brandy. Over time, traders began cutting the wine with about one part brandy to four parts wine. The resulting product had a 20 percent alcohol level, as compared with 12 percent for table wine. But no one complained. Thus was born Port, a sweet wine that the British public, especially the upper class, soon learned to love. In 1703, the two countries signed a trade treaty that gave Portugal export advantages over France and encouraged even more British consumption of Portuguese wines. The economists Adam Smith and David Ricardo in their writings later used the flourishing trade of Portuguese wine for English cloth as an example of the benefits of free trade. If each country concentrated on what it produced best—cloth for the English, wine for the Portuguese—then they could trade their surplus cloth and wine to the other and end up with more of each product than if each tried to make both products. That theory of comparative advantage remains the foundation of world trade.

The British were not content just to drink Port; they also wanted to control the trade of it. Already in the seventeenth century, British companies such as Croft, Warre's, and Taylor Fladgate established operations in the small town of Vila Nova de Gaia near where the Douro River flows into the Atlantic and across the river from the city of Porto. Unwilling to live in the hostile conditions upriver where grapes are grown, British companies built large warehouses along the waterfront that became known as Port lodges. Since overland transportation was impossible, unfinished wine was shipped in barrels down the Douro in colorful sailboats known as *barco rabelos* or riverboats to Vila Nova de Gaia, where winemakers completed vinification and stored the wine in huge wooden vats for aging until it was shipped to England. Winemakers also discovered that wines matured better in the cooler and more humid climate of Vila Nova de Gaia, rather than upriver. Port aged in the upper Douro sometimes had a hint of vinegar that was called the taste of the Douro. Big English companies soon ruled the Port business, buying their grapes from thousands of small growers who farmed only an acre or so of vines and sold them to traders, who controlled the price and were mostly English, although there were a few Dutch and Germans as well.

Wine production in the Douro Valley, which until then had been only for local consumption, greatly expanded, and fields that had been previously planted with grains were turned over to vines. The boom in international consumption, however, also led to the doctoring of wines as unprincipled Port producers began adding other fruit juices to them as well as low-quality wine from other regions. To avoid a scandal and protect the country's biggest business, a Royal Charter on September 10, 1756, set the borders of the Douro region. Regulators planted 335 stone posts in the ground to mark the areas where Port could be produced, ranking vineyards in quality from A to F. It was only the second such wine regulation in history after Tokaji in Hungary, and half a century before France established similar production controls.

For the next two centuries, the English dominated the heavily regulated Port business. There was no incentive to change anything because the rules benefited those who participated in what was basically a sanctioned monopoly. The Port bureaucracy determined levels of production for each winery based on overall market demand, so companies didn't have to worry that surplus wine would come on the market and drive down prices. Any wine not made into Port had to be turned into the brandy needed to make Port, and regulations required Port makers to buy brandy from the official Port Wine Institute. The arrangement was a nice, tight little cartel. One of the most restrictive rules required that all wine shipped out of the country had to be exported by one of the Port companies based in Vila Nova de Gaia. The Portuguese government, run by kings or dictators for centuries, saw no need to rock the Port boats. The oidium and phylloxera natural disasters in vineyards during the nineteenth century also drove many Portuguese wineries in the Douro region out of business, thus reducing competition even more.

As a result of all this, Port remained a sleepy business in a sleepy country. It was a standardized product, where brands were all-important; and the market was both established and stable. The English bought high-quality Vintage Port, which carried a date on the bottle and was produced only in years when conditions were particularly good, while the French, Dutch, and Germans bought lower-quality blends from lesser nonvintage years. Port required patience above all. It was aged much longer than table wines, often for forty years or more. To maintain its consistency, the *provador,* the man who made the Port blend, was the most important person in the winery, and he often held his job for decades to assure a consistent blend. Insiders told me with wry smiles that in those olden days, the Port industry didn't work after lunch.

Two giants towered over the nineteenth-century golden age of Port. The first was English-born Joseph James Forrester, who waged a diligent battle against fraudulent wine and was the first person to map the region. Visitors today can still see reproductions of his famous 10-foot-long, richly illustrated map of the Upper Douro. In appreciation for his work, King Pedro V in 1855 made Forrester a baron. The other was Dona Antónia Adelaide Ferreira. After being widowed with two young children, she took over the family firm and managed it for thirty-three years, planting many new vineyards in the Douro and at one point owning half of all the vineyards. In 1862, Forrester and Dona António were sailing together when their riverboat capsized in a dangerous rapid. The baron and a servant who tried to rescue him were both quickly pulled underwater. It was widely believed that Forrester was carrying on him a large amount of gold to pay his workers, and the heavy metal became an anchor that dragged him to the bottom. Dona António's crinoline petticoats, though, buoyed her up until rescuers could reach her. Douro Valley winemakers are still anxious to brag about their family relationship to Dona António.

In the late 1980s and through the 1990s, however, the Douro Valley wine business went through dramatic changes. The most important stimulus for reform was the Carnation Revolution of 1974 that overthrew the last dictator and set the stage for Portugal to become a democracy and enter the European Union. The stagnant Port market also stimulated a reexamination of the old business. Thanks to production controls, Port was never in a crisis, but growth was extremely slow. The British upper-class market was dying off and not enough new Port drinkers were coming along to replace them. As one veteran of the business told me, "No one has ever found out how to attract young people to Port." Some of the old British companies were sold, often to more innovative Portuguese corporations. The result of all these developments was finally a loosening of the rules governing Port production and a new era for Douro table wines.

The Douro has always had a unique collection of grapes and wines. Some three hundred different grape varieties grow there, and under regulations only eighty of them can be used to make Port. Five grapes, though, dominate production: Touriga Nacional, Tinta Barroca, Touriga Franca, Tinta Roriz (the Portuguese version of Spain's Tempranillo), and Tinto Cão. Most Portuguese vineyards are a crazy quilt of those varieties and more. Growers have little idea exactly what their vineyards contain, and when one vine dies they simply plant another in its place and hope it will do well. Winemakers looking to mix different kinds of grapes to improve the wine's overall quality call it a "field blend."

A law passed in May 1986 overturned the old rule that all wine exports had to go through Vila Nova de Gaia and allowed Douro producers to export as long as they complied with rules on the production and storage of Port. The restrictions, though, did not apply to regular table wine. Another change eliminated the requirement that producers turn wine not used for making Port over to the industry to go into brandy, which opened the way for wineries to make more profitable table wines. In a matter of only four or five years, the Douro Valley wine business, which had changed little in three centuries, became a hotbed of new people doing new things and making new wines. Much of the innovative thinking came out of a wine school started in 1988 in the Douro Valley town of Vila Real. The graduating classes each year had only ten or so students, but they were the area's first locally trained enologists and they challenged the old ways.

Table wine had always been made in the Douro, and there was even a model of a great Douro red table wine first made in the 1950s. The wine was **Barca-Velha**, and it was one of those skunkworks projects that sometimes develop at wineries willing to experiment. After a visit to Bordeaux in the late 1940s, Fernando Nicolau de Almeida, the Port maker at Ferreira, Dona Antónia's company, returned home determined to make a dry red wine similar to what he had seen made in France. In those days before widespread refrigeration and air-conditioning, it was a technical challenge to make table wine in the Douro's hot climate, and Nicolau de Almeida had to take such extreme measures as trucking in blocks of ice to keep the temperature down during fermentation. He experimented with a variety of grapes before ending up with Tinta Roriz as the main variety for his new wine. It was then aged for several years in French oak. The first vintage of Barca-Velha was 1952, and the wine has been made only sporadically since then when conditions were right—three times in both the 1950s and 1960s, and only once in the 1970s. Nicolau de Almeida urged his fellow winemakers to "take what's good from the traditional and adapt what's good from the modern."

France's Pascal Chatonnet, who consulted with the winery Quinta do Portal in the Douro on making table wines, concluded it wasn't possible just to use the same grapes that went into Port to make dry red wines. Tinta Barocca, a good grape for making Port, he felt, did not work as well for table wine. Winemakers had to discover which grapes and in which ratio worked best for table wines. Chatonnet concluded that the most interesting varieties were Tinta Roriz, Touriga Franca, and especially Touriga Nacional.

This young generation of winemakers recognized the profit potential of table wines, since the time it took to get them into the hands of consumers was much shorter than it was for Port. A table wine might go on sale in two or three years after harvest.

Innovation in table wines came from small companies, rather than from the big English brands, though they eventually joined the trend once it became successful. Today all Port producers, with the exception of Taylor's, also make table wines.

Many of the movement's early leaders were young members of old Port families who were searching for something new. In 2002, five of those wineries, **Quinta do Vale Meão**, **Quinta do Crasto**, **Quinta do Vale Dona Maria**, **Niepoort**, and **Quinta do Vallado**, formed a marketing group called the Douro Boys. According to an oft-repeated story, the group got its name when the five founders were on a promotional tour abroad and one day enjoyed too much of their own product before returning late to the rest of the group. While the others were kept waiting, they complained bitterly about "those Douro Boys," and the name stuck.

João Ferreira Álvares Ribeiro was one of the founders and now runs Quinta do Vallado with his cousin Francisco Spratley Ferreira, who is a winemaker. Both trace their family roots back to Dona Antónia, who once owned the winery. João proudly says that the famous Barca-Velha was first served in 1956 at his mother's wedding. The Douro Boys got together in hopes of getting a bigger bang from their individual marketing dollars and to promote the table wines they were all making. "We realized we faced the same challenge, which was to get Douro table wines known in the world," he says. While he hails from a Port family, João came to wine after a career in banking. He and other family members remade Vallado starting in 1993, when they first reached out to enology experts to help them upgrade their 173 acres of vineyards. The old style of field blends was gradually abandoned in favor of grape-specific planting, and the winery is now marketing a line of both red and white grape-specific wines as well as some based on old hodgepodge grapes.

The other Douro Boys have similar stories. A Dutch family started Niepoort in 1842. Dirk van der Niepoort, who was born in 1964, has developed a line of dry wines that carry names like Redoma, Batuta, and Charme as well as simple wines that have such flip labels as Drink Me. Quinta do Crasto's heritage goes back to 1615 and today is owned by the Jorge Roquette family, which in 1994 brought in Australia's Dominic Morris to help it with dry red wines. Roquette in 2002 also joined Jean-Michel Cazes of Bordeaux's Château Lynch-Bages to produce Douro wines sold under the brand Xisto. A 2005 Quinta do Crasto Reserve Old Vines ranked third in *Wine Spectator's* Top 100 in 2008. Cristiano van Zeller left his family's Quinta do Noval in 1993 to start Quinta do Vale Dona Maria and has been slowly buying up vineyards as they become available. It has been marketing wines since the 1997 vintage. Quinta do Vale Dona Maria has a woman enologist, Sandra Tavares da Silva, which is still a rare occurrence in the Douro. Francisco Olazabal, Dona Antónia's great-great-grandson, left his job at A.A. Ferreira in 1998 to run the historic Quinta do Vale Meão with his son. Its vineyards once provided many of the grapes that went into Barca-Velha. Robert Parker reviewed eight of its wines from 2000 to 2005, giving all of them scores in the 90s with one exception—and that was an 89.

Despite the excitement of the outstanding new dry wines, a variety of factors are holding back the development of wine tourism in the Douro Valley, and it will probably never flourish as much as in the Napa Valley or Margaret River. The first problem is history. The Douro was always a poor rural area with extreme temperatures that never attracted many visitors. So until recently, there was no tradition of tourism. Moreover, the Douro Valley's steep hillsides make it hard to build roads or hotels. Since 2001, the Upper Douro has also been a UNESCO World Heritage site, which limits the amount of economic development that can occur there now and in the future. Finally, many Portuguese do not want much tourism, fearing that their beautiful area could someday be turned into what they call "another Algarve." As recently as the early 1970s, the Algarve was a pristine area of sand and sun in southern Portugal, but a decade later it became a playground for international jet-setters and was overrun with high-rise hotels and golf courses. Douro Valley people want to avoid that experience by concentrating on what they call "quality tourism," rather than what they deride as "mass tourism."

Wine tourists can get to the Douro Valley in one of three ways, and I've taken all of them. The oldest mode of transportation is to go by boat. Rest assured, the trip today is much safer than it was in the days of Baron Forrester. Two major companies run boats that carry more than a hundred people on trips that can range from a day to a week. There are few hotels in the Douro, so the boats eliminate the need to find a bed since travelers sleep and eat aboard. The boats make a few stops along the way so passengers can visit wineries and other attractions. Wineries such as **Quinta do Tedo**, which has a tasting room that can seat a hundred people, are happy to open their doors and cellars to boat tours. Casa de Mateus, a restored seventeenth-century manor house in Vila Real, is another popular stop. Visitors arrive at both those destinations by taking a bus from the riverfront. The shortcoming of a boat trip is that visitors are limited in the number of wineries they can visit. Several Portuguese winemakers complained to me that the trips were a cultural or landscape experience of the Douro, but not a wine experience.

Another popular way to visit the valley is by train. Scheduled service leaves from downtown Porto, bringing passengers to Pinhão and other stops in the valley. Travelers enjoy beautiful views as they ride along the riverbank. There is also an antique steam train that makes tours during the summer. People often ride a train to a major railroad station and then get around the area by cab. But that can get complicated and limits the number of wineries one is likely to visit. Some tours also combine boat and train transportation.

The third way to visit the Douro is to drive there from Porto. The drive is now an easy ninety-minute trip. It used to be much longer and tedious, going through many small towns; but a new highway made travel shorter and less fatiguing. Tourists then have the freedom to travel along the *Rota do Vinho do Porto* (Port Wine Route) visiting one winery after another all over the region. Neither the roads nor the wine route are particularly well marked, and the roads are mostly two-lane and tough to negotiate as they twist and turn through valleys. Car travelers willing to overlook those problems, however, will have the most extensive and enjoyable tour of Portugal's leading wine region.

While the Douro Valley has limited accommodations, things are improving. Two small hotels have opened in the past few years that offer a maximum of luxury, but at a high price. The more spectacular and private of the two is Romaneira, which is owned by French investors with ties to the AXA insurance group, who use the facility as their personal resort. They own another two ultra-luxury resorts in southern Morocco. Romaneira consists of nineteen suites and apartments on a secluded 1,000-acre property. Prices start at $1,300 per night, so this appeals to people who demand privacy and don't worry much about what it costs.

The second new hotel is the Aquapura Douro Valley, a five-star accommodation started by a Portuguese company that has another resort in Brazil. It is much less expensive and has fifty rooms and suites, plus twenty-one villas. Aquapura is located just off the Douro River overlooking both the river and a minor tributary. The centerpiece of the hotel complex is a nineteenth-century manor house. Added to that are new buildings that house three restaurants, two bars, a wine-tasting room, the 24,000-square-foot spa, and villas where people can buy a time-share ownership.

Taylor's, a Port company, fifteen years ago opened the Vintage House, the first modern hotel in the Douro Valley. Originally an eighteenth-century wine estate, it has plenty of old-country charm. The small CS chain of hotels now owns it, and renamed it the CS Vintage House. Located only a few steps from the Pinhão train station, it has a terrace with wonderful views of vineyards across the river. There is also a wine shop with a good selection of Ports and table wines from all around the valley. The shop and a nearby library bar both offer wine tastings.

The big British companies that populated the Vila Nova de Gaia until recently thought their job was only to make Port and not promote wine tourism. But the new wineries driving the table wine movement see tourism as an integral part of their business plans. As a result, some of the nicest places to stay in the valley are at *quintas* that have built small guest facilities and sometime also offer meals.

Another advantage of staying at a *quinta,* if you are lucky enough to be in the Douro Valley in late September, is to participate in the annual stomping of the grapes. Not only is this part of Douro wine culture, but many winemakers also consider it to be the gentlest way to crush grapes. So stomping is still practiced with alacrity in the Douro. Vineyard hands put a ton or so of grapes into a shallow rectangular container made of granite, called a *lagar,* and then a group of barefoot men line up on one side, hook their arms around each other's shoulders, and begin stomping to the beat of the person calling out the count. Often the men break into song. This may go on for several hours, and the group may come back the next day for a second stomping. It's a performance not to be missed.

João Ferreira Álvares Ribeiro at Quinta do Vallado was a believer in wine tourism from the beginning. "In every business you try to touch the emotions of your clients. I thought the best way to do that was through wine tourism," he says. "The first visitors were our importers. If one of them stays here a week, he will never forget us. That's true of importers, but also of retail customers."

With a banker's instinct for seeking out a government program that might help him, João Ferreira Álvares Ribeiro found one designed to help wineries renovate old manor houses. So he redid the late-nineteenth-century home on his estate into a small luxury hotel with four double rooms and one suite. When fully built out, there will be fifteen rooms. Vallado puts together visits suited to the interests of its guests. A typical couple stays for three or four days, spending one day learning about local food and wine, a second day on the river in a small boat, a third on the steam railroad, and a fourth just lounging around the winery's swimming pool. He says the most popular activity outside of wine is the boat trip, which he insists is not at all like the big boat trips. "The small boat trips are fantastic," he says with enthusiasm. "The boat takes only fourteen people, and you can water ski, swim, or fish. Or you can simply go into a cove or up a tributary and stop and listen to the birds." The renovated house and winery, which are now painted a colorful orange with white trim, are a nice mix of old and new. Guests can take some meals in the manor house's formal dining room.

Vallado has a relatively broad range of dry wines, including red, white, and rosé. It produces just one Port. Parker gives them scores in the 80s and 90s. Wrote *Wine Spectator*'s Kim Marcus after a visit, "I've always liked Vallado wines for their fresh flavors, good value and the high quality of both the reds and whites."

One drawback at Vallado, as with many other Douro wineries, is the lack of good signs leading to its front door. When visiting the Douro, don't book yourself on too tight a schedule because you are likely to have some trouble finding the next place on your itinerary.

Quinta do Portal is one of many Douro Valley wineries that are hard to visit without a car. It's located back from the river on a mainly two-lane road that can test a driver's nerves. But *Revista de Vinhos,* the Portuguese wine magazine, named it the winery of the year in 2007. It recently hired Álvaro Siza Vieira, the Pritzker Prize–winning architect, who created the officially unofficial Port wineglass that has a dimple in the stem, to design a new cellar for its wines. Portal has become popular with weekenders looking for a comfortable and quiet place to relax. Its Casa das Pipas guesthouse overlooking acres of vineyards in all directions has only fourteen rooms, but a large swimming pool and a gym. The winery regularly has special events such as an evening that pairs its wines with the local Serra cheese, and winter dinners when the staff dramatically opens bottles of Port in the traditional way: using heated prongs to snap off the neck just below the cork. Sure, it's showmanship, but it's fun.

Quinta do Portal's young winemaker Paulo Coutinho hangs around talking with guests more often than you find at most wineries. He started making wine with his father when he was fourteen, but then took advantage of the new enology program at Vila Real to become the first member of his family to get a formal wine education. Consultant Pascal Chatonnet helped improve the Quinta do Portal wines. Coutinho's Muscatel is a delightful white wine from an uncommon grape variety.

Ruy de Brito e Cunha spent most of his career in Port marketing but now runs a resort that has just four small houses with two rooms each at

Quinta de S. José. It is located on the south bank of the Douro amid a plethora of vineyards and almost directly across the river from the ultra-luxury Romaneira. The setting is spectacular, with uninterrupted valley views. The Quinta is located only 50 yards above the river.

Ruy de Brito e Cunha bought the property when it was in ruins in 2000 and then spent two years modernizing it. His concept was to have a small place where people could enjoy an intimate experience of the Douro, its culture, and its wines. And to do that, he says, you need time. "As we say in Portugal, you must eat the place." A minimum three-day visit is required. Guests normally have breakfast at the main house, go off for a day of exploring the region, and then come back and have dinner with him or other family members. Dinner starts with a White Port aperitif and ends with a glass of Vintage Port. The night I had dinner with Ruy de Brito e Cunha, he ended the meal by pulling out a bottle of 1890 Port. He said the hint of the Douro taste indicated that it had been aged in the warmer upriver region rather than in Vila Nova de Gaia. He bought the Port in 1994 and has been serving it in thimblefuls since then in order to make the magic last. The Port was light in color, but rich in flavor. There was something truly humbling about drinking a wine nearly 120 years old.

As we talked after dinner, my host told me he urges visitors to experience everything the Douro has to offer, not just the wine. Two other activities he recommends are a trip in a small boat that leaves from his dock and a visit to the prehistoric cave drawings in nearby Vila Nova de Foz Côa.

Many members of the *Rota do Vinho do Porto* organization have started bed-and-breakfasts. One of them is the winery **Casal Agrícola de Cevêr** in the village of Sarnadelo, which is in the hills far back from the Douro River. These smaller places away from the tourist centers give visitors a sense of what life was like for centuries for small grape growers. The winery sells 90 percent of its grape production to the Port maker Sandeman, keeping only enough to produce 4,000 bottles of table wine, which it sells to visitors. It rents out five rooms, and during the harvest guests can stomp grapes.

Tourists traveling to the Douro should spend a day in Vila Nova de Gaia across from Porto, where they can see many of the ancient Port lodges and enjoy a few glasses of Port. After not paying attention to tourists for hundreds of years, some of the big companies are now opening their doors wide. Many of the tasting rooms are located up steep streets above the river, so be prepared for heavy puffing. Up the hill, but worth the walk, is **Taylor's**, the best Port show in town. My guide told me before we started the tour that her goal was to "demystify Port." The trip through the caves, with their huge old barrels, can take from a half hour to an hour depending on how many questions visitors ask. Taylor's welcomes 35,000 people a year, but is not open on weekends, which are reserved for parties and weddings. Both the tour and samples of two Port wines at the end are free. Taylor's has special events all day long that vary from opening a bottle of Vintage Port with hot tongs to Port and chocolate pairings. Some are free, but there's a modest charge for others. The restaurant at Taylor's is the top one in Vila Nova de Gaia and offers a great view across the river to Porto. The company has begun construction of a luxury wine spa and hotel that will have eighty-five rooms and is slated to open in September 2010. It will be the first wine spa run by a Port house.

Just down the hill a short walk from Taylor's is the **Croft** tasting room. This is the city's most popular, attracting some 50,000 visitors a year. It doesn't offer as many activities as Taylor's, but the tasting is again free. Croft is excited about its new Pink Port, an attempt to attract young people with a drink designed for casual summer entertaining, served chilled or on the rocks.

On the riverfront, a number of Port lodges have simple tasting rooms or tastings and tours. **Sandeman** has one of the best. There's a charge, but a sample of Ports at the end. The knowledgeable Japanese guide on my tour gave an excellent history of Port and the role Sandeman played in it. The company claims its famous silhouette logo of a man with a cape and broad-brimmed hat is the most recognized in the world.

The Douro, from upriver where the grapes grow to Vila Nova de Gaia where many are still made into Port, is a wine region that is just starting to come alive after a long slumber. The new dry red wines are exciting, and the old Ports remain interesting. The Douro is not as busy as Napa Valley or Rioja, and today there's a youthful atmosphere in one of the world's oldest wine regions.

Diary of a Wine Tourist

April 12

Blending My Own Wine

Blending is far more important in the Douro Valley than it is in New Zealand or California, where wines usually come from a single variety of grapes and often from one vineyard. Most Portuguese vineyards have local wine varieties of at least Touriga Nacional, Tinta Roriz, and Touriga Franca, three grapes not found outside that country. In addition, old Douro vineyards are made up of a potpourri of grapes in field blends. As a result, the best Douro wines often come from the mélange of grapes found in old vineyards that are simply labeled *vinho tinto* (red wine).

One of the popular parts of a visit to Quinta do Vallado is when winemaker Francisco Spratley Ferreira shows visitors how he tastes grapes and makes his final blend and then lets them try their own hand at it. But for even the most experienced wine enthusiasts, this can be a humbling experience.

On a Saturday morning and with no other visitors around, Francisco and I met in his lab to do some tastings and then make a blend. He started by explaining that I'd be trying barrel samples of five wines from the 2006 vintage and then putting them together in a style to match the Reserva wine he had made from the same grapes. The five varieties: Touriga Nacional from nine-year-old vines, the same grapes from twenty-year-old vines, Touriga Franca, Souzão, and a field blend of an estimated thirty grapes from eighty-year-old vines. A sample of each wine was in a small plastic water bottle marked simply with numbers one through five. At the same time, he opened a bottle of 2006 Quinta do Vallado Reserva and placed it on the table. Behind us was a small wooden barrel with a tile top and an opening that was obviously for spitting the samples after tasting.

Francisco started by passing out a scorecard that contained some hints he thought might make identifying wines easier. He pointed out that the Touriga Nacional wine would be elegant and have violet flavors. The Touriga Franca could be spotted for its tannins and fine aromas that would make it expressive without being overpowering. The Souzão would have intense color and high acidity that provides freshness. The Old Vines would have lots of complexity and good structure, including long, firm tannins.

Then we got down to business. Francisco half filled the wineglasses that he had placed in front of each of the plastic bottles and invited me to sample. Giving me another hint, he suggested that I might want to pick out the Souzão because its freshness and acidity should make it the easiest to identify. Following his advice, I took small sips of each of the five, carefully spit them out, and then tried to determine if I could identify the one with more acidity.

After a first round, I went back and tried again, and then confessed, "This is tough." I tried to plead for sympathy by telling Francisco that it might have been easier if we'd tasted grape varieties I knew such as Merlot or Cabernet Sauvignon. After all, I didn't have that much experience with Douro grapes.

Perhaps taking pity on this neophyte, Francisco gave me another hint. "The Souzão has the darkest color." I looked at the wines again and noted that the first wine had a distinctly paler color, but the other four looked similar to me. So I tasted them all once again and then said, "I think it's number three."

"You're right," said Francisco.

"All right!" I replied. At that point I should have retired in glory.

"Now let's try to get the old-vines wine. It will have a different mouth feel, with long tannins and will be more full-bodied."

I tasted the four remaining samples and was totally stumped. They all tasted the same. I picked up a stronger nose in one wine, but the taste seemed the same as the others. One had lots of tannins, but none of them, for me, had the long finish that he said was distinct in an old-vine wine.

Since I was clearly stumped, he suggested I try to identify the two Touriga Nacional wines, which should have a darker color. After some hesitation, I finally got those two.

Now down to the final two: the Old Vines and the Touriga Franca.

Ever helpful, Francisco once more gave me some tips: "The Old Vines has lots of long tannins, a more spicy character, and is more complex. The Touriga Franca has more intense fruit."

I thought I picked up some spiciness in one of the two and guessed that must be the Old Vines or field blend, so the other would be the Touriga Franca.

Wrong.

Final test. Which is the older Touriga Nacional? Again a tip: "The older one will have better mouth structure and will be more intense. The younger one will have too much vigor and will not be balanced."

After just smelling them, I made a guess.

Then Francisco said, "I'm not saying you're right, and I'm not saying you're wrong. I'm not going to help you. But now taste them both."

From the taste one wine seemed more round and soft. So I switched my vote.

"You're right."

Now on to the blend. Francisco took the young Touriga Nacional out of the competition and asked me to make a blend of just the four wines. He also offered another tip: "We want a wine that has character and a lot of intensity." He suggested that I make two blends with differing amounts of wine. Then he told me to pour each wine into a glass beaker that had measuring marks etched into the side. I figured his tip indicated that the blend probably had a lot of the Old Vines, so I put 40 percent of that in one blend and 50 percent in the other. Just to have a clear difference between the two I had 5 percent Souzão in one, and 20 percent in the other. Finally I put similar amounts of Touriga Nacional and Touriga Franca in each sample.

"Now taste your two samples and our Reserva," said Francisco. "Which is best?"

"Yours without a doubt," I replied.

"Thanks, but let me try them."

After tasting my two samples, he said, "Touriga Nacional stands out too strongly in one, and you have too much Souzão in the other. You only need a little bit of that."

Following the Quinta do Vallado test, I decided I'd stick to writing and leave the blending to Francisco and other talented winemakers.

CHAPTER TEN

Tuscany, Italy

Three American couples in a Wine Tours of Tuscany van pulled up to the **Fattoria di Pietrafitta** winery, a short distance outside the medieval city of San Gimignano. Two of the couples were from Florida, and one was from New Jersey. The man who appeared to be the leader of the group introduced himself as Willis King and said their trip had been arranged by a woman in Short Hills, New Jersey, who had done previous wine vacations for them to places such as Bordeaux, Burgundy, and Napa Valley. The trips were often built around a theme such as wine and yoga or wine and cooking. This year it was wine and the great Tuscany cities of Florence and Siena. This would be the only wine stop of the day, and later they would go to Siena. The group would tour the winery and then have lunch on a veranda overlooking the Pietrafitta vineyards. A highlight of the visit was going to be trying the winery's Vernaccia, a specialty of San Gimignano, and perhaps also some Vin Santo, the Italian sweet wine.

Before lunch, though, they would tour the cellars. The Pietrafitta winemaker, speaking through the interpreter from Wine Tours of Tuscany, asked the group to follow him as he climbed a steep walkway. At the top of the path King looked out at the Tuscan countryside of rolling, lush green hills, with yellow houses on hilltops, and rows of stately cypress trees lined up like soldiers ready for inspection. "Look at that view," King said in awe. "That's what wine tourism is all about!" The group went on to take the tour, which included seeing the room where Vin Santo grapes were drying, and enjoyed a Tuscan lunch with plenty of wine; but nothing they experienced that day was going to be beat that view.

Tuscany, on the western coast of the Italian boot about 100 miles

north of Rome, has long been a favorite subject for such giants of painting as Giotto and Michelangelo. Foreign authors still run off to live
there and then write lovingly about the area and its people: Frances
Mayes in *Under the Tuscan Sun* and Ference Mate in *A Vineyard in Tuscany* come to mind. Wild vines grew in Tuscany before the Etruscans
occupied the area in the eighth century BC, and they were still making
wine in the third century BC, when the Romans took over.

In medieval times, Florence and Siena became important city-states
and major population centers, while the countryside around them
remained a fertile center for the production of wine, olive oil, and
wheat. Members of the Florence wine trade in 1292 founded the Arte
dei Vinattieri, a guild that set strict rules over the business such as that
wine was not to be served to anyone under fifteen. At that time, the average Florentine drank about a gallon per week. Florence and Siena were
bitter rivals, waging constant wars against each other. Florence eventually dominated, and under the rule of the Medicis became a major center of political, artistic, and financial power from the thirteenth to the
seventeenth centuries. The Tuscan language replaced Latin and became
the national tongue after such writers as Dante Alighieri, Petrarch, and
Boccaccio wrote their great works in it.

Tuscan wine in those days was mostly consumed locally. Unlike
French or Portuguese wine, it was rarely exported to northern Europe,
mainly because only sweet wines could make the ocean voyage without
spoiling. Tuscan wines were then generally of poor quality. Winemaking practices had not changed much since Roman days, and as late
as the nineteenth century, grapes were still grown haphazardly in trees
rather than on low-lying vines.

Red wines did better than white ones in Tuscany's hilly landscape
and Mediterranean climate. Sangiovese was by far the most widely
planted grape, but other local red grape varieties included Mam-
molo, Canaiolo, and Colorino. A few Tuscans planted grapes from
other countries such as Cabernet Sauvignon from France more than
250 years ago, but until recently they were not widely used. The most
common white grape was Trebbiano, which made a poor-quality wine
that was added to red blends. Other whites included Vernaccia di San
Gimignano and Malvasia.

In 1963, Italy introduced a wine classification system similar to the French one and based on the place of origin. The Italians again overhauled their rules in 1992 as a result of the adoption of European Union–wide wine regulation. Tuscany has six designated wines in the top *Denominazione di Origine Controllata e Garantita* (DOCG) classification, which means they have met the highest quality and production standards, five reds and one white: Chianti, Chianti Classico, Brunello di Montalcino, Vino Nobile di Montepulciano, Carmignano, and Vernaccia di San Gimignano. Additional regulations govern the amount of time a wine has to be aged in wooden barrels before it can carry the title Riserva.

Chianti is Tuscany's most famous wine and became known the world over as the wine that came in a *fiasco,* a wicker basket that protected the fragile glass during transportation. The *fiasco* became the universal symbol of Italian wine as well as a handy candleholder in Italian restaurants or dorm rooms. Regulators set out the limits of the first Chianti region in 1716, and the boundaries have been changed many times since then. Chianti was originally made with only Sangiovese grapes, but as its popularity grew Canaiolo, Malvasia, Trebbiano, and other grapes were added to increase output and make the wines more drinkable at an early age. Production requirements on grape yield, vines per hectare, and other criteria are more stringent for Chianti Classico than for plain Chianti. Classico is grown only in the wine's traditional area between Siena and Florence, while plain Chianti comes from a larger area of Florence, Siena, Pistoia, Pisa, and Arezzo. Winemakers of both products in recent years have been using less white wine and more Sangiovese.

Carmignano is produced in small quantities from an area about 12 miles west of Florence. It has long been popular because it is less acidic than Chianti, and received its separate status in the fifteenth century. Carmignano is predominantly based on Sangiovese, but has also long been a blend that included the French grapes Cabernet Sauvignon and Cabernet Franc as well as the Italian Canaiolo.

Vernaccia di San Gimignano, the only Tuscan white wine to have DOCG status, can come solely from the hill town of San Gimignano, which is located about 18 miles from Siena. References to the grape can be found in local records going back to the thirteenth century, and Dante's *Divine Comedy* in the fourteenth century mentions Vernaccia by name. Trebbiano and Malvasia, which produced more abundant crops of lesser-quality grapes, upstaged Vernaccia for many centuries, which only made a comeback starting in the 1960s.

Vino Nobile di Montepulciano has long been one of Tuscany's most prized wines. In 1549, the cellar master for Pope Paul III called it "most perfect, fit for a gentleman." Francesco Redi, a renowned doctor and poet, wrote in his 1685 poem *Bacchus in Tuscany,* "Montepulciano of all wines is king." The wine has had its noble name since the late eighteenth century. Regulations state that Montepulciano has to be 60 to 80 percent Sangiovese Grosso, 10 to 20 percent Canaiolo Nero, and no more than 20 percent approved lesser grapes. In addition, it is not supposed to contain more than 10 percent white grapes, although few producers actually use white grapes. The wine is aged in large oak barrels for a minimum of two years, three for a Riserva. Montepulciano, along with all the Tuscan hill towns, started off as a defense castle that grew into a village. The higher elevation means that Sangiovese grapes ripen better and faster than those going into Chianti, which gives Montepulciano both a richer taste and higher alcohol level.

The brightest star of Tuscany's wine constellation is the relatively new Brunello di Montalcino, which many consumers rank with the French First Growths and California's icon wines as the best in the world. The hilltop fortress town of Montalcino was a stop-off point for pilgrims in the Middle Ages on their way to Rome just as Rioja was for those on the road to Santiago de Compostela. Travelers enjoyed the local wine, which seemed better than others made in nearby areas because its vines grew on the town's higher ground. The hillside vineyards were free of fog, ice, and late frost, which could harm grapes grown in the valleys. Since the vines here, like Montepulciano, matured early, the wines again were richer and had a higher alcohol level.

Ferruccio Biondi Santi, a Montalcino winemaker, in 1888 released a new wine that his grandfather Clemente Santi started to make but he died before it was ready to market. While replanting the family vineyards after the phylloxera epidemic, Santi had isolated the Sangiovese Grosso or Brunello clone, which produced a particularly intense red wine in the warmer area of Montalcino. He then replanted the family vineyards with just that clone. The wine contained no other grape varieties, and was initially aged for more than a decade in wooden casks and then still longer in bottles. Ferruccio called the wine Brunello, a name that had been previously used for a quality wine. Also in 1888, he opened a wine shop, or *enoteca,* in Montalcino's main square as a way to promote his wines. **Biondi Santi,** though, made Brunello only in exceptional years, and in its first fifty-seven years it was only produced four times—in 1888, 1891, 1925, and 1945.

Given how long it took to make and age Brunello, initially not many winemakers followed Biondi Santi's lead. Others wanted a fast turnaround on their investment of time and money and weren't patient enough to wait for all that aging. Tuscany until the late 1960s was still a dirt-poor area, and many young people in those days left to make a better life abroad. In 1960, only twelve Montalcino winemakers produced Brunello di Montalcino. But wine consumers around the world slowly learned about its wonders and began demanding it.

♆ ♆ ♆

Tuscans have outsmarted a host of invaders and occupiers over the centuries by developing a talent for simply ignoring the rules others set and going about their own business. In early 2008, investigators looked into allegations that dozens of Brunello producers were violating rules by using nonapproved grapes. Disdain for rules during the last quarter-century, however, led to the important development of Super Tuscan wines outside the strict confines of the Italian wine regulation system.

Italy's upper classes always had a haughty attitude toward their own country's wines, preferring to drink the best Bordeaux. But Marchese Mario Incisa della Rocchetta, who traced his noble roots back to the Holy Roman Empire, set out during World War II to make a Bordeaux wine in Italy on an estate he owned in Bolgheri, on the coast of Tuscany far from the main grape-growing region. In about 1940, no one knows for sure exactly when, he planted Cabernet Sauvignon grapes from Bordeaux there and began making wine. The first vintages were not great, but he kept at it and in 1965 planted two more vineyards, this time of Cabernet Sauvignon and Cabernet Franc. Over time he adopted some French winemaking techniques, such as aging the wine in small French oak barrels, and the quality of his wines gradually improved. The blend eventually settled down to at least 85 percent Cabernet Sauvignon, and up to 15 percent Cabernet Franc. The marchese at first didn't sell the wines; he simply gave bottles to friends and relatives. He called the wine **Sassicaia**, and only began selling it to the public in 1968. Since it contained French grapes, Incisa della Rocchetta had to put on the label the lowest classification in the Italian hierarchy of wine: *vino da tavola,* or table wine. Sassicaia was the first of the wines that journalists later called Super Tuscans.

The Antinori family was already making wine in Tuscany in 1180, although some clan members were into banking and silk weaving in Florence. The family often innovated by ignoring winemaking conventions. Niccolò Antinori shocked the local wine industry in 1924 by putting Bordeaux grapes into his Chianti blend. Later, Marchese Mario Incisa della Rocchetta sent bottles of Sassicaia to his nephew Marchese Piero Antinori, who succeeded his father, Niccolò, as head of the family firm and continued its trendsetting winemaking. Sassicaia provided the inspiration to Piero for how to get around the restrictive wine regulations that he felt were degrading Chianti and impeding new developments. In 1971, Antinori made his first vintage of a new Chianti that contained more Sangiovese than was allowed and no white wine. He also followed French and New World viticulture methods, aging the wine in small wooden barrels. Since the wine did not conform to the rules for Chianti, he too had to call it simply a *vino da tavola.* After several years of tinkering with the blend, Antinori in 1982 settled on 85 percent Sangiovese, 10 percent Cabernet Sauvignon, and 5 percent Cabernet Franc. He called the wine **Tignanello,** after the estate where it was made.

Soon many other winemakers were following Mario Incisa della Rocchetta and Piero Antinori, coming up with their own rule-breaking wines that they sold as *vino da tavola.* Some of the wines were predominantly Sangiovese, but others combined it with Merlot or Cabernet Sauvignon. The blend of grapes was never listed on the label. International wine enthusiasts loved them and could care less that they were called table wine. The high prices the wines demanded were proof that consumers considered them to be far more than just table wines.

Italians always had close relations with winemakers and the product that is the centerpiece of their culture. Following an old Italian tradition, people from Florence, Rome, and other cities went out to the countryside once a year and bought wine directly from the producer in a wicker-covered demijohn that contained fifty liters of wine and looked like a giant *fiasco*. Handwritten signs along highways read *Se Vende Vino* (Wine for Sale). Winemakers usually put a coating of olive oil inside the demijohns to prevent oxidation. Once people got the demijohns home, they rebottled the wine into standard bottles. Peasant winemakers, though, were always private people who, as one Tuscan saying goes, "had thick soles on their shoes, but very sharp minds." Few wineries moved beyond those basic sales to build up anything like today's wine tourism.

Still, most Italian wines were not highly regarded outside the country in 1970, when John and Harry Mariani, brothers who owned a wine importing business in New York, made a visit to Biondi Santi, the birthplace of Brunello di Montalcino. Their father, John Mariani Sr., had started a wine import company in 1919. He was born in the United States to Italian immigrants, but grew up in Milan under the firm thumb of his aunt Teodolinda Banfi, who later ran the Vatican staff of Pope Pius XI. Among her duties was selecting the pope's wines. When Mariani founded his company, he named it **Banfi** after his aunt. Banfi struggled through Prohibition, but as soon as that was over Mariani was back in Europe buying wines in Italy, France, and Germany.

John Mariani Sr. in 1964 turned the business over to his two sons. John Jr. became chairman and chief executive officer, while Harry ran day-to-day operations as president and chief operating officer. Four years later, they scored a major success as the American importer of Riunite wine, a slightly fizzy Lambrusco they helped develop. Eventually Riunite became the top-selling wine in the United States, a position it held from 1975 to 2000. At the time of the 1970 trip, the brothers were still in the early days of the Riunite success, but they were already seeking out unfashionable areas around the world where they could discover little-known wines with great potential. At the time, Biondi Santi was not exporting Brunello di Montalcino to the United States. After tasting the 1961 and 1964 vintages, John Mariani and Franco Biondi Santi shook hands on an agreement that Banfi would begin importing the wine with an initial order of fifty cases. The logistics of bringing wine into the United States, however, proved too complicated, and Biondi Santi never shipped the wine to Banfi.

The Marianis didn't forget Brunello di Montalcino. By the late 1970s, John was back in Italy, and this time he didn't just want to buy wine to import. With sales of Riunite soaring, he had plans to start making his own wine there for export to the United States, and for him Brunello di Montalcino was the epitome of a great Italian red. His goal was bold: to produce quality wine on a scale never seen in Italy. Mariani hired the top Italian winemaker Ezio Rivella first as a consultant, and then in 1977 as Banfi's winemaker. At the time, Montalcino was just starting to stir, and a couple dozen winemakers were producing annually about 50,000 cases of Brunello di Montalcino.

It was a tense political period for Italy. The country had been stunned in May 1978, when the Marxist Red Brigade took former Prime Minister Aldo Moro hostage and then executed him, leaving his body in the trunk of a car. Many land-rich Italians were also looking to raise cash by selling property after seeing the ancient system of sharecropping collapse with land reforms after World War II.

An old Italian maxim holds that buying a vineyard is the third fastest way to lose money, after lavishing it on women and betting on horses. But with Rivella's help in handling the negotiations as well as his management of winemaking, the Mariani brothers thought they could do it. Banfi in 1978 first bought 4,500 acres of prime Montalcino land and then an adjacent estate of 2,600 acres. Grapes had never been grown there. Wheat and olives were being cultivated in some parts of the property, and woods and scrub covered the rest. Rivella, though, saw the potential for a large quality vineyard. Forty million years ago, the land had been under the sea, and that had left a calcium-rich soil ideal for growing grapes. As proof of the land's heritage, researchers in March 2007 found an 11-foot skeleton of a prehistoric whale on the property. After completing negotiations for the two land sales, Rivella began the major vineyard-planting program. Then in 1982, he started work on a $100 million winery that incorporated all the latest technology, including both large casks of Slavonian oak from south central Europe and small oak barrels from France. Banfi also supported moves to simplify the names of Montalcino wines from Brunello di Montalcino to simply Brunello and from Rosso dei Vigneti di Brunello to Rosso di Montalcino.

At about this same time, the Mariani brothers also started week-long tours of Tuscany, not only for members of the wine trade but also for college students and professors. John had graduated from Cornell University in 1954 and always kept close ties to its School of Hotel Administration and endowed its first chair of wine education and management. Believing that it was important to educate future leaders of the hospitality industry about wine, Banfi gave scholarships to more than two hundred students and teachers for monthlong cultural and gastronomic trips to Italy that included stays at the Banfi property. The wine-trade visitors and students were the forerunners of Banfi's wine tourism, which developed piece by piece starting in the early 1980s and only reached its full development in the first decade of the new century. Wine and tourism just seemed like a magic combination. Says Fabio Datteroni, Banfi's hospitality director, "When you fall in love with wine, you want to see where the wine comes from. You don't have the same feeling about whiskey or gin or beer. I don't understand it, but it's true."

The first step in Banfi's development of wine tourism was to buy the eleventh-century Poggio alle Mura castle. It had originally been part of the property Banfi acquired, but the owners at first wanted to sell only the land and not the buildings. They finally did, though, in 1984. The Marianis renamed it Castello Banfi and drew up plans for making it the company's public showpiece. But first the Marianis had to renovate the rundown buildings.

Banfi was already getting a stream of visitors and needed a restaurant where both the staff and guests could eat. In the early 1980s, the wife of the vineyard manager began cooking simple meals for everyone, and people ate together at long tables as in a refectory. Then the winery in 2001 started the casual-dining Taverna Banfi. The following year Banfi established the goal of becoming a destination for people searching for a culinary experience. Heinz Beck, a Michelin three-star chef in Rome, suggested that the winery hire one of his protégés, Guido Haverkock, who signed his employment agreement on a bench outside a McDonald's. The new restaurant was called Ristorante Castello Banfi, and it won a star in the 2004 Michelin guide. When Haverkock left the estate, he was replaced by another Beck protégé, Massimiliano Blasone. Beck now also gives cooking courses to visitors at Castello Banfi.

A wine shop opened in 1997 that offered not only Banfi wines but also a broad range of Tuscan products from pasta and balsamic vinegar to soaps and ceramics. Tours that start in the wine shop now attract 60,000 people a year. A unique part of the tour is the visit to the Balsameria, the room where small barrels of balsamic vinegar age in a scene that looks much like a wine barrel cellar. Visitors also get a chance to sample the vinegar. Banfi offers separate tours of its museum, which is located in the thirteenth-century wing of the castle and traces the evolution of glass wine containers from the fifth century BC to the present.

Just outside the front gate of the castle when Banfi bought it was a small collection of buildings and people that might have stepped right out of the feudal ages. The settlement was informally called Il Borgo (the village) and had grown up over centuries in the shadow of the castle to service the landowners who lived there. In Il Borgo were a half-dozen buildings, comprised of two churches plus a school, and a citizenry that included a priest, farmers, a baker who managed the communal oven and made bread for residents, and an artisan who stoked the many fireplaces in the castle. They were now gone, but the village remained. Over the years, Banfi had renovated the buildings one by one, but without any overall plan. Then in 2003, John Mariani decided to turn the area into a small luxury hotel that he named simply Il Borgo. Opened in spring 2007, it has nine bedrooms and five suites.

Etruscans who lived in Tuscany before the Romans were famous for their luxurious lifestyle, and Castello Banfi continues the tradition. In addition to drinking great Brunello and dining at a Michelin-star restaurant, visitors can test-drive a Ferrari or rent one for their stay. Boasts the hotel in promotional material, "If you can dream it, it can happen, and for you alone in a customized, one-of-a-kind itinerary."

Wine production and sales remain at the heart of Castello Banfi. The winery now produces 185,000 cases annually, which makes it the largest winery in Montalcino. The United States and Italy are the two largest markets for the Brunello, each taking about 40 percent of production. *Wine Spectator* regularly gives Banfi Brunello scores in the 90s.

Despite Banfi's big push into wine tourism, the rest of Tuscany, in fact all of Italy, has been slow in coming to it. In the early 1990s, however, Donatella Cinelli Colombini set out to bring people into wineries first in Tuscany and then later all over Italy. She has become such a major figure that in the Tuscan wine world, everyone calls her simply by her first name, Donatella. Other people may share the name, but there is no other like her. Alessandro Gallo, the head of the Movimento Turismo del Vino (Wine Tourism Movement) and director of Castello d'Albola, in Radda in Chianti, says, "Donatella is the Mamma. How do you explain the role of the Mamma? Her importance was huge; she invented everything."

Donatella was born into wine. Her family has been in agriculture since 1352 and in 1790 bought **Fattoria dei Barbi** (the Barbi Farm), a highly regarded winery in Montalcino that went on to become one of the early and best producers of Brunello di Montalcino. In the 1960s, Francesca Cinelli Colombini, Donatella's mother, became the driving force behind Fattoria dei Barbi. The nickname of the high-profile woman: "The Lady of Brunello." Her two children both became active at the winery, son, Stefano, as the winemaker, while daughter, Donatella, handled marketing and built up direct wine sales, accommodations, and a restaurant.

The Cinelli Colombini family in 1998 went through the inevitable, and sometimes difficult, transfer of ownership to the next generation. Stefano inherited the family's main property, Fattoria dei Barbi, while Donatella received two lesser estates, **Casato Prime Donne** (Prima Donna Family), a 50-acre winery in Montalcino, and **Fattoria del Colle** (Farm on the Hill), a 57-acre one in the nearby town of Trequanda. Fattoria dei Barbi had a crest displaying four doves, and Donatella borrowed them for her own labels, which show doves flying away to symbolize her own departure from the family winery.

Based on her marketing work at Fattoria dei Barbi, Donatella became convinced there was a great untapped market for wine tourism. She told me her goal was to identify the "passionate wine consumer." She wasn't interested in the person who came to the winery looking to buy cheap wines. She wanted to get in touch with the new wine consumer, aged thirty-five to forty-four, who lived in a big city and paid less attention to price and more to quality. She believed such wine *aficionados* did not get their views on wines from the press or television, but from their friends and from personal experiences at wineries.

Donatella had no model when she set out to build wine tourism in Tuscany. She has never visited Napa Valley and paid little attention to international wine hot spots. Italy's agrotourism, which promotes farm stays for vacationers, had some of the elements she was looking for, but agrotourism is mainly about an inexpensive vacation. Donatella was interested in the sale of sometimes-expensive wine as well as other trappings of hotels and restaurants that combined to produce the total wine experience.

Armed with a few instinctive assumptions but not much data to back them up, Donatella first decided to start an organization to support wine tourism. In April 1993, a few wineries met on the fringes of the annual Vinitaly wine show in Verona and formed the Wine Tourism Movement. Donatella was both the founder and first president. Then she commissioned a survey asking twenty wineries already active in tourism what specific activities they were offering. At the time she suspected some twenty-five wineries in the whole country had only about $300,000 in annual sales as a result of tourism. She turned the results of the survey over to researchers at Bocconi University in Milan, who documented the potential business wine tourism could create.

Even though she was still in the early days of establishing her own two wineries, Donatella somehow found time to get a hundred Tuscan wineries to participate in her first *Cantine Aperte* (Open Wineries) Day. Some of the best plans are the simplest, and this one was simple. All participating wineries promised to stay open one Sunday, a day when most would have been closed, and in addition the owners agreed to be there personally to give tours and pour wine. She believed it was important for tourists to meet the proprietor and hear the winery's story directly. The first *Cantine Aperte* took place on Sunday, May 9, 1993.

Banfi was one of the participating wineries, and Elizabeth Koenig, then the hospitality director, still remembers the day. "The weather was miserable, and we were all wearing ski jackets trying to stay warm. At first no one came, but eventually they did, and we were still there at nine p.m. pouring wines."

While perhaps only 5,000 people showed up to taste wines, the press picked up the story and played it big. Only a few months later, winemakers in Piedmont in northwest Italy did their own Open Wineries Day and printed a map for tourists to follow. Shortly after that, winemakers in Alto Adige on the Austrian border also did an open day. The second year, fourteen regions participated, and there were 150,000 visitors. Since the third year in 1995 wineries all over Italy have been opening their cellars to as many as 1 million people on the last Sunday in May, and the event is now firmly established on the annual calendar of Italian wineries. The Wine Tourism Movement now has nearly 150 members, although 800 wineries participated in the latest Open Wineries Day. Italy also has 140 different wine routes.

On the basis of her work with Open Wineries Day, leaders of the local government in Siena asked Donatella to take over the three-day-a-week job as director of tourism for the area. One of her first projects for the crowded metropolitan area was a new type of city walk that she called "urban trekking," which cities around the world have since copied. "I don't know why, but it's easy for me to invent something new," she says modestly.

In 2001, Donatella resigned as head of the Wine Tourism Movement, although she remains active in it and other wine groups. She outlined her experiences and suggestions for others to follow in the 2007 book *Il marketing del turismo del vino* (Marketing Wine Tourism).

Now in her mid-fifties with a banker husband and a daughter, Violante, in her mid-twenties, Donatella does not at first glance seem like a person to lead a popular movement. With gray hair and gentle, warm eyes, she speaks softly but carries strong opinions. She obviously inherited much of her drive from her mother, who had already blazed a path for women in wine in Tuscany, and believes strongly in empowering women. Donatella told me she looks forward to passing her two wineries along to her daughter.

The properties are located near each other and share many of the same, mostly female staffs. Donatella says that when she was putting the winery staffs together, she went to the enology school in Siena and asked about recommendations for a woman winemaker. The men there told her there weren't any qualified candidates. She found that outrageous and set out to change the winemaking scene, at least in Tuscany. Her two wineries today claim their entire winemaking staff is female, although there is a male cellar master and some men have been spotted working in the field. The wineries have a combined annual production of about 170,000 bottles and sell half of that abroad. Casato Prime Donne makes only red wines, while Fattoria del Colle makes a Super Tuscan and Chianti reds plus one white, a Vin Santo. Donatella's favorite wine is the Brunello di Montalcino Progetto Prime Donne, which the winery calls "the first important red wine chosen by female tasters." The same four women wine experts from four different countries, Britain, Germany, Italy, and the United States, get together once a year and make the blend, which is New World in style and gets high marks from critics.

Both of the wineries have extensive programs for visitors and also offer lodging and meals. The more developed program is at Fattoria del Colle, which has nineteen apartments. In the rustic atmosphere of a working farm and village that stretches out over 830 acres, Fattoria offers tennis, walking tours, swimming, truffle hunts, cooking courses, and much more. There is also a full restaurant staffed entirely by women.

Alessandro Gallo, Donatella's successor as head of the Wine Tourism Movement, says that Italian wineries now face a fundamental question of how much they want to promote to visitors. "When we started the Movement fifteen years ago, a visit to the cellar was enough, but now people want to have dinner in the cellar and more." His own **Castello**

d'Albola cut back on wine tourism in 2007, because it was getting more visitors than it could comfortably handle—about 25,000 people a year. "You can actually lose by having too many people because visitors leave unhappy," says Gallo. The winery is now targeting groups of fewer than ten, which he says is a good number for a dinner with a winemaker. "But if it's a bus with fifty people, you can't have the same kind of experience."

If Gallo could have one wish fulfilled, it would be to find a way to efficiently send wine home with tourists. Many wineries around the world are struggling with the issue, which has become difficult because of antiterrorism measures restricting carry-on luggage. Tourists often want to buy a case or so of wine at a winery even if they can get it cheaper at home. "People want to put the wine on the table at dinner and say that they just brought it back from Tuscany," he says. Gallo is searching for a way to offer cost-effective shipping to his organization's members, but so far hasn't found it.

The most innovative Tuscan wineries are not necessarily the biggest. Morisfarms, Avignonesi, and Tenuta Poggio Verrano are only three of many small or modest Italian wineries doing interesting wine tourism. **Morisfarms** is located at the end of a long road lined with stately cypress trees in the southern Tuscan village of Cura Nuova. Manager Adolfo Parentini is always happy to greet visitors and has a ready answer for the question everybody asks: Where did that English name come from? He explains patiently that his wife is a Moris from the Spanish side of the family that spells the name with one "r" and not two, as the English do. Morisfarms has been selling wine to visitors only since 2005, and Parentini and his son still have the family touch. Framed on one side of the tasting room is an aging photocopy of a Robert Parker review from 1994, when he gave a Morisfarms wine 90 points, but unnoted are the many other Parker reviews where its Super Tuscans have done even better. Large and comfortable chairs stand in front of a nineteenth-century fireplace that just begs visitors to sit and enjoy a glass of wine. Morisfarms offers Tuscan history, culture, and unpretentious wine tourism at its best.

Avignonesi is just outside Montepulciano and gets its name from the people who returned to Italy with the pope in 1376 after the papacy ended its sixty-eight-year stay in Avignon, France. The winery is best known for its Vin Santo, which it stores for ten years in a special room in barrels sealed with wax. Each May the staff opens all the barrels in a great celebration and then bottles the wine. Avignonesi produces 3,000 half-bottles a year. *Wine Spectator* awarded a perfect 100 points to the 1990 Avignonesi Vin Santo, and Parker gave 96 points to the 1993. The winery each day offers about ten visitors a fixed-price menu at its restaurant overlooking the Tuscan hill cities. Price of either lunch or dinner is $95 per person.

In the summer of 2008, the Falvo family that founded Avignonesi sold majority ownership to the director of a Belgian shipping company. Both sides, as always, promised no changes would be made, and Falvo family members will be staying on for five years to manage the winery.

The Bolla family created a lot of Italian wine history, most notably launching Amarone in the 1950s, a wine made with partly dried grapes. After selling his family's nineteenth-century winery, Francesco Bolla hired the esteemed winemaker Carlo Ferrini to help him make a new Super Tuscan in Maremma near the Tyrrhenian Sea that separates the Italian mainland from Sardinia and Sicily. From the top of the vineyard visitors can see the water 10 miles away. **Tenuta Poggio Verrano**, a mostly underground stone winery, is the antithesis of a traditional Italian winery. Everything there is fresh and modern. Resident winemaker Nicola Vaglini and his American wife, Olivia, who moved to Italy in hopes of becoming an opera star, run things on a day-to-day basis and give tours. Poggio Verrano makes only one wine, Dròmos, which is made from Cabernet Sauvignon, Merlot, Sangiovese, Cabernet Franc, and Alicante grapes. The first vintage of 2003 won good reviews, as have subsequent ones. The wine is destined for greatness, and the modern winery is an interesting juxtaposition to ancient Tuscany.

Visitors are warmly welcomed at Tenuta Poggio Verrano, which is not the case at some wineries making the most famous Super Tuscans. In Boston they used to say that the Cabots only talked to the Lodges, and the Lodges only talked to God. Viviana Rosa, the marketing manager at Tenuta dell'Ornellaia, a maker of overpriced wines made with mostly French grapes, gives the impression she doesn't even speak to God and certainly not to many tourists. She specifically said that if anyone ever called and said that they were having a vacation at a nearby beach and wanted to spend a day at the winery, she would not give the person a reservation since he was obviously not serious! Only five years ago, Ornellaia first began accepting nontrade visitors. The few people who make it through the strict screening procedure can pay $100 for a buffet or $150 for a lunch at the winery. It may be easier to break into the Banca d'Italia than it is to get past the tight security at Ornellaia. They might as well put a big sign at the main gate: Visitors Not Welcome.

Two aspects of wine tourism in Tuscany are special and set it apart from other wine centers I visited. The first is the numerous fortified hill towns such as Montalcino, where you are transported back in time and the mystery of history overwhelms you. These are wonderful places to spend an hour or a half-day just walking and soaking up the atmosphere and stopping for a glass of wine. Other wine capitals may have one or two similar spots, but in Tuscany they are everywhere. The second is the food-wine combination. Other areas do it, but no other region combines magnificent splendor with casual flair and turns an average meal into *la dolce vita*.

DIARY OF A WINE TOURIST

APRIL 17–20

COOKING CLASSES IN A

THOUSAND-YEAR-OLD MONASTERY

Florence's Catherine de' Medici married France's Henry II in 1533 and later became queen of that country, where she introduced fine cuisine, into what was then a culinary backwater. French utensils at the time did not even include the spoon, which she brought along with her. French cooking, of course, flourished and became the envy of the world. Italy's regional cooking, however, never lost its reputation and following.

More than two decades ago, Lorenza de' Medici founded a cooking school at Badia a Coltibuono on a hilltop 43 miles south of Florence. It is housed in a former monastery founded in 1051, that includes a Romanesque church and several stone buildings constructed around a central courtyard. Benedictine monks lived there until Napoléon's army chased them out in 1810. A wing of the Medici family took over the monastery in 1838.

Lorenza is an internationally famous chef who has published more than thirty cookbooks on Italian cuisine and appeared in a thirteen-part series on Italian cooking for American public television. Today her son Guido Stucchi-Prinetti, who learned his craft at his mother's apron and is now regularly a guest chef in restaurants around the world, runs the cooking school. Near the former monastery the family also produces olive oil and has a winery, also named **Badia a Coltibuono**. Its most famous wines are Chianti Classico Riserva; Sangioveto, a pure Sangiovese; and Vin Santo del Chianti Classico.

The cooking school offers programs lasting from one day to a week. At each lesson as many as a dozen students work around a large marble table preparing a four-course meal in the well-appointed kitchen, and then sit down to enjoy the lunch or dinner.

One of the highlights of enrolling in the school is living in a monastery nearly one thousand years old. The small church where the monks used to attend Mass still holds religious services and is in remarkably good condition. As you walk down the cold stone monastery corridors, a visitor sees waves of architecture through the centuries pass by—gothic here, renaissance there. Bells that used to call the monks to prayer still ring out on the hour, but fortunately no longer peal after 8:00 p.m. Bedrooms are located in expanded cells where monks once lived, and it is impossible not to think about what it must have been like to live there centuries ago. Well-preserved frescoes cover many walls, and the ones in the beautifully restored refectory are particularly lovely.

My talents in cooking are limited to making microwave popcorn, but I eagerly signed up for the three-day cooking course at Badia a Coltibuono. The program also offered either a visit to the market in a nearby town to buy local cheeses and salamis or a tour and tasting at the estate's winery.

After a buffet breakfast of fresh fruit and baked goods, students gathered in the kitchen at 9:00 a.m. for the first lesson of the day. Both Guido and the students wore green aprons, and he began explaining the basics of the cuisine we would be learning over the next few days. He stressed that there is no such thing as "Italian cooking" outside of Italian restaurants in the United States. There are only regional dishes that vary from Tuscany and Rome to Palermo and Naples. We would be preparing Tuscan cuisine, and the building blocks of it are wine, olive oil, and bread. Guido stressed that it is much less complicated than classical French cooking and included none of what he called "heavy brown sauces."

Each class included a bread, a first course, a second course, a vegetable, and a dessert, or *il dolce*. The first bread was the deceptively easy Tuscan bread, which Guido repeatedly pointed out was made without salt. Later we also made flatbread with rosemary and milk bread.

Among the first courses were potato gnocchi with fresh gorgonzola cheese, which was creamier than any I had ever experienced, tagliatelle pasta with vegetable ragout, orecchiette pasta with tomato sauce and ricotta cheese, Florentine crêpes with an eggplant filling, and fennel and orange soup. Stars of the second courses were veal rolls with sage, lamb fricassée, as well as pork tenderloin with a bread-and-bacon crust. Among the delicious vegetables were artichokes alla Romana, roast potatoes with fennel seeds, and cannellini beans with tomato and sage. Finally *I dolci* were an orange-scented ricotta tart, pears cooked in red wine with custard and wine sauce, and chocolate and olive oil mousse.

Several times in a lesson Guido asked for a volunteer to work directly with him on one aspect of preparing a dish. I stepped up when we were making the crust for the orange-scented ricotta tart. I couldn't remember the last time I had made a crust, if I ever had, but now was the time to try. With his guidance, I first worked the flour into a ball with sugar, butter, and egg, rolled out the chilled crust, and then gently laid it into the baking pan. Then I stepped back and looked at my work with the same pride that Michelangelo must have had when he first examined his *David*.

Repeatedly Guido talked about the importance of fresh products. Local farmers provide him daily with meat, cheese, and vegetables. He also grows most of his herbs in the monastery's garden. He said that without fresh ingredients, good Tuscan cooking was simply impossible.

I was unprepared for the lavish use of olive oil. Guido put it on everything and in great quantities. Just as Americans might put salt and pepper on food, often without even thinking, Guido was always reaching for the bottle of his own olive oil and sprinkling it on whatever he was preparing. I had never heard of including olive oil in a chocolate mousse until he made one that turned out wonderfully.

The best part of the cooking school for me, though, was the wines. Guido reached generously into the family's cellar to bring out a selection of both young and old vintages to enjoy with meals. In the three evenings I was there, all the guests retired from the table to sit in front of a large fireplace that might have been a thousand years old and sampled both Badia a Coltibuono Grappa and Vin Santo. It was the perfect way to end a perfect Tuscan day.

CHAPTER ELEVEN

Bordeaux, France

Of the twelve countries I visited in my search of Bacchus, France was where it was most difficult to select the best region. So many interesting areas make great wine, and local people have developed innovative ways to attract visitors. Over the years, I have visited many wine regions in France and retain fond memories of them all. Champagne produces its own special wine that never goes out of fashion, and the big Champagne producers have built wonderful programs that educate people about its history and its wine. The cathedral of Reims, where French kings were once crowned, is interesting to visit again and again and makes a nice side trip when Champagne tasting.

The Route des Vins in Alsace, which runs for some 75 miles on the eastern side of the Vosges Mountains from just outside Strasbourg in the north to the city of Thann in the south, offers exciting wineries to visit and wonderful wines to taste. Residents of little towns such as Ribeauvillé, Kaysersberg, and Bergheim always seem to be smiling. Few wine experiences can beat pilgrimages to Kientzheim to visit Domaine Paul Blanck or to Turckheim to taste Olivier Zind-Humbrecht's wines. And if you get palate fatigue, you can always move over to the Route du Fromage in the Munster Valley and enjoy fresh, unpasteurized Munster cheese.

Burgundy, with its many small wineries and crazy-quilt vineyards dating back nearly two thousand years, is a perfect place for a leisurely stroll, and you can stop along the way to enjoy both great food and great wine. The region has a wonderful three-day wine festival each November built around the Hospices de Beaune auction that has been appropriately nicknamed Les Trois Glorieuses. If you ever get a chance to attend, don't pass it up.

I will never forget the Loire Valley, where I first experienced French wines as a college student. My friends and I used to ride bicycles up and down the valley from Tours, stopping to visit such magnificent châteaux as Chenonceau, Azay-le-Rideau, and Blois as well as to enjoy wines with vintners in Vouvray, Anjou, and Chinon. Sancerre and Pouilly-Fumé were also favorite destinations.

The Côtes du Rhône and its wines were popular with both Thomas Jefferson and Robert Louis Stevenson. Jefferson loved the Viognier of Château Grillet, while Stevenson was a fan of Hermitage. The steep hillsides and ancient ruins never cease to fascinate visitors. And who doesn't love the city of Avignon?

Yet as I pondered my final choice, I kept coming back to Bordeaux, the wine capital of the world. It was here that I had to go to experience not only the best wines France produces, although Burgundians would surely challenge that, but also to see how the Bordelais are developing wine tourism.

Bordeaux is a large wine region that includes fifty-seven appellations, or geographic wine regions, and vines cover just over 300,000 acres, which makes it seven times bigger than the Napa Valley and five times the size of Burgundy. Bordeaux today produces 25 percent of France's appellation wine. About 90 percent of its wines are red and 10 percent white or rosé, but as late as the 1960s, the region was still making more whites than reds. The red wines come from Merlot, Cabernet Sauvignon, Cabernet Franc, Malbec, Carmenère, and Petit Verdot grapes. The first three, though, dominate. The whites are made with Sauvignon Blanc, Sémillon, Muscadelle, Ugni Blanc, Colombard, Merlot Blanc, Mauzac, and Ondenc, with the first three again being the most important. The great majority of Bordeaux wines, whether red or white, are blends, and it's unusual for one to be made from a single variety.

The topography of Bordeaux is different from that of the Napa Valley or Stellenbosch, where mountains dominate the landscape. Bordeaux is mainly flat with only minor variations in altitude. That difference, though, can be important, and the price of wine from a slightly higher region may be several times more than one from a nearby vineyard only a few feet lower. The dominant geographical feature is the Gironde, a muddy river that flows 357 miles from its headwaters in the Spanish Pyrenees, past the city of Bordeaux, and then joins with the Dordogne River to form the Gironde Estuary, which empties into the Atlantic Ocean, 47 miles away.

The city of Bordeaux, which only two decades ago was dirty and run-down, has gone through a major renovation in recent years and is now a UNESCO World Heritage site. City planners tore down warehouses that used to block the view of the Gironde, and the waterfront is now a broad, open promenade complete with dramatic fountains. Buildings dating back to the eighteenth century have been scrubbed clean. For the first time in decades Bordeaux again has a top hotel, the Regent, which is located on the city's main square facing the opera. In the past, one had to go to Biarritz 105 miles away to find luxury accommodations. The Regent's management has brought in a top chef from Brussels and promises to soon be collecting Michelin stars. The menu emphasizes seafood, and the *pièce de résistance* is lobster.

Bordeaux *négociants,* the dealers who for centuries have handled the sale of most wines, are based in the city. Wineries generally only produce wines and then sell them to *négociants,* who handle the marketing. Some *négociants* also buy wine in bulk and then blend it and sell it under their own brands. It's a system that exists in no other wine-producing country, but it works for the French. There are today some four hundred Bordeaux *négociants,* about the same number as there were in the nineteenth century. From the seventeenth to the nineteenth centuries, English and Irish traders were major players among the *négociants* since the main export market was England; and names such as Barton, Lynch, and Talbot are found on many famous Bordeaux châteaux. Many foreigners later married into French families and became members of the class that Bordeaux-born author François Mauriac called the "cork aristocrats."

Bordeaux was already a major port in Roman times, when its name was Burdigala, and the Roman historian Pliny the Elder in AD 71 wrote of vineyards being cultivated there, noting that they are "never liable to injury, as they do not come before the west wind of early spring and can withstand wine and rain." Bordeaux developed a special relationship with England because of the wine trade. In the twelfth century, the marriage between Eleanor of Aquitaine, the duchy in which Bordeaux is located, and the future Henry II of England united the two regions. The

English looked to Bordeaux for their wine, at least when the two countries were not waging war against each other. In the fourteenth century,
75 percent of all Bordeaux wine production was shipped to England,
where they called Bordeaux red wine "claret." The name may have come
from the claret or clairet grape, a common vine in the Middle Ages, or
more likely from the light red, almost rosé, color of Bordeaux wines up
until the eighteenth century.

Vineyards surround the city of Bordeaux on three sides, and only the
western side is not cultivated. The vineyards are divided into five sub-
regions, each with its own history and style of wine. The most famous
of the five is Médoc, where most, but not all, of the top châteaux are
located. Driving along the generally two-lane road called the D2, a visitor feels he is riding through French wine history, passing wineries with
such famous names as Lafite, Margaux, Latour, and many more. The
road is informally called the Route des Châteaux. Majestic stone castles
stand in silence as monuments to the glory of France. The circuit is the
wine equivalent of the Hollywood homes-of-the-stars tour. The best
vineyards are in the upper part of the peninsula, where winemakers in
such sleepy villages as Margaux, St.-Estèphe, and Pauillac produce some
of the world's best wines. Vineyards are located in a strip of land directly
north of Bordeaux for about 50 miles between the coastal marshes on
the banks of the Gironde Estuary and pine forests about 8 miles inland.
It was only in the seventeenth century that Dutch engineers came to
Bordeaux and used their dike-making technology to drain marshland
used for grazing animals and turn it into vineyards. Newly prosperous
wine aristocrats built the great châteaux in the eighteenth and nineteenth centuries, launching Bordeaux's modern era.

The château owners in those days didn't consider traveling to the
right bank of the Gironde Estuary because of the complications of making the trip by boat. As a result, the wine growing areas of the left and
right banks developed differently. While Cabernet Sauvignon grapes
rule the left bank, Merlot is more prominent on the right bank. Médoc
also differs from other parts of Bordeaux by the size of properties. The
five First Growths of the left bank average 183 acres, while a typical
Bordeaux vineyard is only about 30 acres.

It was only after World War II that the right bank began to enjoy the success it long deserved. The main wine region on the right bank is St.-Émilion, which is located 25 miles from the city of Bordeaux; but it includes much more than the village of that name that has only three hundred residents. The Benedictine monk Émilian, who had moved there from Brittany, founded the town in the eighth century. Many of its historic treasures, including an entire church, are located underground. Eleanor of Aquitaine and Henry II established the basic structure of St.-Émilion wine that still exists today. Because the area was settled so long ago and the vineyards on the right bank have been divided among many heirs over the centuries, the average winery is only 15 acres of vines. Château Ausone is only 17.3 acres and produces fewer than 2,000 cases a year. In 1999, UNESCO put St.-Émilion and its vineyards on its World Heritage list. It was the first time the organization had given the honor to vineyards. Many visitors come to St.-Émilion for the wines, without realizing the village's great cultural heritage. Unfortunately, the village has only five hotels and fewer than two dozen restaurants.

The right bank, though, is about more than just St.-Émilion. Pomerol is a nondescript little village with a single church spire rising up out of the flat countryside. Only a small ditch that a visitor would be hard pressed to find separates this appellation from St.-Émilion. But within the confines of Pomerol are such wineries as Châteaux Le Pin, Pétrus, and Lafleur. The region was long dismissed by wine connoisseurs, but gradually, starting in the 1920s, Pomerol became better known first in France and then in northern Europe. After World War II, Harry Waugh, a British wine writer and merchant, brought Pomerol to the attention of British and American wine consumers. Dominique Renard, the general director of the *négociant* Bordeaux Millésimes and a resident of St.-Émilion, walked with me into the vineyard of **Château Pétrus** to admire the quality of the clay soil. "The soil has three types of clay that hold water better than other areas. That's the magic of the Merlot you can grow here." Vineyards in Pomerol are generally even smaller than in St.-Émilion. **Château Lafleur** has only 9.9 acres and produces just 1,000 cases each year; Château Pétrus has 28.2 acres and makes at most 2,500 cases.

Also on the right bank is Fronsac, once a highly esteemed wine region and still perhaps the prettiest part of Bordeaux. Charlemagne and Cardinal Richelieu both loved Fronsac wines. In the twentieth century, the wines fell out of fashion with consumers, but that may be changing. Patrick Leon, the former winemaker at Château Mouton Rothschild and Napa Valley's Opus One, is making wine in Fronsac at **Château Les Trois Croix**, and flying winemaker Michel Rolland has **Château Fontenil**.

South of the city of Bordeaux on the left bank of the Gironde is the region of Graves, where some of Bordeaux's oldest wineries are located. From its gravelly soils come both excellent red and dry white wines. **Château Pape Clément**, the first named winery in Bordeaux, makes both, as does its neighbor **Château Haut-Brion**. Graves has suffered over the centuries from creeping urbanization, and many vineyards are now virtually in Bordeaux city. It takes a lot of determination to make wines in this area, but Denis Dubourdieu, a Bordeaux University professor as well as winemaker, produces an excellent **Clos Floridène**, also red and white, on a 44-acre property.

If Médoc is home to the aristocracy of Bordeaux, then Entre-Deux-Mers (Between Two Seas) is working-class Bordeaux. Located between the Gironde and Dordogne rivers, it is also between Graves and St.-Émilion. Once major producers of Bordeaux white wines, vintners there switched mainly to red in the 1960s and 1970s. Entre-Deux-Mers is the main producer of simple Bordeaux appellation wines. Some 2,000 wineries make 15 million bottles a year, but the average winery has only 74 acres. Cooperatives are a big part of the business, and most wineries sell 70 percent of their production to cooperatives and keep only 30 percent to market under their own brand names. **Château du Payre** in Cardan is a typical producer trying to make a go of it far from the madding crowds of Médoc and St.-Émilion. Valerie Labruse, a member of the owner's family, studied marketing, and handles much of the promotion. The winery rents three rooms to overnight guests and welcomes drop-in visitors from 9:00 a.m. to 12:00 p.m. and 2:00 p.m. to 6:00 p.m. Its tasting room offers a full range of products from sparkling Bordeaux to nonalcoholic grape juice. The blends are mainly Merlot. "We have to be like sheep with five feet and sell everything we can to survive," Labruse says. That kind of attitude and historic structures such as the ruins of the eleventh-century Sauve-Majeure Abbey make Entre-Deux-Mers an interesting place to visit. Because of its gently rolling hills, the area has become a favorite destination for bicycle tourists.

In the southern part of Bordeaux, in Sauternes and Barsac, nature plays some tricks that allow winemakers to produce the nectar of the gods. At the end of summer, grapevines turn gold in color, and in the morning thick fog and cool breezes roll in. There is also usually little rain. The conditions conspire to produce a botrytis fungus nicknamed "noble rot," which shrinks grapes on the vine and concentrates the natural sugar. Bunches of white grapes look rotten to the untrained eye, but the wine made from them is delightful. Unfortunately for Sauternes and Barsac producers, sweet wines, which before World War I were more highly priced than dry red ones, have gone out of fashion, and so prices are relatively low. A top Médoc red, for example the 2005 **Château Latour**, costs $2,000 a bottle, but an equal-rated Sauternes, **Château La Tour Blanche**, sells for less than $50.

As far back as the mid-seventeenth century, Bordeaux wine merchants had an informal system for ranking the region's wines based solely on the price the market was willing to pay. Thomas Jefferson in his diaries refers to this system, and even tried his hand at making his own variation. In preparation for a world's fair in Paris in 1855, Emperor Napoléon III asked the Bordeaux Chamber of Commerce to come up with a list of the best local wines to exhibit. The chamber passed the job along to the Bordeaux wine brokers. Using the same procedure of basing the selection on historic price, the group chose sixty-one red wines and twenty-six sweet white wines for the exhibition. The reds were put into five categories called Crus, or Growths, while the whites fell into three. All the reds, with one exception, Château Haut-Brion, came from the Médoc region. The white wines were all from Sauternes and Barsac. Since 1855, the classification has been changed only once: Château Mouton Rothschild in 1973 went from being a Second Growth to a First Growth. It took Baron Philippe de Rothschild nearly fifty years of lobbying Paris officials to get the upgrade, and the decision to correct history was justified again on the grounds of comparative prices.

The 1855 wines still command premium prices around the world even though the 1855 listings are clearly out of date. Bordeaux places heavy emphasis on the importance of *terroir,* the hard-to-define term that emphasizes the location where the grapes are grown. But there have been changes in the vineyards of Grand Cru wineries over the years, and some châteaux don't have the same land as they had in 1855. Talents of winemakers also don't remain static. Some wines are rated lower than they really should be, and some should not even be on the list. Nonetheless, the 1855 classification lives on as a convenient, if flawed, scorecard for Médoc wines.

Exactly a century later in 1955, St.-Émilion came up with its own official classification. The plan was to update the list periodically to reflect the changing quality of the wines. Being on the list is a great boon to producers, who can sell all their wine and at higher prices. The first classification came out in June 1955 and was revised in August and then again in September of that year. The final list included seventy-five wines. Revisions were made in 1969, 1985, 1996, and 2006. The last one demoted eleven properties, which appealed the decision in a battle that reached the highest court in France and the French Senate. A French Court of Appeals scrapped the 2006 classification, but in May 2009 the French government tacked a footnote onto a new agriculture law reinstating the 1996 classification and permitting eight châteaux that had been promoted in 2006 to claim their higher ranking on their labels. This revised classification will last until 2011. By that time, it is hoped that a new, and less controversial, way of updating the St.-Émilion classification will have been established. Battles over promoting—and demoting—wines, though, are likely to continue.

In 1959, Graves producers established a classification for their wines, both reds and dry whites. This list now consists of thirteen reds and nine whites, and several wineries have both reds and whites on the Graves list. Château Haut-Brion is a member of both the 1855 classification and the Graves one.

Some of Bordeaux's best wines come from Pomerol, which does not have a classified list. Château Pétrus, for example, is more expensive than the most costly Médoc. But since Pomerol winemakers quickly sell out of their wines at the high prices they demand, they have no interest in a Pomerol list or being included in any of the existing classifications.

The various Bordeaux classified wines and the leading Pomerol ones make up only about 5 percent of total Bordeaux sales, and those wineries have little problem selling all their production year after year. The other 95 percent of the business, though, faces tougher and tougher competition in global wine markets from both New World producers such as California and Australia and from surging European ones in Spain, Italy, and Portugal. Many Bordeaux wine people are concerned about the future of that 95 percent.

Bordeaux historically had little interest in wine tourism. The *négociants* handled marketing, and French wines, after all, were considered the best in the world, so why bother? Winemakers felt they didn't need to attract visitors, who only got in the way of making wine. I'll never forget the sign I saw in the summer of 2006 on the white picket fence outside Château Bellegrave. It summed up in no uncertain terms the attitude of many in Bordeaux toward wine tourism, stating "Private Property" first in French, and then in English "No Visitors."

Two twentieth-century leaders of the Bordeaux wine world tried to introduce a friendlier attitude toward tourists, but their attempts at the time had little impact. The first was Baron Philippe de Rothschild. Nathaniel de Rothschild in 1853 bought the winery then named Brane-Mouton, only two years before it was ruled a Second Growth under the 1855 classification, and renamed it **Château Mouton Rothschild**. The judges were never totally clear why they gave it that ranking, but it may have been partly because the winery was in bad repair and perhaps also because its new owner was both English and Jewish. Mouton continued to decline until 1922, when Philippe de Rothschild, the great-grandson of Nathaniel, inherited a joint share and took over management of the property. Baron Philippe later wrote, "I was staggered at the mess and neglect I found everywhere." Nonetheless, he threw himself into rescuing Mouton and took the unusual step of moving to Pauillac, the sleepy Bordeaux village where it was located, although he escaped frequently to Paris to continue his busy social life.

Baron Philippe also began entertaining in Bordeaux. He hired a

Parisian stage designer to plan the interior of the winery in a manner that included plenty of dramatic lighting. In 1926, Rothschild built a 109-yard-long cellar for barrels in the first year of aging, which attracted great attention and made the winery a favorite of visitors. Starting in the 1950s, he began collecting pieces of wine history and culture and then built the best wine museum in Bordeaux. André Malraux, French president de Gaulle's minister of culture, inaugurated it in 1962. In his autobiography, Baron Philippe wrote enthusiastically, "On the drawing board there are new projects, a reception room for tourists, arriving each year in increasing numbers . . . Ideas for the future are still bubbling in my brain . . . a Mouton village, with shops, covered walkways, a restaurant and a *salle des fêtes,* lakes, garden, trees." While he had the vision, Mouton in Baron Philippe's lifetime never enjoyed huge crowds, receiving only five or six visitors on some days.

In September 1976, when I was a reporter for *Time,* I was fortunate to visit Mouton as part of a press visit that Baron Philippe arranged for American and British journalists in Paris. We toured the cellar and the museum and then enjoyed a long dinner, during which the baron pulled out some of his favorite old wines. Ever the attentive host, he moved from table to table talking about his wines and the special pleasure of drinking the vintage of your birth year. Rothschild died in 1988.

Alexis Lichine, a contemporary of Baron Philippe, was a Russian-American-Frenchman who taught Americans about wine after World War II through his 1951 book *Wines of France.* Born in Moscow before the Soviet revolution, his family escaped first to the United States and then moved to France to join the large White Russian community there. After American Prohibition ended, Lichine moved to the United States and got into the wine business, first in a retail store and then as an importer. During World War II, he served in U.S. Army Military Intelligence and was on General Dwight Eisenhower's staff as his wine advisor. After the war, Lichine divided his time between the United States and France, and in 1951 he bought the run-down winery Château Prieuré-Cantenac, a Fourth Growth by the 1855 classification, which he renamed **Château Prieuré-Lichine**. He also became a partner in **Château Lascombes**, a Second Growth.

Lichine was an iconoclast. In 1959, he was a member of a commit-
tee of shippers, growers, and brokers formed to update the 1855 classification. The group never could agree on any changes, so in 1962 he
published his own list of Bordeaux's top 136 red wines, including those
from Médoc, Graves, St.-Émilion, and Pomerol. In addition, he instituted fixed visiting hours at Prieuré-Lichine and Lascombes and put up
large billboards in vineyards inviting people to tour his wineries. The
local wine establishment was shocked by what it considered undignified
promotions, and few followed his lead.

Jean-Michel Cazes of **Château Lynch-Bages**, however, has been
able to achieve some of the goals of Baron Philippe de Rothschild and
Alexis Lichine. Cazes is a believer in wine tourism, although he hates
the French word for it—*enotourism.* "It's a combination of a Greek root
(eno) and a Latin one (tornare). A professor once told me never to
combine the two."

Along with many Bordelais of his generation, Cazes headed off for a
different field at the age of eighteen in 1953 because he didn't see much
of a future in wine. "Lots of wineries were then going bankrupt," he
recalls. So he went to Paris to the École des Mines with the intention of
becoming a petroleum engineer and continued his studies at the University of Texas. "Yes, I'm a longhorn," he told me. When he couldn't
find an interesting job in the oil business, he parlayed his knowledge of
English and computers into a job with IBM in Paris, where he worked
for twelve years. Then in 1972, after his grandfather died, Jean-Michel
returned to the family business in Pauillac at age thirty-eight. Lynch-
Bages is only a Fifth Growth wine, but has good neighbors such as
Château Latour and Château Pichon-Longueville.

As soon as he was home, Cazes saw tourism as something that could
"be a big plus," especially in the American market, which was just wak-
ing up to French wine. "I thought the winery was a good place to communicate our message. Visitors would become our ambassadors." Cazes
still remembers the first American who showed up unannounced. His
name was Sherwood Deutsch, and he owned Century Liquor & Wine
in Rochester, New York. Deutsch soon became a major buyer of Lynch-
Bages wines. Before long, Jean-Michel and his wife, Thereza, were inviting visitors home to lunch or dinner nearly every day of the week. In

1978, Cazes went to Napa and met with Robert Mondavi to talk about wine and tourism. "That inspired me a lot," Cazes recalls. Later he sent his oldest daughter there to check on developments.

During the late 1970s, Cazes and his new wine director, Daniel Llose, began raising the quality of Lynch-Bages beyond its Fifth Growth status, and by Bordeaux's glorious decade of the 1980s experts considered it to be on a par with a Second Growth.

Once his wines were in top form, Cazes set out to expand his palette of wine tourism offerings. He bought in 1987 the neighboring seventeenth-century Château Cordeillan-Bages, and two years later had turned it into a hotel with twenty-four rooms and four suites that was considered Médoc's best. Then in 1997, he hired Thierry Marx, a young chef who had worked at the three-star Taillevent restaurant in Paris. Cazes's goal was to make the restaurant a destination for wine-and-food lovers from around the world. Marx got his first Michelin star in 1997 and a second in 2000. An added benefit of the restaurant was that the Cazes family no longer had to entertain visitors at home.

With business booming in 2000, Lynch-Bages needed to expand the winery's cellar. Cazes's architect proposed tearing down several buildings and putting up a large new one for the cellar. Cazes, though, didn't like the idea. He had grown up in the little hamlet of Bages on the outskirts of Pauillac and felt a responsibility to it. Thierry Marx had also told him that he was having trouble buying quality bread and pastries and suggested that maybe the winery should open a bakery. For all those reasons, Cazes sent the architect back to his drawing board, telling him to create a village like the one he had known in his youth.

Today the restored village of Bages is a reality. In addition to the Château Lynch-Bages winery, which offers wine tours, tastings, and courses in wine appreciation, the hamlet also includes Bages's Bazaar, a boutique offering Cazes wines plus a collection of wine and food accessories and books; Café Lavinal, a brasserie-style restaurant; Au Baba d'Andréa, a bakery; Les Ateliers de Bages, two workshops, one with master basket weavers and one for painters; and École des Saveurs, a cooking school. Nearby at Château Cordeillan-Bages are also a hotel and restaurant.

The village of Bages has become one of the top tourist destinations in Médoc, receiving 20,000 visitors a year. But Cazes was dissatisfied that there wasn't more life in the village. So he decided St. Antoine would be the village's patron saint in order to have a festival in his honor each year on June 12. That was so successful he added another festival in December for St. Barbara. The village also stages the Médoc Marathon, a literary competition, and various single events such as a performance by a New Orleans jazz pianist. In everything he does at the Bages Village, Cazes has two rules: "It must give a quality image that corresponds with what we have in a bottle of Lynch-Bages wine, and it is important to bring life back to this village." So far, he's succeeding on both counts.

Only a short distance from the village of Bages is La Winery, one of Bordeaux's most innovative efforts in wine tourism. Located at the Rond-point des Vendangeurs, the first major traffic circle and a half-hour drive from Bordeaux, La Winery was built with the wine tourist in mind. Its slogan: "A New Approach to Wine." Owner Philippe Raoux comes from a wine family, and owns four properties in Bordeaux. He is perhaps best known for his tenacity. In the 1990s, he waged a nine-year war with wine regulators to get his winery **Château d'Arsac** designated a Margaux appellation, a battle he eventually won.

For four generations the family had a wine business in Algeria. But after that country's independence from France in 1962, they moved to Bordeaux and built a successful mail-order business selling mainly inexpensive wine. That kind of wine consumption started declining in the 1980s as people began drinking less but better-quality wine. At the same time, urban renewal in Bordeaux was forcing the family's company out of the city. Then after the election in 1981 of Socialist François Mitterrand as president of France, Raoux's father became concerned about the outlook for business in France. So following a time-honored French tradition, the family started looking into how they might get money out of France by investing abroad.

Coincidentally, Philippe Raoux was looking to compete in his first marathon. In August 1981, he flew to San Francisco to run one there, which he was happy to see was cosponsored by Paul Masson wines. After finishing the marathon in 3 hours and 37 minutes, and at his father's request, Philippe stayed a little longer to investigate possible investments in the Napa Valley. While there, he visited Sterling Vineyards, Clos Pegase, Sebastiani Vineyards, "and of course" the Robert Mondavi Winery. He later returned to Napa several times, but never found the right investment and eventually dropped the idea.

Raoux is one of the millions of Frenchmen who, despite their national reputation for being anti-American, are fascinated by many aspects of American life. Jerry Lewis, for example, is a national idol in France. Raoux liked what he saw in Napa Valley and thought a lot about it in the late 1990s, when he was refocusing his business away from mail-order wines. He first wanted to find a location that would bring thousands of people past his front door, just as Route 29 does in Napa. That brought his attention to the Rond-point des Vendangeurs traffic circle; some 18,000 people drive around it daily. Then he built a showy glass-and-steel structure at the property's main entrance on the circle and put in front of it a six-ton, orange, stainless steel sculpture called Sun Tree, made by Japanese artist Susumu Shingu. Tipping his hat again to America, he called the new business **La Winery**, and opened the $27 million venture in March 2007.

In addition to its good location and the sculpture, La Winery came up with a unique offering to attract visitors: a chance to discover their enological sign, a wine variation of a horoscope. Visitors do this by taking a blind tasting of six wines, one white and five reds. A computer records the reactions and then determines what types of wines the person likes and gives him one of sixty-four taste profiles and an enological sign such as "sensual" or "powerful." Raoux insists this is not "un gadget," but actually works and helps customers buy wines that they can know in advance they will like.

Armed with that knowledge, visitors can then make their purchases at La Winery's large retail store, which carries more than one thousand wines from around the world. Unlike most wine shops in Bordeaux that offer mostly local products, La Winery also stocks such big international brands as Cloudy Bay from Marlborough, New Zealand, Vega Sicilia from Ribera del Duero in Spain, and Rubicon from Napa Valley. The store displays the enological signs for the wines it carries. Cloudy Bay, for example, is listed as "easy to drink," while Château Lagrange is "powerful."

La Winery's panoply of activities to keep visitors busy also includes several wine tastings, a restaurant, Sunday afternoon concerts, and rotating art shows. Raoux is hoping to get 100,000 visitors annually, but the early traffic has been much less than that. He remains confident, though, that his "new way to discover wine" will be successful.

Château Smith Haut Lafitte in Pessac-Léognan, just south of Bordeaux, has a different approach to wines and wine tourism. It pampers them in the lap of luxury. Daniel Cathiard and his wife, Florence, who met in the 1960s when both were members of the national ski team, bought the winery in 1990, after each had enjoyed successful careers that included running a large chain of supermarkets and sporting goods stores for him, and advertising for her. At the time, Château Smith Haut Lafitte, which makes both red and white wines though only the red is a classified Graves, was on the skids. But they invested heavily and brought both the winery and an eighteenth-century manor house back to their former glory. They also put eye-catching sculptures, including a giant leaping rabbit, out among the vines.

Now located on the property in addition to the winery are a hotel, a spa, and two restaurants. The small (forty-nine rooms) luxury hotel opened in 1995, and Florence has been quoted as saying, "We didn't want the only great wine resorts to be in the Napa Valley." Rooms are furnished with antiques, and no two of them are the same. One suite is in a fisherman's hut built on stilts in a small, artificial lake. The hotel has two restaurants, the bistro-style La Table du Lavoir, and the gourmet-level La Grand'Vigne, which serves classical, high-calorie selections as well as low-fat *cuisine minceur*. The French Paradox bar offers many of Bordeaux's best wines by the glass. There's also a cooking school associated with the hotel.

Smith Haut Lafitte's unique contribution to wine tourism is Les Sources de Caudalie, a spa built around grape-based cosmetics. The Cathiards' daughter Mathilde and her husband, Bertrand Thomas, who worked for the French cosmetics company L'Oréal, came up with the concept with the help of a University of Bordeaux professor who was doing research on how grapes slow signs of the skin's aging. Visitors can enjoy such Vinothérapie treatments as a Merlot wrap and a Cabernet body scrub. The products and spas are spreading worldwide. The spa opened in 2000 and now receives 15,000 customers a year, including women who come for postpartum vacations to regain their figures after childbirth. The spa recommends at least six days of treatment for that.

Visitors can go to Smith Haut Lafitte for the wine, the food, the hotel, or the spa. Some combine all the activities, while others take part in just one. The only requirement is to bring your credit card, with a generous line of credit, with you.

Today, Bordeaux wineries generally disagree with the sign that shouted "No Visitors." Officials estimate that the city of Bordeaux now gets 700,000 tourists annually, with one-fifth of them coming for the wine. The four-day Bordeaux Wine Festival, held every other year in late June, attracts thousands of people to the banks of the Gironde for parades, games, food, and, naturally, wine. Dominique Renard of Bordeaux Millésimes told me that the best way to get in the door of some of the most exclusive châteaux is the "Weekend des Grands Amateurs," held each year in May. The Bordeaux Union of Grands Crus, which includes more than a hundred top wineries, puts on the events that include tastings, tours, vineyard visits, brunches, and dinners.

One of the most interesting new initiatives in Bordeaux is Les Médocaines (Médoc Women), started by the daughters of four Médoc châteaux owners. The wineries: **Châteaux Paloumey**, **La Tour de Bessan**, **du Taillan**, and **Loudenne**. Shortly before the 2005 harvest, the four created a wine route. They run a series of small group (no more than fifteen people) workshops at their wineries on a rotating basis, and during harvest there's something going on each week. Florence Lafragette of Château Loudenne, who once did an internship at Joseph Phelps Vineyards in the Napa Valley, said the four got together because they wanted to pool their energies and talents. The group now receives 10,000 visitors per year, almost all during the summer and fall. As members of the Internet generation, their prime way of promoting programs is via the Web (www.lesmedocaines.com).

Despite the professed enthusiasm for wine tourism, however, there remains some lingering reluctance to embrace it. Jean-François Quenin in St.-Émilion is a first-generation winemaker who worked in accounting before buying the fifteenth-century winery **Château de Pressac**, where the English and the French signed the treaty ending the Hundred

Years War. At the age of forty-eight, he went to school in Bordeaux to learn the fundamentals of winemaking in a class with teenagers. He mastered his lessons and now owns two wineries, the second being **Château Pavillon Bel-Air** in Lalande-de-Pomerol. Quenin has only one employee who works with him in the cellar.

Quenin admits to being conflicted about wine tourism. On the one hand, he knows he should be doing it. "More and more people are coming, and we have to find a way to welcome them." But on the other hand he honestly doesn't like it. "If we become too professional, we'll lose our heritage and our soul."

Château de Pressac has too few visitors—only a couple of groups a week—to hire someone to give tours, so Quenin does them himself. Since antiterrorism regulations now restrict what air passengers can take in the cabin on commercial flights, his sales to tourists have been cut in half, and he now sells only about one thousand bottles a year at the winery. "I give a free tour and visit for an hour and a half, and the person might buy one bottle," he says ruefully.

Quenin explained to me that the day before we met, a travel agent had berated him on the phone because he wouldn't open the cellar for a group on Sunday. "I work six days a week in the winery, and my grandchildren, whom I haven't seen in six months, are coming on Sunday. I'm sorry, but I want to see them." Quenin thinks he's typical, and most wineries in St.-Émilion are too small to get into wine tourism. Of the some 800 wineries in St.-Émilion, only 101 participate in the local tourism office's wine program for receiving visitors, and just 30 have signed a new agreement to be open at specified times.

Quenin hopes the wine trade group can come up with a plan that would allow three or four wineries to share the time when at least one of them would be open. "I don't like to keep saying no, but we are family-owned and can't work the seventh day of the week to sell only one bottle out of the cellar."

Many French winemakers along with Quenin continue to worry about losing their "soul" and the "culture of wine" to tourism. The essence of French wine is tradition, which ultimately sets it apart. This will remain a benefit to visitors who travel to France and accept the country and its people on their own terms.

Diary of a Wine Tourist

September 2–7

Walking Through Burgundy

The ideal speed for wine tourism is either hiking or biking. If you're driving, you're going too fast and miss the pleasure of gazing out at the countryside or studying vineyards in detail. It's also easier to stop on a bike or during a walk to get up-close and personal with a winemaker or people working in the fields.

Arblaster & Clarke has been conducting wine trips around the world since 1987. Before they started, Lynette Arblaster was working for a London travel agency, while her future husband, Tim Clarke, had worked in wine shops and was looking for some job in wine that was going to be more rewarding than retail. Their first wine trip was to Champagne, still their most popular destination, and they have since been to all parts of the wine world. They have been doing a walking tour of Burgundy since 1994. Looking back at the growth of wine tourism, Clarke told me, "We picked up a ripple on a surfboard twenty-one years ago that has now turned into a great tsunami."

On a warm Sunday evening, the fourteen participants in the Burgundy trip met on the terrace of the Hôtel les Grands Crus just outside the wine village of Gevrey-Chambertin, which is best known for its delicious Pinot Noirs. All the others in the group were British, as was the guide, who is married to a French woman and works in Burgundy for a French barrel maker. As people introduced themselves after drink orders were taken, it quickly became clear the group was quite diverse.

It included a man in his eighties who had been on one of the first Arblaster & Clarke tours, as well as several people in their twenties, who were on their first trip. The guide gave a brief overview of the trip, which was going to last until Friday night and would end in the wine village of Puligny-Montrachet, noted for its Chardonnay.

Quickly, the group fell into a routine. Up early for a generous breakfast, then a walk for an hour or so followed by a visit to a winery for a tasting, then perhaps a picnic lunch of local foods and wines near a vineyard, another walk or two in the afternoon, and another visit and tasting before either a free evening or a dinner together. On any given day we never walked more than 10 miles, with much of the distance on vineyard lanes high above the valley floor and the main highway going south from Dijon. If the distance got too far for people or if they just didn't want to walk, a bus was always there to pick them up and also to carry the bottles of wine the group started collecting along the way. We stayed in three hotels during the six nights, which meant that we weren't packing and unpacking each day. The highlight of the entire walk was probably the visit to **Clos de Vougeot**, Burgundy's most famous vineyard and home to the Tastevin wine brotherhood.

The obvious benefit of going on such a trip is that the tour company, if it is any good, can open doors of wineries that an off-the-street tourist could never visit. We visited seven wineries for tours and tastings that might last two hours. Lunch the second day was at **Domaine Armelle et Bernard Rion**, where Armelle kept bringing out more and better wines to go with the Burgundian dishes she served. It went on and on, but no one complained. The staffs at **Domaine Comte Senard** in Aloxe-Corton and at **Domaine des Lambrays** in Morey-St.-Denis opened their best wines. After tasting both the 2000 and the 2001 Grand Cru Clos des Lambrays, we walked by the vineyard where the grapes are grown.

The experience of walking next to the hallowed vineyards of Burgundy—and maybe slipping into the rows to pick a grape or two—is special. After turning down one narrow path, I saw chiseled in the rock a sign saying that this was the **Domaine de la Romanée-Conti**, and later we passed a sign indicating that the vineyard was the **Clos des Mouches**. Those are two of France's great vineyards. The guide kept up a steady chatter of wine education as we walked, pointing out how there were sometimes different soils on two sides of the same path, which explains why a wine from one side may cost more than wine from the other. He said that simple village wines mostly come from vineyards on the flat areas near the highway, while Premier Cru and Grand Cru ones are made with grapes grown on the hillsides where they get more sunshine. At one point we walked down a path that had a Montrachet vineyard on one side and a Bâtard-Montrachet on the other.

At each stop we could buy wines we had just tasted, although there was no pressure to do so. We were a knowledgeable, but tough, crowd. The group was particularly unimpressed at one winery in Gevrey-Chambertin, and no one purchased even a single bottle. At most wineries, though, walkers after the first few days were trying to decide whether they could pack just one more bottle in their luggage. The happiest people on the tour were a couple who had their own car and kept buying more and more wine to take home. This was their third wine tour, so they knew the routine.

On Friday, the last night of the tour, the group dined at the one-star Michelin restaurant of the Hotel Le Montrachet in Puligny-Montrachet. The guide said that he was already over his budget for the tour's wines, but we just had to have one that he saw on the list. I hope he didn't get into too much trouble for ordering a bottle of 2005 Domaine Sylvain Langoureau Meursault-Blagny Premier Cru. It was delicious. As the group lingered over the last sips of wine, people told one another what a great tour it had been and how we should get together to do another one. The trips are addictive, and many people come back time after time. Perhaps our paths would cross again, who knows? In any case, we all hoped to enjoy the wines of the week again sometime, somewhere, and with someone special.

CHAPTER TWELVE

Rheingau and Middle Mosel, Germany

The Rhine and Mosel rivers and valleys are the birthplace of Germany's romantic heritage. High on the hilltops stand the remains of former castles and monasteries, some dating back a thousand years, although many were destroyed by the wars of the twentieth century and rebuilt. The most famous spot on the Rhine is the Loreley. According to legend, a beautiful maiden there used to entice sailors to their deaths with her seductive calls. The rocky cliff, which somewhat resembles a woman's face if you have a good imagination, reaches down 130 yards to the river below. Sailors often ventured too close to the cliff in order to hear her provocative cries and ended up crashing their ships on the unforgiving rocks. Historians now believe the sounds came from a small waterfall that later dried up, but stories of sailors and a beautiful maiden have long survived in folklore and poetry. The Roman poet Ausonius in about AD 370 celebrated the beauty and life along the Mosel that still exists today in the poem *Mosella*: "Rocks on sunny heights, cliffs, and mounds of earth are covered with vines as if nature built its own theatre." Goethe, in the nineteenth century, wrote a poem celebrating the Mosel where "the vine prospered to be its very best." Heinrich Heine, a major romantic poet, also wrote a famous tribute to the Loreley: "The summit of the mountain sparkles in the evening sunshine."

The Rhine and Mosel rivers are like two superhighways that sweep through central western Germany. On a map, the waterways resemble a person's intestines, twisting and turning back and forth. The Rhine starts in the Swiss Alps near Basel and flows 820 miles to the Netherlands, where it joins the Meuse River, and then flows into the Atlantic Ocean at the port of Rotterdam. The headwaters of the 339-mile

Mosel River are in the Vosges Mountains, and it flows through eastern France and Luxembourg before entering Germany at the city of Trier. The Mosel then winds its way northeast to join the Rhine at Koblenz. Unlike Portugal's lightly traveled Douro River, the two German rivers are vibrant arteries of Germany's economic and social life. A steady flotilla of boats carries cargo and travelers north toward Rotterdam or south in the direction of Basel. The Mosel has somewhat less traffic, although it is still significant.

The heart of Germany's wine country is the Rheingau section of the Rhine, a 25-mile stretch between Wiesbaden and Rüdesheim, and the Middle Mosel, a section between the villages of Zell in the north and Schweich in the south that is only 25 miles as the crow flies but is much farther on the winding road along the river. The epicenter of the Rheingau is in a string of villages from Geisenheim to Erbach, while the unofficial capital of the Middle Mosel is Bernkastel-Kues. The two areas are only about an hour's drive apart. In both places vineyards grow at gravity-defying steepness in slate-heavy soils and the vines reach down almost to the river below. The vines seem at first glance to have been haphazardly planted, but after a while it becomes clear that the locations are not accidental at all. Centuries ago, winemakers planted vines facing south and southwest to get the maximum amount of sunshine as the river changes direction. In the Middle Mosel the great Doktor and Sonnenuhr vineyards are on the east side of the river above the villages of Bernkastel and Wehlen. Only a short distance up the Mosel the prized Brauneberger Juffer vineyard is on the opposite side. The same happens on the Rhine.

Small towns dot the banks of both rivers. Villages such as Rüdesheim on the Rhine or Bernkastel-Kues on the Mosel are normally packed on warm afternoons with people walking, riding bikes or motorcycles, in cars, or taking a boat ride up or down the river or simply crossing by barge from one side of the river to the other. Railroad lines run along both banks of the Rhine, but not on the Mosel. Especially on Sunday afternoons from spring through fall, the Rhine and the Mosel are vibrantly alive. Wine festivals take place all year long, when villages turn into colorful, crowded, happy markets.

Rhine and Mosel winemakers are largely devoted to just one grape variety: Riesling. That's because the dominating factor in winemaking there is the generally cool climate. Since the region is so far north, enologists struggle to get grapes to ripen enough to produce sugar that can be turned into alcohol. Harvests are much later than in other wine areas, and many winemakers traditionally added sugar to fermenting grape juice to raise alcohol levels. Winemaking, though, was not always so restricted. For centuries, growers cultivated both red and white grape varieties. But over time and with trial and error they discovered that white wines did better than reds, and Riesling grew best of all. Winemakers cultivated the white Elbling grape in the area from Roman times until the early twentieth century, but it produced an acidic, low-alcohol wine and largely fell out of popularity except for sparkling wine. In the late nineteenth century, Hermann Müller, a scientist working at Research Institute Geisenheim in the Rheingau, combined Riesling and Madeleine Royale cuttings to make a white variety he called Müller-Thurgau, which ripened earlier than Riesling and became popular for a while in Germany and other northern climates. The wine it produced, though, was flabby, had a mousy aroma, and was often tasteless. As a result, in recent years it has been in decline. Today twice as much Riesling is planted in Germany as Müller-Thurgau, the second most common grape. In the past two decades, domestic demand for red wines encouraged winemakers to plant Pinot Noir, which the Germans call Spätburgunder. The wine, though, pales in color and quality when compared to red Burgundy. The parents of the communist philosopher Karl Marx owned vineyards on the banks of the Ruwer River, a subsidiary of the Mosel, and today Weingut Erben von Beulwitz, near Trier, produces a Spätburgunder with the Karl Marx label for those who want to advertise their politics through the wine they drink.

Germany is best known internationally for its sweet Rieslings. In ascending order of quality and price, these are Spätlese (late harvest), Auslese (select harvest), Beerenauslese (berry selection), Eiswein (ice wine), and Trockenbeerenauslese (dry berry selection). Beerenauslese and Trockenbeerenauslese are made with the same noble rot as are Sauternes. Prior to World War I, members of the British upper class were big fans of German wines. Britain's Queen Victoria visited the Rheingau in 1845, where she fell in love with Riesling from the village of

Hochheim. The British then shortened the name and called all German wines Hock. In the late nineteenth century, auction prices in Britain for the best Hock were higher than those for top claret. As sweet wines have gone out of fashion, though, Hock prices have not kept up with those paid internationally for the best dry red wines. Nonetheless, there remains a small, but devoted, following for Rhine and Mosel sweet wines, in particular for Eiswein and Trockenbeerenauslese, which often cost $100 for a half-bottle.

Unfortunately for Rhine and Mosel winemakers, the popularity in the 1950s and 1960s of a wine called Liebfraumilch, which means "beloved lady's milk," badly damaged the reputation of all German white wines. Big producers used a variety of inexpensive grapes, mainly Müller-Thurgau, to make huge volumes of a sickly sweet white wine that sold under such brands as Blue Nun and Black Tower. And if nature didn't make the wine sweet enough, producers just added more sugar. Liebfraumilch became popular with new wine drinkers, who liked both its sweetness and its low level of alcohol. Many consumers, though, confused Liebfraumilch with quality Riesling and as a result turned away from all German white wines. Eventually even Blue Nun stopped calling itself Liebfraumilch, although the quality didn't improve. Liebfraumilch still accounts for more than half of German wine exports. In recent years, however, quality Riesling has been making a strong comeback, in part because of some outstanding wines of that variety coming out of Alsace, Australia's Eden Valley, and other New World locations. The best Rhine and Mosel Riesling producers are doing better, but the Liebfraumilch image problem lingers on.

While grapes grew in Germany in prehistoric times, it was the Romans who developed vineyards in a big way. Julius Caesar conquered the region in 58 BC, and his grandnephew, Augustus Caesar, established Augusta Treverorum (the City of Augustus), modern-day Trier. From 293 to 395, the emperors of the Western Roman Empire resided in Trier, the largest city north of the Alps, which was called the "Rome of the North." The Rhine and Mosel eventually became the first line of defense against barbaric Germanic tribes from the north. It is not certain when the Romans planted their first grapes, but in about 280 the Roman emperor Marcus Aurelius Probus lifted the imperial ban on making wine outside Italy, making it legal to grow vines on the banks of the Rhine and Mosel. The quality and style of wines made there at that time remain a mystery, but by 570 the Roman poet Venantius Fortunatus wrote homages to German red wines. After the fall of the Roman Empire in the fifth century, however, trade declined sharply, and northern Europeans had to make all the wine for their own consumption.

Charlemagne, who first conquered and then united much of Western Europe in the eighth century, played a major role in the development of wine in the Rhine and Mosel areas. Since he supported Christianity over pagan religions, monasteries flourished and religious orders became major wine developers along both rivers. Many techniques for winemaking migrated east from Burgundy, where monks first discovered them. Charlemagne had one of his many castles in the Rhineland town of Ingelheim, and he noticed that the snow melted first on a certain hill near there and concluded that it would be a good place to plant vines. So in 817, Charlemagne's bastard son Louis the Pious planted a vineyard on that spot in the Rheingau and made more than 1,500 gallons of wine annually.

During the first decade of the twelfth century, Benedictine monks built their first monastery in the Rheingau at the same place where Louis the Pious had planted his vineyard. The monks named the basilica after St. John the Baptist, and both the castle and the town took on the name Johannisberg (John's Mountain). They soon began expanding the vineyards and furthering their winemaking skills. Two monasteries, **Schloss Johannisberg** and **Kloster Eberbach**, for centuries were the best Rhine wineries.

The Benedictines abandoned Schloss Johannisberg in 1563, and the property went into private hands. For more than six hundred years, Schloss Johannisberg primarily made red wines, but in the first half of the eighteenth century it began a gradual shift toward the production of Riesling. In 1720, the Baron of Fulda, the owner, planted the world's first Riesling vineyard there and it became the center for cultivating that grape. In 1755, Schloss Johannisberg produced the first Spätlese wine, in 1787 the first Auslese, and in 1858 the first Eiswein. Goethe was a great fan of the winery. Looking out at it from the garret of the Brömser Castle in Rüdesheim on August 15, 1814, he wrote, "Johannisberg dominates everything." As just one indication of the long shadow it cast on wine history, California winemakers in the 1960s were still giving the name Johannisberg Riesling to their Rieslings. In 1802, as part of the upheavals of the Napoléonic era, the state took over the winery, and in 1815 the Congress of Vienna gave to it the family of Austrian foreign minister Prince von Metternich, which still owns it today. For more than two centuries, Schloss Johannisberg made only Riesling, but today it produces 85 percent Riesling and 15 percent Spätburgunder.

Just up the road from Schloss Johannisberg, Burgundy's Bernard of Clairvaux, a French abbot in the Cistercian order, in 1136 founded the monastery Kloster Eberbach above the village of Eltville. The monks brought Pinot Noir vines with them and found they did well in the Rhineland, even though the slate soil there is different from that in Burgundy. The Kloster Eberbach monks built a stone wall around an 80-acre piece of prime property for growing grapes and named the vineyard Steinberg. Today it remains one of the Rheingau's best vineyards. Nearly three hundred years ago, Eberbach monks also switched to Riesling. The abbey, though, was dissolved in 1803 during the antireligion movement fostered by the Napoléonic wars, and Eberbach has been in public hands since then. The current owner is the German state of Hesse, although government officials play no role in running Germany's largest winery.

Schloss Johannisberg and Kloster Eberbach remain the two most prestigious wineries in the Rheingau and also have the best wine tourism. Schloss Johannisberg in the hills above Rüdesheim, was virtually destroyed in an air attack on August 13, 1942, but has been totally rebuilt. It offers a wide variety of wine-related activities, and receives 200,000 visitors a year. The grounds are large, so there's no sense of big crowds. It annually stages nearly fifty concerts featuring all types of music, and the view from the Johannisberg tasting room down on the Rheingau is spectacular. The highlight of any visit is a tour and tasting in the wine cellar, which dates back to 1728. Lighting in the cellar is dim and comes from candles, and the floor is covered with gravel. The walls and ceiling have a blanket of natural mold. There's no charge for a simple tour, although there is for a tour and tasting of three wines, usually a dry, a half-dry, and a sweet one. The visit includes a look at the wine library, where the oldest bottle is vintage 1748. The library includes wine from every year from 1801 to the present, and the staff changes the corks every twenty-five years to protect the wines.

Kloster Eberbach may be the most beautiful medieval monastery in Europe and includes examples of Romanesque, Gothic, and Baroque architecture. It annually gets 150,000 visitors, but most tourists go to see the monastery rather than to taste the wine. While the area right along the Rhine River can sometimes feel congested, up at Kloster Eberbach a visitor can be quickly lost in a quiet, sylvan wonderland. The monastery was not badly damaged during World War II and since then has been well maintained with generous state support. The interior filming for the 1986 movie *The Name of the Rose* took place there. At its peak in the Middle Ages, the vineyards encompassed 741 acres, but today the winery cultivates only 519 acres and not all of them are located at the monastery. The walled Steinberg vineyard still exists, and one of the special treats at Kloster Eberbach is to pick up a light lunch at the Black House café, which is near the Steinberg, and then sit outside and gaze down at the vineyard and the Rhine Valley.

The original winery has been turned into a museum, which has an extensive and excellent collection of old wooden presses. A new winery is located mainly underground near the Steinberg vineyard. Just as at Schloss Johannisberg, the most interesting part of a tour is the old cellar, which was built between 1240 and 1250 and contains bottles of wine dating back to 1706. The winery recorks bottles every twenty years and at the same time tastes the wines to see if they have survived. Some of the old wines are sold at a semiannual wine auction, and the buyer receives the tasting notes from the last recorking. The winery also gives a quality guarantee for the old wines. After opening a 1706 bottle, the winery director said simply, "You know it was once wine." It was not offered for sale. But winemaker Ralf Bengel told me that wines as old as 1893 are "still perfect, still tasting like honey." A bottle of 1920 Steinberg Trockenbeerenauslese in 2006 sold at auction for €10,300 ($14,420).

The Kloster Eberbach Foundation, which the government established to keep up the property and support the wine culture, hosts a
wide range of activities from concerts to wine tastings. One of the most
popular events involves drinking wines at six different locations in the
monastery. Most of the tours are in small groups of fewer than fifteen
people. Large corporations hold special events at the monastery, and
there are also accommodations for overnight guests.

The Benedictine Abbey of St. Hildegard in the hills above Rüdesheim
follows the millennium-old Rheingau tradition that links wine and
monasteries. The founder, Hildegard of Bingen, who was born in 1098,
entered a community of Benedictine nuns at age eight and in 1150
built her first monastery on the east side of the Rhine near Bingen. She
later moved to a bigger location on the western side in Eibingen near
Rüdesheim. During her life, Hildegard became a leading church figure
and a counselor to popes. She also wrote extensively on religious topics
as well as guidelines for healthy living. Wine, of course, was an important part of the monastery's work, and she once wrote: "A wine that is
pure cleanses the blood of its drinker." Hildegard died in 1179 and has
never actually been canonized a saint but is commonly given the title.

The Abbey of St. Hildegard faced the same fate during the Napoléonic
wars as Schloss Johannisberg and Kloster Eberbach, and the state took
it over in 1803. But in the late nineteenth century, Prince Karl of Löw-
enstein helped reestablish the monastery, which opened in 1908 in a
new complex of buildings. In 1941, the Gestapo expelled the 115 nuns
residing there, and the property became a military hospital for the rest
of World War II. Before the nuns left, though, they built a false wall
in the cellar and sealed away most of their wine behind it. When they
reclaimed the abbey in 1945, the wine was still there.

In recent times, Hildegard has become an icon for both feminists
and the New Age movement. The nine hundredth anniversary of her
birth in 1998 turned into a yearlong celebration that brought thousands
of tourists from around the world to the abbey. Hildegard's writings,

especially those on spirituality and natural health, are still published and today many follow her ancient precepts. Her continuing popularity makes the abbey a popular tourist destination.

The abbey now has fifty-five nuns, aged twenty-seven to ninety-five. Prayer and work are the two basic principles of the Benedictine order, so the nuns have active lives doing historic restoration, ceramics, gold-smithing, and research. Sister Thekla Baumgart runs the **St. Hildegard** winery. Shortly after joining the abbey, she was given the job of taking over winemaking from an elderly nun and has now been doing it for more than seventeen years. Raised in the northern Germany city of Bremen, which is noted for its beer rather than its wine, she had no background in either viticulture or enology when she joined the convent. But she studied both subjects at the nearby Research Institute Geisenheim, and a local winemaker now helps the nuns. Two young nuns are currently in training at Geisenheim, which will give the winery more depth in winemaking talent, and St. Hildegard has been upgrading its enology equipment.

The Abbey of St. Hildegard has only 16 acres of vineyards in several locations around Rüdesheim. That is enough to produce annually 40,000 to 50,000 bottles. All but one of the dozen wines it makes are Rieslings. The sole red is a Spätburgunder. Sister Thekla says people claim to like dry wines, but she finds they actually buy more off-dry or sweet wines than dry ones. From time to time, she makes a Spätlese. The nun says that since she's been a winemaker, people have been generally drinking younger, more aromatic wines, which is the kind she now makes. About 50 percent of sales are made at the winery, and that accounts for a quarter of what the abbey needs to support its work. "We must be clever," Sister Thekla told me. "But we get a lot of information from the shop, where we sell both wine and other things such as books, so we know what people like."

The abbey also runs a guesthouse with sixteen rooms, which has about 350 overnight stays a year. The guesthouse, though, is reserved for visitors who come for religious activities. People of any religious belief can stay for up to a week and follow the rituals of the monastic life. Some people also come regularly in the fall to help with the harvest, when all the monastery's able-bodied nuns are out in the fields picking grapes. St. Hildegard must be the only winery in the world where field hands periodically stop their work during harvest and go to the abbey's church for the prayer services that are an integral part of monastic life. At the end of the harvest, three pickers are named wine princesses and receive a crown of vines.

Wine tourism has long existed in the Rheingau because of the old German tradition of traveling there once a year to stock up on wine. Germany also has a program that allows a winemaker to supplement his income by running a small inn, or *strausswirtschaft,* where he can serve wine and simple foods, usually regional dishes, for four months a year without having to comply with the standard restaurant regulations.

Stefan Rumpf's family started making wine in 1708 and since 1792 has been living in the village of Münster-Sarmsheim on the Nahe River only a short distance from where it flows into the Rhine at Bingen. Stefan developed some ambitious goals for the family winery in 1978, when he spent six months in California working for three wineries in Sonoma and Monterey counties. Stefan left for the United States without speaking any English but still traveled on a Greyhound bus from New York City to California. Wine tourism there was then in its early stages, but he returned home with plenty of plans. He was particularly impressed by what he calls the "California attitude"—that a person could do anything he wanted, which stood in sharp contrast to the conservative traditionalism Stefan had learned at home.

Helping Stefan develop his plans was his soon-to-be wife, Cornelia, who at an early age had decided she wanted to get into either hotel or restaurant management. The first time she visited the Rumpf family's wine inn, she told Stefan that this was a place where she could build her dreams. After they married, the two set out on separate tracks toward the same goal of developing a wine business that would be bigger than just the wine. In 1984, he took over the vineyards and winemaking from his parents and set out to improve both the size of the holdings and the quality of the wine. Previously the family had sold almost all its wine in bulk to well-known producers. Stefan, though, began bottling and selling it under the **Weingut Kruger-Rumpf** label. At the same time, he was buying up small vineyards as they became available. He inherited only 20 acres, but now owns 50 acres. Winemaking techniques were improved with increased attention paid to the ripeness of the fruit and picking grapes several times a season as they reached their peak. The winery now produces some 18,000 cases annually, with 70 percent of that Riesling.

Meanwhile, Cornelia was building up the wine inn with quality décor and food. Weingut Kruger-Rumpf became the first wine inn to be listed in the *Gault Millau Guide to German Wines*. The winery entered the German organization of quality producers in 1992, and two years later upgraded its wine pub to a full restaurant. A banking friend came to Stefan just before they opened it and urged him, as both a banker and a friend, not to go ahead with the project, saying it was too risky. But the restaurant was a success from the first day, and Cornelia now has three cooks on staff, although she still creates the menus. The banker friend has become a regular guest at the restaurant, which serves only dinner and is fully booked most evenings. Wine tourism now makes up about 25 percent of Weingut Kruger-Rumpf's income.

Stefan thinks a key to their success is that he and Cornelia are always around the restaurant and the winery. "People want to see me and my wife here," he told me. "And they like the fact that the restaurant hasn't been hired out to an outside manager. People want to experience together wine, food, and historic buildings." Customers who come for the food, he says, soon take an interest in the wine, and many of those who come for wine stay for the food. Every night except Monday, when the restaurant is closed, Cornelia can be found in the dining room explaining the day's specials and taking orders, while Stefan, the amiable host, moves from table to table talking with guests. With a quick smile flashing frequently across his face, he's a natural.

Now the Rumpfs want to move on to the next stage of wine tourism. Stefan thinks his area of the Rheingau has a shortage of small, quality hotels. Good networks of roads and trains as well as inexpensive flights bring thousands of people to the area, but there are not enough hotels to serve the demanding international wine tourists. So in the summer of 2008, Stefan and his wife bought a building across the street from the winery with plans of turning it into a hotel with ten to fifteen rooms. It will take three or four years to complete construction. They have also started work on expanding the restaurant area with several rooms that can host groups of a few people or as many as sixty.

Stefan sees the possibility of providing more tourism opportunities to his visitors. "Wine tourism needs to be more than wine," he says. People want to enjoy local architecture, take a cruise on the Rhine, or hike in the vineyards. Small wineries such as his, he believes, must let visitors know about similar ones nearby. "People need help in finding out more about the area, and they will be grateful to you, and come back to you, if you recommend another winery," he says. "But it's hard to break the old kind of thinking that you shouldn't help your competition."

With their new ventures just getting started, the next Rumpf generation is set to take over the winery. The couple has three sons and a daughter. The sons have all joined the business, while the daughter is still in school in Ireland. The family winery is fortunately now big enough to provide jobs for all of them.

♆ ♆ ♆

While it takes less than an hour to drive from the Rheingau to the Middle Mosel, the wine tourism scene is different there in dozens of small ways. For starters, Rhine wine traditionally comes in brown bottles, while Mosel wine is in green ones. While the Rhine is massive and majestic, the Mosel is intense and intimate. Everything seems smaller and quieter. Village roads are generally narrower and more winding. Everywhere you look on the Mosel are signs at wineries and restaurants reading *Zimmer Frei* (Room for Rent), and there are few hotels. War damage was not as great in the Mosel, and there are also more historic half-timbered houses. Several towns have double names, such as Bernkastel-Kues, because they were originally two separate villages on opposite sides of the river that have now been joined.

Outside the village of Bremm, the Mosel River makes a hairpin turn. Just before the bend stands Calmont, the steepest vineyard in the world with a 65° incline. The top of the vineyard is at an altitude of 240 yards, while the bottom is at 100 yards. The soil is composed of soft slate and sandstone rock. Along with many other vineyards in Germany, the 30-acre plot was divided among scores of winemakers over the centuries. It was possible to work the land only with slow, hand labor, and starting in the 1950s vintners began abandoning the property and moving on to more hospitable terrain. By the beginning of the new century, most of the vineyard was overrun with thorns and wild blackberry bushes.

The vineyard, though, was still blessed with valuable southern exposure that had attracted winemakers since Roman times. When Ulrich Franzen inherited **Weingut Reinhold Franzen** from his father, it had only 5 acres of vines. But in 2002, Franzen negotiated a complex deal to buy from fifty different owners 112 parcels in the Calmont vineyard totaling 10 acres. Most of the land hadn't been farmed in decades. Franzen then began clearing the property and preparing it for new planting. It was killing labor on almost impossible slopes. It soon became clear to Franzen that he had to figure out a more efficient way to get workers and their tools up and down the mountain. The answer was a Swiss-made monorail that required laying 550 yards of rail track. The cog-rail car looks like a lurching sled as it carries passengers on a bumpy, hair-raising ride up or down the slope. As I learned from riding the rail, the trip can be slightly terrifying, especially going down. By the spring of 2003, the vineyard was finally cleared, and over the next two years Franzen and his crew planted 7,000 vines and completed another section of the monorail. Today Franzen produces four wines from the Calmont vineyard, three dry Rieslings selling for between €9.50 ($13.30) and €16 ($22.40), and a half-bottle of Beerenauslese for €150 ($196).

Ulrich Franzen was born with an innate sense of marketing. When the steepest vineyard in the world was just about finished, he came up with the idea of selling individual vines at the top of the plantings for €150 ($210) each. For that price, vine owners get one bottle of Calmont Riesling each year for ten years and a certificate of ownership. They also get their names and country on a piece of slate that hangs on a trellis in front of their vine. By the time I visited the Calmont vineyard, Franzen had sold 450 vines, with most of them going to Germans, although 130 Japanese have also bought them. Down in the village of Bremm, Franzen has a wine shop where he happily recounts the story of building the Calmont vineyard and sells both his wines and pieces of blue slate. Looking at his thick, calloused hands and powerful arms, you know he does the vineyard work himself.

The most famous name in Mosel wine is Prüm, and members of that family have been making wine there since 1156. Several wineries have the name on their labels, and **J. J. Prüm** is the most widely distributed. Sebastian Alois Prüm founded **Weingut S. A. Prüm** in 1911, and Raimund Prüm took over the family property in 1971. He now spends much of his time traveling the world selling his wine, which has given him an opportunity to see what other countries are doing in wine tourism. He says the main lesson he learned is that it's difficult to transfer what works in one region or country to another.

During the past four decades, Prüm has seen many changes in the way people visit the Mosel. In the old days most of the tourists were Germans, and they came by car once a year to buy wine at a less-expensive price than they could get it at home. Today people arrive from all over the world, and they are interested in more than just drinking wine and looking at the beautiful scenery. Now they want active vacations that might include bike riding or hiking. "On any weekend you can count thousands of people on bikes," says Prüm. "It's wonderful."

The decade from the mid-1980s to the mid-1990s, he says, was a difficult time for German wines. Liebfraumilch was damaging the reputation of quality Rhine and Mosel wines, and an Austrian scandal involving glycol in wine spilled over into Germany and hurt sales abroad. Even in those bad times, though, Prüm searched hard for ways to deepen his relationship with customers. Eventually he came up with a two-pronged strategy. First he started a series of monthly events to attract visitors. There wasn't much need for programs in the high-season months of August, September, and October. But in the off-season, especially in November and December, he needed some special draw. In 1984, he started the Open Cellars weekend that ran from Thursday to Sunday night. He also tried to attract visitors coming to the famous Christmas

Market in Bernkastel-Kues. He later added an event in the spring, when the first wines of the new vintage are released. Often he worked with other wineries in the area or with local restaurants. Then he built an upscale accommodation at the winery. The old standards of a simple room, with the shared bathroom down the hall, are no longer good enough for today's affluent Germans and foreign guests, who expect creature comforts, even at a winery. He built a new guesthouse with eight double rooms as well as facilities where companies could hold small business meetings. One of the pleasures of staying at S. A. Prüm is breakfast on the terrace of the main house, which looks across the Mosel. Spread out in front is the historic Sonnenuhr vineyard, while off to both the right and left are vineyards as far as the eye can see. The river's only suspension bridge is on the left, decked out with flags of the world. An occasional car passes on the opposite bank, and barges chug up and down the waterway. The scene is so beautiful that one is tempted to stay there all day, sipping a cup of coffee or a glass of S. A. Prüm Riesling.

A popular tourist destination on the Mosel is **Weingut Dr. Pauly-Bergweiler**, which is located on the riverfront in Bernkastel near the bridge that unites the original twin villages of Bernkastel and Kues. It gets some 10,000 visitors a year, with a heavy contingent from Scandinavia, one of its biggest markets. The winery produces 12,000 cases a year and sells about 20 percent to visitors.

The Dr. Pauly winery handles both group tours and individuals, and the serious wine geek can get a free tasting that will last two hours and include twenty wines. The winery grows or buys grapes from some of the best vineyards in the Mosel, including such historic properties as Bernkasteler Badstube and Wehlener Sonnenuhr. *Wine Spectator* gave Weingut Dr. Pauly's 2005 Wehlener Sonnenuhr Auslese 96 points, and called the 2007 Bernkasteler Badstube Riesling Spätlese a "hot wine" and awarded it 94 points.

The winery entered wine tourism thirty years ago, at a time when few places were doing much. In 1982, it moved its production operations from the middle of town to the outskirts and devoted the old facilities mainly to visitors. Weingut Dr. Pauly now gives excellent tours of its ancient cellars. The winery also built a classic tasting room that will soon be renovated. "We want to provide even more for the tourist market," Stefan Pauly, whose family has owned the winery for generations, told me.

A traveler to the Rhine and Mosel who wants to experience the true romance of the two historic rivers should spend at least one night in one of the castle hotels that cling to the top of cliffs overlooking the valleys. My favorite is the Schönburg Castle in Oberwesel, which was built between 951 and 1166. I have been going there since the early 1970s and have never been disappointed. Schönburg is a place where you can be king for a day. Walk or drive your way through vineyards up the hill to the massive stone structure that includes a drawbridge and turrets. It was recently totally renovated and offers impeccable services, including a fine restaurant. There are only twenty-two rooms, most of which are small, but the views from the ancient windows are spectacular. Directly ahead are beautiful Rheingau vineyards. Looking down on the river, you can spot a tower in the middle of the water where boats once had to stop and pay a tax before they were allowed to continue on their journey. Boats still glide slowly up and down the river. And if a traveler ever gets bored, he can always visit the Schönburg prison tower.

At Burghotel Auf Schönburg some of Germany's romantic legends were born and new ones are still being created. The castle hotel brings together in one place the high culture and the wine that make the Rhine and Mosel special. It's a powerful duo, and wine tourists to this region are sure to enjoy many other examples of that classical combination.

Diary of a Wine Tourist

May 8

Biking Along the Banks of the Mosel

The Mosel River area is the perfect place for the visitor who wants to combine wine tourism and cycling. For some 90 miles, a well-marked path for walkers and bikers runs between the main road and the river. This provides a beautiful and relaxing way to experience both the Mosel and its wines at their best. The most popular time for Germans is on a Sunday usually in May, when highways on both sides of the river are closed to cars so that some 120,000 bikers can be kings of the road.

Although either side of the river is fine for biking, residents told me the northern side is better, and it was there that I made my trip one sunny day, cycling from Bernkastel-Kues to Traben-Trarbach, 15 miles up the river. My plan was to rent a bike in Bernkastel, ride to Trarbach, and then return to where I started on one of the tourist boats that frequently travel up and down the Mosel.

I set out shortly after 9:30 a.m., passing the many half-timbered buildings of downtown Bernkastel. Less than fifteen minutes out and across from the village of Wehlen, I stopped to take a picture of the Wehlener Sonnenuhr, perhaps the most famous vineyard on the Mosel after Bernkasteler Doktor. High on the hill was a sundial that provided the time of day in addition to giving the vineyard its name, which literally means Wehlen Sun Dial.

Back on the road, the miles easily melted away, and I frequently looked out at the river where boats passed and swans paddled by. Since the road is right along the riverbank, there are no hills to climb.

A group of Dutch cyclists joined me for a while near the village of Graach, and a short while later, two young and determined Germans in a hurry passed all of us. No one minded, and the Dutch soon stopped at a café. Many cyclists ride for several days in the Mosel Valley, staying at guesthouses along the way and then at the end of their trip get on a train with their bikes and return to where they started. A bus was following the Dutch and would pick them and their bikes up at the end of the day.

About half way to my destination, I made a detour to look at a Roman wine press that had only recently been discovered and underscores the Mosel's role as Germany's oldest wine region.

Before leaving Bernkastel, I decided that somewhere along the way I was going to stop at a *strausswirtschaft,* one of the many wine inns, in order to visit with a local winemaker. It was about eleven o'clock as I rode into the village of Wolf. Out of the corner of my eye, I spotted a display of empty wine bottles promoting **Weingut Günter Comes**, which was only 50 yards up Burggasse, a winding, narrow lane whose name indicates it was once the path up to a castle.

Pulling into the courtyard decked out with tables, the inn looked empty, and I figured I had probably picked the wrong place. As I searched around for signs of life, someone showed up and said he was the neighbor. He explained that the owner was probably either at the doctor's since he had been ill recently or in his fields working. The neighbor quickly added that he could serve me some wine until the owner got back and poured a glass of a Riesling Kabinett, which I noticed on the menu was €1.50 ($2.10).

About a half hour later, the burly Günter Comes arrived sweating profusely and explained that he had been working in the fields. Then with an infectious enthusiasm he began pouring wines that showed the broad range of his production. In addition to several Rieslings both sweet and dry, he also makes a Spätburgunder as well as a Müller-Thurgau. Comes explained his total annual production is between 10,000 and 14,000 bottles, and that comes from his 6.2 acres of vines. This is slightly more than the 4.2-acre average for Mosel winemakers.

Comes said that selling wine from his home is an important part of the business since no distributor would work with such a small winery. Comes receives guests from eleven in the morning until ten at night, but the day before he had only four visitors. He and his wife, Hildegard, have two double rooms in the house that they rent for €45 ($63) each a night. With obvious pride, the winemaker took me down to the cellar. He pointed to five large barrels where Riesling was stored and said that his father had made them. There were also four newer oak barrels filled with Spätburgunder. Comes ended the visit with a quick trip to see his vineyards in a red Volkswagen truck. Along the way, he pointed out that he had vines in the Wolfer Goldgrube vineyard, the best in the village. Just before he finally let me go after an hour and a half, Comes insisted I take a bottle of his 2006 Wolfer Sonnenlay Riesling Spätlese.

I got to Trarbach just in time to catch the 1:30 p.m. boat that would take the rented bike and me back to Bernkastel. Signs all over the boat announced that the new Maibowle, a light sweet wine sold in spring, was on sale for €2 ($2.80) a glass. It was an unexpected surprise to participate in this annual German tradition. Sitting in the bright sunshine on the back deck of the boat, I watched the beautiful vineyards including the Wolfer Goldgrube pass by while I slowly sipped a Maibowle from a classic green Mosel wineglass.

CHAPTER THIRTEEN

Kakheti, Georgia—the Last Frontier

No one knows exactly where or when wine was first made. The Chinese had a drink that may have contained some fermented grape juice along with other ingredients. The Turks claim they are the first wine country, and there is evidence of early winemaking in the Zagros Mountains as well as in the Taurus Mountains areas of Turkey, Syria, Iran, and Iraq. Patrick McGovern, author of *Ancient Wine,* the seminal work on the topic, believes that the wine culture in Georgia and other parts of the Caucasus likely goes back to the Neolithic period of 6000 BC. "We now have chemical evidence for wine inside jars, some of which are decorated with what appear to be grape clusters or celebratory scenes under grape arbors. I have not yet published this evidence, because the samples are very small, and we need additional confirmation by an extremely sensitive chemical technique," McGovern told me. He believes that Georgia could well turn out to be the "vinicultural Garden of Eden."

Georgia is located at the southern side of the Caucasus Mountains that span from the Black Sea in the west to the Caspian Sea in the east. The mountains separate the country from Russia to the north, while in the south and southeast Georgia shares borders with Turkey, Armenia, and Azerbaijan. Almost no matter where you are in the country, the snowcapped Caucasus Mountains loom in the distance.

Many historians believe the first humans coming out of Africa arrived in the region 1.8 million years ago. As proof of that, Georgians point to archeological discoveries made in the 1990s, including *Homo georgicus,* at the site of the ancient city of Dmanis. The first rural settlements were established perhaps in the seventh millennium BC. There is also evidence that humans practiced agriculture in Georgia between 6000 and 5000 BC.

The Georgian weather is mostly temperate, and the soil ancient and fertile. According to legend, when God was distributing parts of the earth to the various peoples, the Georgians were off having a party and drinking hard. When they finally arrived, God told them that all the land had already been given away. But the Georgians explained that they were tardy only because they had been toasting and praising him, so God relented and gave them the fecund land he had been reserving for himself.

Georgia's location where Europe and Asia meet has long been a crossroads for traders traveling the Silk Road. That, however, also condemned the country to endless wars with invading tribes and cultures, often leading to its occupation. St. Nino of Cappadocia is credited with converting Georgia to the Greek Orthodox faith in AD 330, but for all its history the country has been torn between the Muslim and Christian worlds. Politically, the country has always been oriented toward Europe and remained Christian, but Persians and Turks occupied it for centuries. Georgians consider their nation's golden age to have been almost one thousand years ago, from the late eleventh century to the early thirteenth century. In the eighteenth century, Georgia's leaders turned to Russia to protect the country from its neighbors, but that soon turned into Russian domination. In the chaos after the Soviet revolution, the independent Democratic Republic of Georgia was established in 1918, but the Soviet Union in 1921 again took over the country. Georgia and Georgians played major roles in Soviet history. Stalin was an ethnic Georgian as was the head of his secret police, Lavrentiy Beria. Eduard Shevardnadze, Mikhail Gorbachev's longtime foreign minister, was also Georgian. After the breakup of the Soviet Union, Georgia in 1991 again became an independent country, but relations with Russia remained tense. Then in the summer of 2008, Russia invaded the country under the pretense that it was protecting ethnic minorities.

Wine has always played a central role in Georgian culture. The country's most widely reproduced icon shows St. Nino holding a cross made of grapevines and held together by strands of her hair. Gravestones often have carvings of grapevines, and researchers have dug up many bowls, cups, and other utensils used for wine, with some dating back to the third millennium BC. No gathering of Georgians is complete without wine, and the most respected ritual of Georgian life is the feast called the *supra,* where the toastmaster, or *tamada,* makes a series of eloquent and often long toasts late into the night. A meal might last five hours, and there would be between ten and twenty-five toasts. After each one everyone drinks, often to bottoms up. The Georgian word for wine, *gvino,* appears to be the origin of *vin, vino,* and *wein* in French, Italian, and German. According to folklore, wild-grape juice turned into wine after being buried in the ground during the winter. Orthodox Christianity was one of the things that held the people together during the Islamic and Soviet occupations, and wine plays a central role in religious ceremonies. Georgians are proud of their historic monasteries, some of which were built in the fifth and sixth centuries. Most have the remains of major wine production and storage facilities. Georgians even claim that the unique scroll of their alphabet resembles grapevines.

Winemaking, though, developed differently in Georgia than it did in Western Europe. Georgia produces two different styles of wine. One is the modern, international style, which is mainly exported. The other traditional Georgian method goes back perhaps 9,000 years, but is still in widespread use today. Until recently, that kind of wine could only be enjoyed in Georgia, but now some is being exported to the United States. The first question posed either in a restaurant or a private home is whether the guest wants traditional wine, which is brought to the table in a pitcher, or bottled wine. I enjoyed both kinds. But since I would be able, albeit with some difficulty, to get Georgian wine in a bottle when I returned home, I usually had traditional wine. In all cases except one, it was good and interesting with intense flavors and lots of color. Once, though, at a restaurant, it was obviously off. I'm not a wine chemist, so I'm not sure what was wrong, but I drank just one glass— and then only to be polite.

Viticulture is the same for both types of wine. Grapes generally grow on trellises, although some farmers still have them on pergolas as high as 8 feet tall. Traditional winemaking, which is the same for both red wines and white, can vary in different parts of the country, but the most common practice involves crushing bunches of grapes in hollowed-out tree logs about 10 yards long and 2 yards both high and wide. When full, the tree trunks contain up to 2 tons of grapes. Both ends of the log have a flat finish, but one end also has a small hole and funnel so grape juice can flow out. Men and boys, never women or girls, get into the log and stomp the grapes, often to the accompaniment of music. While visiting Georgia, I saw at ancient cave dwellings in Uplistsikhe a large tub carved out of granite that looked exactly like the wooden ones still in use today. My guide told me it was probably carved in the first half of the first millennium BC.

The grape juice flows into a clay jar called a *kvevri* that has already been buried in the ground, or into a container and then transferred to the jar. A *kvevri* can hold as little as 2.5 gallons of juice or as much as 2,000 gallons. Most have a capacity of between 15 and 500 gallons. Winemakers have several sizes of vessels so they don't have to open their entire production at once and can use one, for example, for a special event or party. Only the vessel's upper lip and top stick out of the ground, and folklore maintains that something bad will happen to anyone who walks over a *kvevri*. If handled properly, *kvevris* can be used for hundreds of years. Damage, though, sometimes occurs during earthquakes, which are common in Georgia.

In the village of Shrosha I talked with a pottery maker who still makes the jars. He explained that it takes him about a month to make the biggest ones, which can hold 2 tons of stomped grapes and juice and are 2 yards high. He methodically builds the jar's wall over several weeks by adding 10 inches of new clay a day, but only if the weather is dry. If it's raining, he doesn't add any because the clay won't dry properly. After the *kvevri* dries thoroughly, he glazes and fires it for several days in an oven at 1,500°F. The potter says that Italian researchers bought several large jars from him for an experiment to see how their wine would develop in them.

Once the jars are full of grapes, stems, and juice, spontaneous fermentation starts thanks to natural yeasts that land on the grape skins, a process that continues for at least fourteen days, and sometimes goes on for as long as forty-five days. The winemaker never uses artificial yeasts.

Georgians consider the ideal temperature for fermentation to be 73°F. That is easy to obtain since the jars are underground. Several times a day during this process of grape juice becoming wine, the winemaker uses a stick to punch down the hard cap made of grape seeds and skins that forms at the top of the jar, just as Western winemakers do with red wine production. When the winemaking process finishes, the jar is sealed with a piece of wood and a glob of wet clay and then more wet clay is put around the edges to make it airtight. Sometimes the wine-maker might also place a couple of rocks on the container's top to keep it in place. Wine stays in the jars until the following spring. Lower than 60°F is considered a good storage temperature. This part of the process is different from that in both Europe and the New World, where viticulturists do not leave white wines in contact with the mixture of grape stems, skins, and seeds, and red wines are left in contact only until fermentation finishes in a couple of weeks. From time to time, in late summer until the following spring, the Georgian winemaker opens a jar to see how the wine is progressing. He uses a scoop made from a dried wild pumpkin to take out a small amount of wine to taste.

Traditional Georgian wine is an annual product. There is no attempt to continue aging it in the clay jars. People drink the year's wine from spring of one year to spring of the next, and then begin drinking the new wine.

Herbicides or pesticides are not sprayed on vines in the fields, nor are any chemicals used in winemaking. There is no need to filter or fine these traditional wines because the long period in the *kvevris* clarifies and stabilizes them. Experts recommend burning a little sulfur in the vessels before they are filled to disinfect them, an ancient procedure mentioned in the Bible and used by the Romans.

White wines made in the traditional method look and taste different from Western wines. Because of the long aging on the lees, white wines are light brown and have a fuller, more complex flavor. Red wines are deep in color and fruity. After he opens a jar, the winemaker removes all the contents and puts them into glass or plastic containers that are again sealed tight. Otherwise the leftover wine would oxidize just as it does if left in an open bottle.

Extracting as much as he can out of the grapes, the winemaker distills the remnants of stems, grapes, and seeds left in the jar into *chacha,* a high-alcohol, grappa-like drink also called Georgian vodka.

One of the problems with *kvevri* winemaking is that the jars are hard to clean, even more difficult than wooden barrels. If the jars are not thoroughly cleaned, remaining bacteria can ruin the next vintage. Winemakers use long brushes made from branches to scrub them clean from the top. For particularly large jars, they often lower a small adult into the vessel to scrub the inside.

Vajha Khutzurauli, sixty-eight, and his wife, Tzitzino, sixty-four, started a small bed-and-breakfast (four rooms with a bath down the hall) in the village of Ikalto in eastern Georgia. It's a Spartan, but clean, facility that has a great view of the Caucasus Mountains. The price is $18 a night. Vajha is a typical small Georgian winemaker, working a 3.7-acre plot that his grandfather planted. In his cellar, Vajha has eleven *kvevris* in a variety of sizes. While some have a capacity of 25 gallons, one holds 925 gallons. He makes 80 percent red wines and 20 percent white. Vajha opens clay jars as he needs more wine or for special events. Once the vessel is open, he transfers all the contents to glass demijohns, where the wine remains until he needs it or sells it. Since Vajha produces about 1,500 gallons each year, more wine than he and his family can consume, he sells his surplus to people in his village. He also makes his own *chacha,* which he often barters for cheese.

Georgians have more than five hundred—some even claim more than four thousand—grape varieties, but few people outside the country, even wine experts, have ever heard of any of them. Commercial winemakers can legally use only thirty-eight varieties, but in practice most use about twenty. The grapes come in a broad spectrum of colors from white and green to deep red and black. The name is often a description of the grape: Rkatsiteli (red sprout), Saperavi (paint die), Mtevandidi (large bunch). Small amounts of international grapes such as Cabernet Sauvignon also grow in Georgia. The most common white grape is Rkatsiteli, which is high in acidity and makes both dry and sweet wines. The most popular red variety is the dark and intense Saperavi. Many Georgian wines are blends of several grapes.

Georgia has eighteen appellations and five viticulture zones. The most important province for wine is Kakheti, which starts with a half-hour drive outside the capital of Tbilisi and ends about a three-hour drive away in the Caucasus foothills. Kakheti produces 70 percent of the country's wines. The Alazani Valley in Kakheti is the most fertile area and makes the best wines. Grape-growing conditions there are ideal, with long, dry, hot summers. The eastern Racha-Lechkhumi highland region, the next most productive, is more humid and at a higher altitude.

When it was still part of the Soviet Union, and before Gorbachev instituted a program to pull out grapevines in the name of promoting lower alcohol consumption, Georgia produced some 7 million cases of wine per year. Current output, though, is down substantially from that level. Since outside big cities many Georgians make their own wine or buy surplus wine from friends, Georgians purchase relatively little bottled wine and export most of their production.

During the long decades of Soviet rule, Georgia made wine basically for Russia and other Soviet Republics. Under communism there were only a few large producers, who tailored it for communist tastes. In Telavi, the provincial center of Kakheti, eight Soviet plants with names such as Plant No. 2 each annually produced more than 1 million gallons of wine. Some 90 percent of it went to the Soviet Union. Wineries paid little attention to quality, and farmers planted grapes that had the highest yields, rather than those that made the best wine.

Russians like semisweet red wines, which generally have slightly lower alcohol levels than dry ones. The Georgian way of making them is different from the methods used to produce either Port or Sauternes. Winemakers interrupt the fermentation of sugar into alcohol by dramatically cooling the wine, holding it at a low temperature for a long period, and then filtering it to remove any remaining yeast so fermentation will not start up again when the temperature rises. Nearly half the production of Georgian wineries today is sweet wines, and those remain its most popular wines in the still important East European market. Stalin was a great fan of the semisweet red Khvanchkara, which is made with Mujaretuli and Aleksandrouli grapes primarily in western Georgia. He served large quantities of it to Winston Churchill and Franklin Roosevelt at the Yalta Conference at the end of World War II.

$$\text{♟ ♟ ♟}$$

When the Soviets pulled out of Georgia, they left behind mountains of rusting winemaking equipment. Much of it is still in use today even though it is a shocking eyesore. Following Georgian independence in 1991, several Western companies invested in Georgia in expectation that the country would tap the potential of its vineyards. In 1993, when the country was still going through an undeclared civil war, Pernod Ricard, the French alcohol giant, invested in **Georgian Wines and Spirits**, the biggest producer in the country in Soviet days. Pernod sent Beka Gagunashvili, a young winemaker, to be trained in France and installed a plethora of new equipment, such as an Italian bottling line that stands in stark contrast to ancient Soviet equipment still used at the plant. GWS, as it is called, has been turning out good wines sold under the brands Tamada and Old Tbilisi. Thanks to the Pernod distribution network, the wine sells in twenty-five countries, including the United States, where it retails for about $10 a bottle. By the early 2000s, GWS was producing 5 million bottles annually, but selling nearly half of that to Russia and other former Soviet republics. The company became the driving force behind sales growth that made wine Georgia's second biggest export. It also planted new vineyards for Mukuzani and Kindzmarauli wines.

Badagoni is an ambitious joint venture between Georgian investors and the Italian wine research center Enosis, which the famous agronomist Donato Lanati directs. The name sounds Italian, but it is actually Georgia's ancient god of wine, who predated the Greek Dionysus and the Roman Bacchus. Founded in 2002, the company built a large, modern winery in the village of Zemo Khodasheni in Kakheti and outfitted it with all the latest Italian equipment. The structure was built in the shape of the cross of St. George, which is part of the national flags of both Georgia and England. The winery is Italian in design, and the company brags that it is "producing unique Georgian wine varieties with modern Italian technologies." It claims to be the only large winery in Georgia with entirely new equipment. Italians also are in charge of quality control.

From its own 750 acres of vineyards and with the help of an aggressive program of buying grapes from farmers, Badagoni produces 1.2 million cases per year, making it the largest winery in the Caucasus. Its top-of-the-line Kakhetian Noble wine is made under Lanati's close control with 100 percent Saperavi grapes grown in a vineyard located opposite Alaverdi Cathedral. Badagoni produces nearly two dozen red and white wines, with about 25 percent of them sweet. The best-selling white is Tsinandali, and the top red is Saperavi.

Badagoni designed the winery with visitors in mind and has catwalks high above the production floor, where people can watch wine being made without getting in the way of workers. It offers regularly scheduled daily tours that last an hour and a half and end with a tasting of some fifteen wines. Badagoni also stages a three-day wine festival in October that showcases other wines from Kakheti in addition to its own. It has plans on the drawing board for a hotel to be built next to the winery, and is establishing connections with Alaverdi Cathedral, which was founded in the sixth century and is a top local tourist attraction. Badagoni in 2007 started selling Alaverdi wine made by monks there and has been associated with archeological digs at the church's wine cellar, where researchers found more than forty ancient *kvevris*. In the fall of 2007 the company started Badagoni Tours, which combines wine with food, art, history, and skiing.

Another new winery that did well after independence is **Teliani Valley**, so far the only Georgian wine company that has good distribution in the United States. Twenty-nine Georgian investors with support from the National Bank of Georgia founded the company in 1997. It traces its origins back to Alexander Chavchavadze, a soldier and poet who in the late nineteenth century started the first Western-style winery in Georgia. Chavchavadze recruited viticulture help from Bordeaux in the 1890s and introduced the first Cabernet Sauvignon grapes to the country. Teliani Valley produces more than two dozen wines and two *chachas*. With financial help from the European Bank for Reconstruction and Development, it built a new winery with state-of-the-art equipment that opened in 2006 in the town of Telavi. Winemaker Giorgi Dakishvili is well trained and, with a partner, also has a small winery called Vinoterra that makes only traditional-style wine. Teliani Valley has 370 acres of vineyards, but still buys more than half of its grapes from local farmers. It sells 20 percent of its production in Georgia and exports the rest to twenty-one countries. Ukraine and the Baltic states are its biggest markets.

Teliani Valley has won awards at the London International Wine Fair, the International Wine Challenge, and from *Decanter* magazine. While visiting the winery, I sampled half a dozen Teliani Valley wines in its ultramodern tasting room. The dry wines were good and could have easily passed as a Western product, which is not surprising since they are made with such Western technology as stainless steel tanks. I had an interesting comparison of a 100 percent Saperavi and a 50–50 blend of Cabernet Sauvignon and Saperavi grapes. I liked the single variety better. A white wine made with grapes from western Georgia named Tsolikouri was interesting and could be confused with a Chardonnay. After Dakishvili poured me a semisweet white wine called Tvishi from the 2007 vintage, he said, "I treat my hangovers with this." It had only 11 percent alcohol and 7.2 grams of sugar per liter. We also tried Teliani Valley's Kindzmarauli, a semisweet red with 11.5 percent alcohol and 5.7 grams sugar. In general, the whites seemed better than the reds, but I guess Georgian sweet wines are an acquired taste.

Teliani Valley has been inching its way into wine tourism. After managers made a research trip to Austria, the company built a guesthouse that includes two suites and five double rooms. The double rooms with breakfast are $41 a night, while the suites are $82. Most visitors have been German and Japanese, and they come during the harvest season. People generally learn about Teliani from travel agencies. The winery also offers regular tours and tastings. In mid-September it stages the three-day Teliani Valley Wine Festival; the star of the 2007 show was British rock singer Joe Cocker.

Gela Gamtkitsulashvili and brother, Gia, have started the **Twins Old Cellar**. Their grandfather was a winemaker in the 1930s and had only a 2.5-acre plot of land in the village of Napareuli in Kakheti. But in 1937, the Soviets appropriated the land, took over his farm animals, and told him to start working on a collective farm. After he refused, local communists jailed him and in 1940 sent him to the Soviet Union. The Gamtkitsulashvili family thinks he was killed in World War II, but no one ever heard from him again. He simply vanished. Gela was not as stubborn as his grandfather and worked within the communist system to have a successful career. He became an engineer and worked for the state construction agency putting up buildings such as schools and clubs. "It was constant lying, but I survived," he told me.

The family got its house and land back in the post-Stalin thaw of the mid-1950s, which pleased Gela because some of his earliest memories were of making wine there as a child. After Georgia became independent in 1991, the twins, Gela and Gia, started several new businesses, including a bakery, a meat store, and a construction company. The businesses all did well and cleared the way for the twins to open a winery. They started renovating the property in 2003, and it turned out to be a good place for their aged mother to stay and be looked after. Gela these days works his cell phone constantly just as any international businessman, talking about his various projects—but he says his soul and culture are at the winery.

As soon as I arrived for a visit, Gela took me into a dining room and wine cellar and had a young man pull back the sand and clay covering one of two *kvevris* buried there. Then Gela picked up an empty pitcher, scooped out some wine, and offered me a glass of his traditional white. The highest honor a Georgian can give a visitor is to open a *kvevri* for him. Speaking through his interpreter, Gela welcomed me and quickly showed me pictures of the Georgian president, Mikheil Saakashvili, who has visited the winery three times.

As we walked around the winery complex, Gela explained that he makes two-thirds of his wine in the traditional way and the rest in the European style. The first stop was an open room where many of his eighty-three *kvevris* are buried. All that is visible sticking out above ground are the tops covered with clay and sand. Gela, in 2007, sold wine for the first time, marketing 25,000 gallons. He now starts selling in the spring and opens one *kvevri* after another as the public buys more. He bottles the wine in plastic or glass containers.

Then he took me out to the vineyard, which looks like it did in Soviet times with big, ugly cement posts for trellising the vines. The posts look as if they might double as railroad ties, but are standing up. Gela quickly said he's putting in new and better vines. He also pointed to the place where he will soon build a guesthouse. After that he showed me the distillery that makes *chacha* and a traditional circular bread oven, where loaves are placed against the inside wall to bake.

Following the tour, we returned to the wine cellar for lunch. Gela served both traditional and European wines during the meal, but clearly his heart is with the old-fashioned ones. He said he likes them because they are all-natural. He said that creates a minor problem because the wines sometimes leave sediment in the glass or cup, which might offend a Westerner, although Georgians know there is nothing wrong with it. Some Japanese visitors once liked the traditional wines so much that they asked if they could take some home with them. He reluctantly told them he didn't export that wine because he would have to add chemicals to preserve it during shipping. "Wine is a living creature for me. If you add chemicals, it will die," he told me.

The Twins Old Cellar already offers a full range of programs to visitors who want to learn about Georgian culture and its wine. Gela hopes to expand that once he can open the guesthouse for overnight stays. The visits include a tour of the entire winery, a tasting of four wines, one traditional white to compare with a European white and then a red of each style. Visitors can also see people making *churchkhela,* a national dessert made of grape juice, flour, and walnuts; experience bread making; and eat *khinkalis,* dumplings with spiced meat. The finale is a festive dinner or *supra* with all those foods and drinks.

♥ ♥ ♥

Giorgi Tevzadze, who is thirty-two, epitomizes the new generation of Georgian winemakers who came of age after the country broke away from the dying Soviet Union. He spent the harvests of 2000, 2001, and 2002 as a research scholar at the University of California, Davis, and did internships at Rosenblum Cellars and Bella Vineyards in California.

While in the United States, Tevzadze came up with the idea of starting a small family winery that would target its sales on just Georgia, Britain, and the United States. He called it **Georgian Legend** and made his first vintage in 2003. It was a 100 percent Saperavi, and in 2005 the wine won a silver medal in the World Wine Awards of *Decanter* magazine. He has since sold the brand. Tevzadze has also been a winemaker and head of quality control at Georgian Wines and Spirits. In addition, he was one of six founding members of the Young Winemakers' Union of Georgia, which hopes to influence Georgia's international wine strategy. All of the founders have had some international experience, so they're aware of what is happening in other countries. The day after I met him in Tbilisi, Tevzadze flew off to do some wine consulting in Albania.

Tevzadze insists Georgia should not be building its future on traditional wines, even though they are unique. He says that too much of it is low quality and unstable, so it goes bad easily. "Everyone in Georgia says his wine is good, but a lot of it is not very good," he admits. The better approach, he says, would be his three-pronged program. First, the country's winemakers should concentrate on a few grape varieties so they can become better known around the world. Two, they need to improve their packaging, which is still mainly late-Stalinist in style, and protect their brand names internationally. Three, wineries need to build the infrastructure for wine tourism and link it to the country's rich cultural heritage of ancient monasteries. "No one is doing really good wine tourism in Georgia today," he says.

Despite their shortcomings, Georgian winemakers got off to a good start in improving the quality of their wines in the post-Soviet era and were on track to make a major contribution to the country's economic development. Wine tourism, on the other hand, has not done as well. Outside of the capital city of Tbilisi, there are still few of the amenities Western tourists take for granted. Transportation is only by car, in autos that may be left over from Soviet days and over roads that are often primitive once you get off major highways. Few locals speak any language except Georgian and Russian. There are no Western-style hotels in the wine regions. Restaurants serve tasty local dishes that are interesting, but there's nothing like the *haute cuisine* that tourists expect. A few wineries are trying to start simple lodgings and restaurants, and they will eventually become more prevalent. But for now, wineries have been more interested in expanding their foreign markets.

Nonetheless, Georgian wine tourism has some powerful things going for it. The first is the friendliness of the Georgian people. They genuinely and warmly welcome foreigners since they didn't meet many during the years of Soviet rule and see ties to the West as their way of maintaining their independence. In addition, the ancient Georgian culture, as seen most prominently in its monasteries with their architecture, music, and rituals, is unique. The third attraction is the interesting Georgian wines, especially the traditional ones. European-style wines are getting better, but *kvevri* ones are best enjoyed on the spot in Georgia. Every wine lover should have a chance to drink them at least once.

Progress toward better wines and more wine tourism, though, has been held back by the political struggle between Moscow and Tbilisi. Starting in the early 2000s, Russian leader Vladimir Putin became increasingly aggressive toward all the former Soviet republics by applying economic pressure to slow their diplomatic moves toward the European Union and the United States. He cut off transportation between Russia and Georgia, more than doubled the price of natural gas exports, and in March 2006 blocked the import of all Georgian wines, a heavy blow to producers just starting to increase their quality and expand their markets. In the summer of 2008, Russian troops invaded the country under the pretext of protecting pro-Russian ethnic groups. They temporarily occupied a large part of the country, but then settled into what appears to be a long-term stay in two disputed zones.

The impact of Russian pressure has been devastating. Wine sales to Russia disappeared overnight. Exports by the large Georgia Wine and Spirits company took a particularly heavy hit. Sixty percent of the 3.5 million bottles it produces used to go to Russia, and those fell to virtually zero. When I visited the winery in May 2008, whole buildings were empty and looked as if they had been abandoned. The place resembled a ghost factory. Badagoni, on the other hand, was lucky because it had never counted on Russia to be a major market and had not yet attempted to build business there. Since Twins Old Cellar doesn't export, it has also not been affected by the blockade. Overall, Georgian wine exports dropped from 56 million bottles annually to about 10 million, and it was probably only a bureaucratic snafu that let those few get through. Winemakers have been trying to find alternative markets in the United States, Western Europe, and former Soviet Republics. In the Ukraine, Georgian companies advertise, "Try the Wine of Freedom." But it has been impossible to replace the large Russian market overnight.

The effects were felt down to the smallest winery. Three Khareba brothers started the **Khareba** winery in western Georgia in 1995, but got off to a slow start, and then in 2003 went through financial reorganization. The winery has an international approach to business, and all the signs at its facility near the city of Kutaisi, the country's second city and western capital, are in both English and Georgian. To underscore their ties to the nation's heritage, the founders built an Orthodox church just inside the main gate. The company's business plan was to sell wine primarily to Russia since it was the country's traditional and largest export market.

Khareba, though, had only shipped one truckload of wine there in 2006, when Putin's boycott took effect. The day I visited the company two years later, only a skeleton staff was on duty. The Italian-made bottling line can handle one thousand bottles an hour, but that and other equipment weren't operating. Khareba's sales director told me he is now struggling to find new markets for its wines, perhaps in Ukraine, but so far he hasn't succeeded. Khareba is selling only a small amount of wine at the winery and through one store in Tbilisi.

At the plant's main entrance off a major road linking Kutaisi to the capital of Tbilisi stands Khareba's well-equipped tasting room. When I walked in, two men were standing behind the bar, but they clearly were there only because I was expected. They proudly explained their line of sixteen wines, saying that they made only Western-style ones, both dry and sweet, and two types of sparkling wine, semi-dry and brut, and *chacha*. Prices ranged from $3 to $17 a bottle. The staff said they aged their red wines in Hungarian oak. Seventy percent of Khareba's production is white wine, since the market seems to prefer its whites. As I left the tasting room, I could only conclude that Khareba appeared to be on its way to failure, a victim of international power politics.

Long-term relations between Russia and Georgia remain an open question, and politics will determine the development of wine tourism in the small country. Tourists of any kind don't like to get into situations that could turn into armed conflicts and catch them in the crossfire. It is likely that Russia will continue trying to get Georgia back to its status during the Soviet era or at least turn it into a vassal state. Moscow will probably continue applying economic pressure such as the boycott of Georgian wines. A strong majority of Georgians, however, appears to be anxious to continue moving closer to the European Union and the United States.

Anyone looking for a truly unique experience in wine tourism should at least consider Georgia, although a trip there involves additional levels of uncertainty. There is simply nothing like it. The political and military situation in the Caucasus region could flare up again at any moment and for unexpected reasons. Maybe that's a reason to have some Georgian wine around to calm everyone's nerves, perhaps even Stalin's favorite, Khvanchkara.

DIARY OF A WINE TOURIST

MAY 16

A *SUPRA* WITH A FAMILY OF WINEMAKERS

Two women from the Sharvazeebi family enthusiastically greeted me as my car rolled through the gate at a winery outside the village of Koreti. They quickly began explaining that their extended family of thirty people owned a dozen wine cellars where they have been making wine for centuries in the ancient Georgian style. No one knows exactly for how long. Even the nearly one hundred years of Soviet rule of Georgia had not changed the family's business, and they continued making wines both for themselves and for selling to neighbors.

All the wineries are similar, consisting of three-sided buildings filled with ancient winemaking equipment. Since the family has several separate vineyards, they make and store wine in different locations so they don't have to transport the grapes far after picking. At each place there is at least one hollowed-out tree trunk with a hole at the end, where at harvest time they stomp grapes to get juice for making wine. The two women said they could easily get 1 ton of grapes into a tree trunk. First the boys walk on the grapes, and then the older and heavier men crush them harder. Girls and women join in the harvests by singing and dancing, but only males are permitted to stomp. It takes about two hours to finish the job. Turpa, one of the women, proudly pointed to one tree trunk and said the family had been using it for three centuries. Buried in the ground in front of the opening at each winery were the tops of *kvevris* that each holds about 50 gallons of juice. The women explained they had been sealed after fermentation ended the previous October and were waiting there for someone to open them and try the wine. All I could see was a mound of earth about 3 feet wide that was covered with a piece of roofing sheet metal.

In honor of my arrival, Vasili, a thickly built man who appeared to be in his sixties and had heavy fists gained from years of work in the vineyards, opened one of the jars. First he took off the piece of metal and exposed the jar's top. Then he scraped aside by hand some dirt on the neck and used a flat shovel to dig out the damp clay that sealed the vessel. After removing the clay, he pulled out a piece of wood that had been placed in the neck to block it. Turpa explained that they regularly pour water on the clay to keep the top moist and the seal tight.

After touring several of the family cellars, Turpa directed me to a larger, one-room building nearby. At the back of it was a fireplace. On both the mantel and the walls were faded pictures of deceased family members. To the right was a tombstone. Already laid out on a table were the first dishes for lunch, and three women were soon bringing in more plates of food. Then Vasili arrived with the first pitcher of white wine and quickly filled everyone's glass. Minutes later he was back with another pitcher—this time with red wine. The *supra,* or feast, was beginning.

One of the women brought out a 6-inch-wide silver cup. With a deep sense of pride, she explained that King Erekle II had given it to the family in the eighteenth century. I was a bit skeptical that a poor family like this would receive such a gift from a king and asked for the story behind it. The woman explained that at the time the family was part of the nobility and that the king had once stayed overnight with them and gave it to them in appreciation. Decorated with the fine scroll of the day, it was the family's most prized heirloom.

I soon started eating from the spread that included several different kinds of meat, including chicken and beef, fresh homemade cheeses, *khachapuri,* a popular cheese pastry, plus plenty of fresh tomatoes and cucumbers. More and more plates kept coming. Soon a man named Otari arrived and immediately asked if there was already a *tamada,* the master of the table who leads the toasts at a traditional Georgian celebration. When no one spoke up, he assumed the role. Picking up his glass of wine that he pointed toward me, he said, "Let your foot be welcome in my house." The toasts then started coming more and more quickly, with Vasili filling up glasses in between. We toasted peace, and Georgia, and people who do good things for others, and the earth.

Lunch had been going about an hour, when Otari's cell phone rang. After talking briefly, he turned off the phone, saying it was just a neighbor wondering who was visiting them. Neighbors are always nosy. Then Otari picked up a traditional clay wine bowl, filled it with white wine, and passed it to me. "We will toast our ancestors," he said. My translator had given me some tips about toasting customs, and I knew that I was expected to drink the entire bowl of wine without putting it down. Sipping slowly but steadily, I drank to the bottom.

With a twinkle, Otari said I wasn't drinking enough. He explained that when they open a wine jar for a guest, everyone had to finish it. That meant drinking more than 50 gallons!

Soon the silver Erekle cup was being passed from person to person around the table, with each drinking all the wine at one time. Then the cup was refilled and passed along. When it reached me, I toasted, "To our parents. If we didn't have good parents, we wouldn't be here."

No one was counting, but there must have been twenty toasts before Otari stood up to make what was obviously going to be the last one. "To Georgian-American friendship," he said with a strong voice and then everyone repeated after him. Finally, shortly before 3:00 p.m., we all got up from the table and stepped out into the crisp, late-spring sunlight. The lunch had taken more than two hours, and I doubt that anyone did much work that afternoon. But I had enjoyed an intimate glimpse of Georgian life.

Conclusion

After I returned home from my six-month, worldwide search for Bacchus, friends immediately began asking me which of the many places I had visited was my favorite. The answer was unfortunately not simple. It would be a little like having Gaston Lenôtre, the great French pastry chef, prepare twelve of his top desserts and then ask you to select the one you liked best. I'm sure I couldn't do it.

I had, however, come to a few generalizations that were important, at least for me. All the areas were drop-dead beautiful, but each in its own way. The deep and steep valleys of the Douro are different from the rolling hills of Tuscany with its stately cypress trees. Which is more beautiful? Take your pick.

Remote destinations may be harder to reach, but once there you usually don't have to fight crowds. Napa is only an hour's drive from San Francisco, so it was the easiest of all the places to visit, but also the most packed with people. Margaret River is a long drive from Perth, which is already far from everywhere. The flight to South Africa from North America takes the better part of twenty-four hours, which automatically reduces the number of people going there. The payoff from traveling to a remote place is that it's your private reserve.

Another advantage of hard-to-reach places is that the owner or winemaker is more likely to be around. It's rare these days to meet one in a tasting room in the Napa Valley. But in Chile's Colchagua Valley or Spain's Rioja it's more likely to happen.

Popular places naturally have more established tourism infrastructure—more and different restaurants and many, varied places to stay. Georgia truly is the last frontier, and the Russian invasion during the summer of 2008 has certainly set back tourism. Anyone venturing there must be prepared to rough it a bit by staying at a fairly basic bed-and-breakfast. But that also makes the Georgian wine tourism experience unique and wonderful. I will fondly remember my time and the people I met there. Central Otago, on the other hand, is a remote destination with a great tourist infrastructure because it was already built for the skiers and adventure-sport fans when wine tourists started arriving.

Today, wine tourism is vital to the thousands of small wineries around the world that depend on walk-in visitors who wander into a tasting room and buy a bottle or two. Small producers can't get mass distribution so are anxious to make that personal connection with new customers. To cite just one example, New York State now has more than 250 wineries, but probably 200 of them survive solely thanks to tourists.

Good food and good wine go together like love and marriage; as the old song says, you can't have one without the other. All the twelve places I visited are striving to offer food that matches the greatness of their wines, but Italy does the best job. South Africa, on the other hand, still has a long way to go on food. Many wineries there have established their own restaurants, and some of them, such as the one at Rust en Vrede in Stellenbosch, are outstanding. The old saw of travelers is that you should eat where the truck drivers stop; a variation of that for the wine tourist is to eat at a winery restaurant because it has already made a commitment to the food-and-wine combination.

I also learned that it's important that the destination offers more than just wine. Even the most fanatic wine geek needs a break from wine tastings and great meals. Central Otago has the most diverse offerings of any wine site thanks to all its adventure tourism. Tuscany has interesting old towns and great art, especially in Florence. In Tuscany you can drink a great Brunello one day, and see Michelangelo's *David* the next.

Language can be a challenge, especially in the smaller wine regions such as the Douro Valley. In Stellenbosch, Napa Valley, Margaret River, and Central Otago, of course, there is no language problem for English speakers. In many other areas travelers can get by fairly easily. I was pleasantly surprised by how many people in Bordeaux now speak English, which is a big change from the mid-1970s when I lived in France. Germans have always been comfortable speaking

English. Generally, the bigger the winery the more likely you are to find someone who speaks English. Lots of people at wineries in Chile and Argentina are ready to converse in English. In Georgia, on the other hand, most people speak either Georgian or Russian. It was the only country I visited where I felt it was essential to have a translator. My driver and I finally discovered that our common language was German, and we communicated well enough to share many glasses of the local *chacha*. Even in countries where you need a translator, though, it always helps to learn a few words in the local language and then use them. People appreciate that you are making an effort to learn their culture. I wrote the phonetic spelling of "thank you" in Georgian (*madlobt*) on the cover of the notebook I used there. Even my broken pronunciation was invariably greeted with a smile.

Your comfort level in the local language will likely determine whether you'll want to get a translator or a driver or go on a guided tour. I had all those experiences. Remember that you'll generally be out in the countryside for a lot of your visits since wineries aren't located in big cities. Many of the places won't have much of an address, so GPS navigation devices may not be helpful. I spent one memorable morning stumbling around southern Tuscany looking for the **Rocca di Montemassi** winery, where I had an appointment. I failed in several attempts to make myself understood to policemen and farmers with hand signs and my few words of Italian. Finally, a roadside vegetable merchant understood me. He telephoned the winery and asked the manager to come pick me up. I followed her to the winery in my car, arriving an hour and a half late.

Driving a rental car on the "other" side of the road in South Africa, Australia, and New Zealand provided another interesting experience. The first day on the road in each country was always the most difficult, but after that it was fairly easy. One tip is to be sure to get a car with an automatic transmission because shifting gears is a headache and distraction that you really don't need.

One night in Queenstown, New Zealand, I had dinner with David Kennedy, the director of Destination Queenstown, the city's tourism service. Several days later, he had to give a public report that said the boom in tourism that the region had enjoyed, thanks to the popularity of the *Lord of the Rings* films, was over. It had been a wonderful ride, he told me, but tourism was returning to normal. Over a bottle of 2006 Black Ridge Pinot Noir, Kennedy and I discussed the future of international tourism.

Kennedy said the type of tourist was changing and the reason people are traveling now is different than it had been. The first generation of mass tourism started in the 1960s, when jet passenger planes opened up the world, especially a distant place like New Zealand, to travelers. Those people had gone first to the world's capitals. Europe was frequently the initial destination, and they wanted to see great cities such as Paris, London, and Rome. Once they had landed, they probably went around the area in a bus, stayed at an international hotel, and had limited contact with the local people. By now, however, those same people are branching out to more remote destinations and look at Europe beyond the major cities.

Today's travelers, Kennedy said, are different. Their parents may have dragged them around Paris in their youth, and so the capitals are old hat. The new generation of travelers wants to go deeper into the culture of an area and to make connections with the people. While both experienced and novice travelers may not call wine tourism educational travel, that is really what they seek. They want stories and a way to connect with the local culture. Just looking at old buildings is no longer enough. In addition, they want a variety of things to do. A place must capture their attention for several days by offering many things new and interesting.

Wine tourism in many ways epitomizes Kennedy's new tourism. Many people bring to it a broad knowledge of wine, but they are there to deepen that understanding of a particular place. The natural beauty is an added benefit, as visitors explore a region by car, train, bike, boat, bus, or on foot. Wine is a subject no one can ever exhaust. No matter how many you've tasted and how many wineries you've visited, there is always something to discover: a new wine, a new vintage, a new winemaker. There's a story in each bottle, and each tale differs slightly. The search for Bacchus is a journey that fortunately never ends. So where in the world is the best wine tourism? Your next destination.

As a travel aid for your trips, here are the toasts that you might use at every stop along the way in the order in which I went about my journey. In some countries a ritual goes along with a toast. In several places it is expected that you will look squarely in the eyes of the people you are toasting. In fact, I was told in South Africa that if you do not, your punishment will be seven years of bad sex. Many of the toasts have to do with health. Some have interesting derivations, such as the Italian one, which seems to be from Chinese and was probably brought home by ancient mariners. The most elaborate, not surprisingly, comes from Georgia, where toasting is an art form. In any language a toast is simply an invitation to enjoy your wine.

A common toast in Napa is a casual *Drink Up*. In bilingual Stellenbosch you could say *Cheers* in English or *Gesondheid* (Health) in Afrikaans. In Argentina it would be *Salud, dinero y amor* (Health, money, and love). In Chile say *A vuestra salud* (To your health). In Margaret River it is *Cheers,* but in New Zealand it is *Good Health.* In Rioja the toast is a simple *Salud* (Health), while in Portugal say *À vossa saúde* (To your health). In Tuscany it is *Cin Cin* (pronounced chin chin). In Bordeaux an informal *À la vôtre* (To yours) will do. In the Rhineland it is *Zum Wohle* (To well being). And in Kakheti, Georgia, the first of what will become a string of many toasts is ᲛᲨᲕᲘᲓᲝᲑᲐᲡ ᲒᲐᲣᲛᲐᲠᲯᲝᲡ ᲛᲗᲔᲚᲡ ᲛᲡᲝᲤᲚᲘᲝᲨᲘ, ᲩᲕᲔᲜᲡ ᲥᲕᲔᲧᲐᲜᲐᲡᲐ ᲓᲐ ᲩᲕᲔᲜᲡ ᲝᲯᲐᲮᲔᲑᲨᲘ (Let's drink for peace all around the world, for peace in our country, and peace in our families).

Appendix

Armchair Traveler

Even if you can't travel to any of the twelve countries I visited for this book, you can still enjoy the wine experience of those places by trying their wines at home. Below are recommendations from each of the countries. I tried to select wines that give a sampling of the vines and styles of that region. With only a few exceptions, I picked wines generally widely available in the United States. I also tried to select a range of prices, so readers could experience a wide gamut. Several Internet sites such as www.winesearcher.com will locate them in case you have trouble. Enjoy the wines and your vicarious travels.

NAPA VALLEY, CALIFORNIA

Robert Mondavi Fumé Blanc	dry white	$15
Domaine Chandon Brut Classic	sparkling white	$20
Beaulieu Vineyard Chardonnay Carneros	dry white	$25
Niebaum-Coppola Edizione Pennino Zinfandel	dry red	$40
Quintessa	dry red	$110

Stellenbosch, South Africa

Goats Do Roam Bored Doe	dry red	$10
Delheim Pinotage	dry red	$20
Rust en Vrede Estate	dry red	$35
Klein Constantia Vin de Constance	sweet white	$50
Ken Forrester FMC Chenin Blanc	dry white	$60

Mendoza, Argentina

Lurton Torrontés	dry white	$10
O. Fournier Urban Uco Malbec	dry red	$10
Familia Zuccardi Q Malbec	dry red	$15
Clos de los Siete	dry red	$15
Achaval-Ferrer Finca Altamira	dry red	$120

Colchagua Valley, Chile

Los Vascos Sauvignon Blanc	dry white	$10
Casa Silva Reserva Chardonnay	dry white	$10
Arboleda Carmenère	dry red	$15
Montes Purple Angel	dry red	$50
Casa Lapostolle Clos Apalta	dry red	$60

Margaret River, Australia

Chateau Xanadu Chardonnay	dry white	$15
Cape Mentelle Chardonnay	dry white	$20
Vasse Felix Shiraz	dry red	$25
Moss Wood Cabernet Sauvignon	dry red	$80
Leeuwin Estate Art Series Chardonnay	dry white	$80

Central Otago, New Zealand

Mt. Difficulty Pinot Gris	dry white	$20
Carrick Riesling	dry white	$20
Amisfield Pinot Noir	dry red	$30
Felton Road Pinot Noir	dry red	$50
Rippon Pinot Noir	dry red	$50

Rioja, Spain

Viña Real Crianza	dry red	$15
R. López de Heredia Viña Gravonia Crianza	dry white	$30
Ysios Vendimia Seleccionada	dry red	$30
Barón de Ley Finca Monasterio	dry red	$50
Torre Muga	dry red	$100

Douro Valley, Portugal

Quinta do Portal Fine White Port	sweet white	$15
Quinta do Vollado Douro Tinto	dry red	$20
Croft LBV Port	sweet red	$20
Quinta do Vale Meão Meandro	dry red	$30
Quinta do Crasto Reserva Old Vines	dry red	$50

Tuscany, Italy

Pietrafitta Vernaccia di San Gimignano	dry white	$15
Avignonese Vino Nobile di Montepulciano	dry red	$30
Badia a Coltibuono Vin Santo	sweet white	$30
Castello Banfi Brunello di Montalcino	dry red	$60
Antinori Tignanello	dry red	$100

Bordeaux, France

Clos Floridène Blanc	dry white	$20
Château Loudenne	dry red	$25
Château de Pressac	dry red	$35
Château Smith Haut Lafitte Blanc	dry white	$60
Château Lynch-Bages	dry red	$90

Rheingau and Middle Mosel, Germany

S. A. Prüm Wehlener Sonnenuhr Kabinett	dry white	$20
Dr. Pauly-Bergweiler Wehlener Sonnenuhr Kabinett	dry white	$25
J. J. Prüm Riesling Kabinett	dry white	$30
Kloster Eberbach Steinberger Spätlese	dry white	$35
Schloss Johannisberg Beerenauslese	sweet white	$100

Kakheti, Georgia

Georgian Royal Estates Saperavi	dry red	$10
Georgian Royal Estates Khvanchkara	sweet red	$20
Teliani Valley Tsinandali	dry white	$10
Tamada Tvishi	sweet white	$15
Teliani Valley Mukuzani	dry red	$20

Bibliography

Allen, H. Warner. *The Romance of Wine*. Miniola, NY: Dover Publications, 1971.

Alvarado, Rodrigo. *Chilean Wine*. Origo Ediciones: Santiago de Chile, 2004.

Andrijich, Frances, Peter Forrestal, and Ray Jordan. *Margaret River*. Fremantle, Australia: Fremantle Arts Centre Press, 2003.

Bell, Ian. *Dreams of Exile*. New York: Henry Holt, 1992.

Briggs, Asa. *Haut-Brion*. London: Faber and Faber, 1994.

Brook, Stephen. *A Century of Wine*. San Francisco: The Wine Appreciation Guild, 2000.

Cathiard, Florence. *Art of the Vine*. Geneva: Aubanel, 2002.

Chilashvili, Levan. *The Vine, Wine and the Georgians*. Tbilisi: Petite Publisher, 2004.

Cinelli Colombini, Donatella. *Il Marketing del Turismo del Vino*. Rome: A.G.R.A., 2007.

Conaway, James. *Napa*. New York: Avon Books, 1990.

Coppola, Eleanor. *Notes on a Life*. New York: Doubleday, 2008.

Cull, Dave. *Vineyards on the Edge*. Dunedin, New Zealand: Longacre Press, 2001.

Dubrule, Paul. Letter. "L'oenotourisme: une valorisation des produits et du patrimoine vitivinicoles." Vitisphere.com. E-lettre #239. May 1, 2007.

Duijker, Hubrecht. *The Wines of Chile*. Utrecht, Netherlands: Het Spectrum, 1999.

Elias Pastor, Luis Vicente. *El Turismo del Vino*. Bilboa: Universidad de Deusto, 2006.

Fleming, Stuart J. *Vinum: The Story of Roman Wine*. Glen Mills, PA: Art Flair, 2001.

Friedman, Alan. *Spider's Web*. New York: Bantam Books, 1993.

Gabler, James M. *Passions*. Baltimore: Bacchus Press, 1995.

Gachechiladze, Levan, and Tamaz Kandelaki. *The Vine, Wine and the Georgians*. Tbilisi: Georgian Wine and Spirits, 2004.

Gladstones, J. S. "The Climate and Soils of Southwestern Australia in Relation to Vine Growing." *Journal of the Australian Institute of Agricultural Science*. December 1965.

———. "Soils and Climate of the Margaret River–Busselton Area: Their Suitability for Wine Grape Production." *Journal of the Australian Institute of Agricultural Science*. April 1966.

Hackett, AJ. *Jump Start*. Auckland: Random House New Zealand, 2006.

Hailman, John. *Thomas Jefferson on Wine*. Jackson, MS: University Press of Mississippi, 2006.

Hall, C. Michael et al. *Wine Tourism Around the World*. Oxford: Butterworth Heinemann, 2000.

Hands, Phyllis, and Dave Hughes. *New World of Wine from the Cape of Good Hope*. Somerset West, South Africa: Stephan Phillips, 2001.

Heintz, William. *California's Napa Valley*. San Francisco: Scottwall Associates, 1999.

Hobley, Stephen. *A Traveller's Wine Guide to Italy*. New York: Interlinks Books, 2002.

Hughes, Eugenio. *Chile a Land of Contrasts*. Pueblo del Inglés, Chile: Mandiola Cia, 2005.

Jefferson, Thomas. *Jefferson Abroad*. Edited by Douglas L. Wilson and Lucia Stanton. New York: Modern Library, 1999.

———. *The Papers of Thomas Jefferson*. Edited by Julian P. Boyd. Vol. 11–13. Princeton, NJ: Princeton University Press, 1955, 1956.

Johnson, Hugh. *The Story of Wine*. London: Mitchell Beazley, 2002.

Johnson, Hugh, and Jancis Robinson. *The World Atlas of Wine* (5th ed). London: Mitchell Beasley, 2001.

Jordan, Ray. *Wine: Western Australia's Best*. Osborne Park WA, Australia: The West Australian, 2002.

Kauffmann, Jean-Paul et al. *Bordeaux Châteaux*. Paris: Éditions Flammarion, 2004.

Kushman, Rick, and Hank Beal. *A Moveable Thirst*. Hoboken, New Jersey: John Wiley & Sons, 2007.

Lichine, Alexis. *Wines of France*. New York: Knopf, 1951.

Littlewood, Joan. *Baron Philippe*. New York: Crown Publishers, 1984.

Locke, John. *The World of John Locke*. Vol. 10. Boston: Adamant Media, 2001.

Lough, John. *Locke's Travels in France 1675–1679*. Cambridge: University Press, 1953.

MacNeil, Karen. *The Wine Bible*. New York: Workman Publishing, 2001.

Markham, Dewsey, Jr. *1855*. New York: John Wiley & Sons, 1998.

Matthews, Sara. *Chile: The Art of Wine*. San Francisco: The Wine Appreciation Guild, 2004.

McGovern, Patrick E. *Ancient Wine*. Princeton, NJ: Princeton University Press, 2003.

Metcalfe, Charles, and Kathryn McWhirter. *The Wine and Food Lover's Guide to Portugal*. London: Inn House Publishing, 2007.

Mondavi, Robert. *Harvests of Joy*. New York: Harcourt Brace & Co, 1998.

Moore, Roy, and Alma Moore. *Thomas Jefferson's Journey to the South of France*. New York: Stewart, Tabori & Chang, 1999.

Oram, Ric. *Pinot Pioneers*. Auckland: New Holland Publishers, 2004.

Parker, Robert M., Jr. *The World's Greatest Wine Estates*. New York: Simon & Schuster, 2005.

Pascual, Jesús Marino. *Dinastía Vivanco Museum of Wine Culture*. Biornes, Spain: Museo de la Cultura del Vino, 2005.

Pellechia, Thomas. *Wine*. New York: Thunder's Mouth Press, 2006.

Pliny the Elder. *Natural History*. Book 14. Cambridge, MA: Harvard University Press, 1952.

Proust, Alain, and Graham Knox. *Wines of South Africa*. Vlaeberg, South Africa: Fernwood Press, 2002.

Ray, Jonathan. *Bloodlines & Grapevines*. London: Conran Octopus, 2004.

Riba D'Ave, Raúl. *Argentine Wines*. Buenos Aires: Maizal, 2002.

Richards, Peter. *The Wines of Chile*. London: Mitchell Beazley, 2006.

Robinson, Jancis. *The Oxford Companion to Wine*. 3rd Edition. Oxford, Oxford University Press, 2006.

Ross, Jamie. *Where Angels Tread*. Santiago, Chile: Montes, 2006.

Shackelford, George Green. *Thomas Jefferson's Travels in Europe, 1784–89*. Baltimore: Johns Hopkins University Press, 1995.

Siler, Julia Flynn. *The House of Mondavi*. New York: Gotham Books, 2007.

Smilie, Robert S. *The Sonoma Mission*. Fresno: Valley Publishers, 1975.

Stabb, Josef, Hans Reinhard Seeliger, and Wolfgang Schleicher. *Schloss Johannisberg*. Mainz: Woschek Verlags.

Stevenson, Robert Louis. *The Silverado Squatters*. St. Helena, CA: Silverado Museum, 1974.

Weber, Lin. *Old Napa Valley*. St. Helena, CA: Wine Ventures Publishing, 1998.

Wolf, Erik. *Culinary Tourism*. Dubuque, Iowa: Kendall/Hunt, 2006.

Woolhouse, Roger. *Locke*. Cambridge: Cambridge University Press, 2007.

Wright, John. Regional Oral History Office. The Bancroft Library, University of California, Berkeley.

Note on Currency and Measurements

During the past two years, as a result of the international economic crisis, the valuations of currencies have increased and decreased, sometimes wildly. This book reports on areas where seven different currencies are used. The valuations of local currencies in all cases are in American dollar terms on the basis of the exchange rate in effect on January 1, 2009. Since the euro is the most widely used currency in countries outside the dollar area, both euro and dollar values are given. All other local money is converted into U.S. dollars.

Countries in this book use either the imperial or the metric system of measurement. For the sake of consistency, all of those numbers are given in the American version of imperial measurement units.

Acknowledgments

Thanks to countless people around the world, this book turned from a captivating, but vague, idea into the words on these pages and an eBook. I owe all of them a deep sense of gratitude, and I dedicate the book to all of them.

The most challenging and complex part of the research had to be done before I ever bought my first airplane ticket. That involved deciding where to visit and whom to see. I started by concluding that I should go to what I thought were the twelve most interesting wine countries in the world. I had already been to eleven of the countries I identified. Only Georgia was going to be virgin territory, but I had read much about archeological studies there showing that it was perhaps the birthplace of wine. I quickly concluded, however, that I couldn't visit every wine region in each country. So I dug into research material and narrowed my focus to just one region per country and then picked up the phone and also began sending e-mails.

Thanks to that basic research, I was able to meet a host of helpful wine experts who shared their local knowledge and helped me come up with an itinerary that took me to the most interesting places in each region. I also had serendipitous meetings along the byways of the twelve regions. The people listed below were crucial. Without them the book would never have come to be. Their backgrounds were very diverse. Some were wine people; some were travel people. All were experts and gladly shared their knowledge with me. They were the Sherpas who helped me get to the summit of the subject. They included Margrit Mondavi in Napa, Rory Callahan and Meryl Weaver in Stellenbosch, Michael Evans in Mendoza, Eduardo Chadwick in Colchagua Valley, Denis Horgan in Margaret River, David Strada for Central Otago, Judy Musa and Thomas Perry in Rioja, Joana Mesquita and Ruy de Brito e Cunha in the Douro Valley, Alioscia Lombardini in Tuscany, Dominique Renard in Bordeaux, Michael Schemmel in the Rhine/Mosel, and Mamuka Tsereteli for Kakheti. In addition, scores of winemakers and winery owners took time to talk with me about what they were doing in wine tourism. Wine is an international fraternity where many people cast competition aside and openly share stories of their past experiences, some failures, and future plans. Many of those insights found their way into this book.

The logistics of travels as complex as mine were monumental. My wife, Jean Taber, turned our house on Block Island, Rhode Island, into Wine Tourism Mission Control, coordinating travel plans that were often changing and also being the backstop when things went wrong. Rekha Arapurakal of Personal Travel in New Jersey, who handled my reservations, was unflappable even on the day I said, "I want to fly from Frankfurt, Germany to Tbilisi, Georgia on a Saturday."

Throughout the preparation of this book, my editors at Scribner, Brant Rumble and Kara Watson, were always there with encouragement as I thrashed my way through the writing underbrush. Then when I was finished, they carefully edited the manuscript, improving it mightily by suggesting ever so gently a nip here and a tuck there.

An endeavor as global and complex as *In Search of Bacchus* threw down great challenges for me in tracking down facts and getting them right. The Internet made it a lot easier than it would have been in the days when people were restricted to telex machines, telephones, and the mail. I tried hard to get it all correct, and I hope I did. Any errors, though, are my sole responsibility. Finally, I hope Bacchus is pleased.

Index

Read on for an excerpt from

TO CORK OR NOT TO CORK
Tradition, Romance, Science, and the Battle for the Wine Bottle

by George M. Taber

Available in paperback from Scribner

CHAPTER ONE

Nature's Nearly Perfect Product

*When Robert Hooke first saw
cork under a microscope,
the structure reminded him
of a monk's cell.*

In the early 1660s, Robert Hooke, the Curator of Experiments for the newly founded Royal Society, a group leading the scientific revolution in England, labored for hours over his new, exciting instrument. It was called a microscope, and just as Galileo had opened new worlds by looking far into space in the early 1600s with a telescope, Hooke was now discovering new worlds in the opposite direction, minute ones that had previously been too small for the human eye to see.

Hooke, a physically unattractive and often unpleasant person who collected enemies as easily as friends, would later be called England's Leonardo da Vinci because of the breadth of his scholarship. After graduating from Oxford in 1663, he worked with scientist Robert Boyle developing the theory of gases that bears his collaborator's name. He also worked with court architect Sir Christopher Wren in the reconstruction of London after the Great Fire of 1666 and on such historic projects as rebuilding St. Paul's Cathedral and the Royal Observatory at Greenwich, where world time starts. In addition, Hooke discovered the spring control of the balance wheel for watches, which finally made accurate time-telling possible, the reflecting telescope, and the pedometer.

Through his microscope, which had a fifty-times magnification, far more than others at the time, Hooke studied some of the most basic natural objects around him: fleas, sponges, bird feathers, and more. Observation Eighteen, as he carefully noted it, particularly fascinated him. It was a piece of cork, a product that had been around for centuries but was only recently being used widespread as a stopper in bottles. He first selected what he described as a "good clear piece" and then with a penknife "sharpened as keen as a razor" cut off a slice to leave "the surface exceedingly smooth." Then he sliced an "exceedingly thin piece" and placed it on a black plate so that the pale cork would stand out in contrast. As he peered at the material through his lens, the cork seemed to take on magical characteristics. He later wrote, "I could exceeding plainly perceive it to be all perforated and porous, much like a honeycomb."

The structure of the piece reminded Hooke of cells where monks in a monastery slept and prayed, and so he called the boxes cells, coining the term since given to the building blocks of all living things. He went on to calculate with awe that there must be "twelve hundred million" cells in a cubic inch of cork. Swept away with the excitement of the moment, Hooke later wrote, "These pores, or cells, were not very deep. . . . I no sooner discerned these (which were indeed the first microscopical pores I ever saw, and perhaps that were ever seen, for I had not met with any writer or person that had made any mention of them before this) but me thought I had with the discovery of them presently hinted to me the true and intelligible reason of all the phenomena of cork."

In 1665, when Hooke was twenty-nine, the Royal Society published his *Micrographia,* a book recounting his experiments, which became a best seller and laid the foundation for using microscopes in biology and medicine. Hooke was also an artist and drew detailed illustrations for the book of what he had seen through his microscope, including the cross section of a cork that indeed resembled a honeycomb. One of his book's early readers was English diarist Samuel Pepys. After working at his job as Secretary to the Admiralty Commission until past midnight on January 21, 1665, Pepys stayed up at home until two in the morning reading what he called "the most ingenious book that ever I read in my life."

People since then have been just as fascinated by cork as Robert Hooke was the day he saw it for the first time under a microscope, for there is no other product in nature quite like it. Later scientists with better microscopes have learned a lot more about cork. The cells that Hooke first saw are fourteen-sided, or tetrakaidecahedrons, so tightly joined together that there is no empty space between them. The cell walls are made up of five layers of material: two outer ones are cellulose; the central one has a woody quality and provides the structure; two inner ones are impermeable. Suberin, a complex fatty acid, is the basic material in cork. Hooke was off only a little on the number of cells; a wine cork contains some 800 million.

Cork cells are filled with microscopic amounts of air. Nearly 90 percent of cork's volume is made up of those tiny, trapped air pockets, and that gives the product its unique buoyancy and compressibility. Air gets into a bottle closed with a cork, but three and a half centuries after Hooke, scientists still don't know how that happens. Some believe it comes through or around the cork, but others think compressed cork cells release it.

Because of the air pockets, cork is among the lightest of all solid substances, which is why it has been used for millennia as floats. If a cork is pushed in one direction, it does not bulge out in another, unlike rubber or plastic. Cork simply contracts. But then it also quickly returns to its original shape because of its unique elastic memory. Even if cork is strongly compacted, it will return to 85 percent of its original volume almost immediately and to 98 percent after a day. In addition, cork can withstand extreme high and low temperatures, but does not conduct either heat or cold. It also absorbs vibration and is extremely long lasting. Cork floors or cork bottle stoppers are good for decades. In 1956, twenty bottles of vintage 1789 wine were found with corks in them in a French cave. The corks were still in fine condition. The wine was slightly brown and obviously overaged, but still well preserved.

Cork comes from the cork oak tree, known to scientists as *Quercus suber*. The tree has two layers of bark. The inner one is alive, while the outer one has died. As successive layers die, the outer bark becomes thicker. This outer layer can be harvested about every decade without doing damage to the inner tree.

Although attempts have been made to cultivate cork elsewhere in the world, it still grows mainly around the western-Mediterranean region. It is thought that cork was originally harvested around the whole basin, but in more recent times it has been grown primarily in the western part on both the northern and southern shores—from Italy to Portugal in the north and from Tunisia to Morocco in the south. The two major cork-producing countries are Portugal and Spain, accounting for more than 80 percent of total world production.

No one knows exactly when the first person put the first cork in a wine container. Archaeologist Patrick McGovern of the University of Pennsylvania and author of *Ancient Wine* is a leading expert on the history of winemaking. According to his research, the Chinese made a product that consisted of wine, beer, honey, and other products about nine thousand years ago. Western wine was first produced about a millennium later somewhere in the mountainous area stretching from eastern Turkey across the Taurus, Caucasus, and Zagros mountains to northern Iran. The first wine was probably made by accident when bunches of grapes were left too long in a container and mysteriously turned into a light, fruity wine. McGovern labels that Stone Age Beaujolais Nouveau, speculating that it was made by carbonic maceration much like the short-lived, but popular, drink now made each fall in France.

The Greek historian Thucydides wrote, "The peoples of the Mediterranean began to emerge from barbarism when they learned to cultivate the olive and the vine." The discovery of pottery in roughly 6000 BC made it possible for people to store wine for the first time, and so the history of pottery coincides with that of wine. Pottery also made wine trade possible. The vast majority of trade in ancient times was in just three products: wine, grain, and olives or olive oil.

Winemakers soon learned that air is the enemy of wine. While some air is crucial to get fermentation started and turn the sugar in grape juice into alcohol, the resulting wine will become vinegar if it stays in contact with air. Ethanol, the intoxicating ingredient in wine, in the presence of the bacterium *Acetobacter aceti* turns into acetic acid, which gives vinegar its astringent smell and taste. The English word *vinegar* comes from the French *vinaigre,* which literally means "sour wine."

Thus winemaking for millennia was an endless struggle to halt the natural process of wine turning into vinegar. Vintners soon developed containers that not only held wine but also kept out most air. The most popular were amphoras made of reddish brown clay, which carried a variety of both dry and liquid products. They remained in use for nearly six thousand years and came in all sizes, with the most popular being about two to three feet high and containing between eight and sixteen gallons of liquid. The larger ones weighed about 130 pounds when full of wine.

Amphoras had two handles and a pointed end, which served as a third handle that helped in carrying and pouring them. They also had long, narrow necks that made it hard for air to enter the container, but during winemaking the amphora's neck had to be left at least partially open so that carbon dioxide, a by-product of fermentation, could escape. Fermentation was a haphazard development that early winemakers could neither understand nor control. They learned from bad experiences that if they sealed amphoras too tight, pressure built up, and the vessels exploded. Early winemakers learned that once fermentation ended, though, they had to seal amphoras to keep out air. This was often done by putting a glob of wet clay onto the top of the neck. Many early winemakers also stored amphoras partly in the ground to keep the contents cooler and thereby slow the change to vinegar.

By 3000 BC, Egypt, the superpower of its day, was the center of wine. At first the Egyptians imported wine, probably from southern Palestine, but eventually they planted their own vines and took the rudimentary craft they inherited to a much higher level. Egyptian methods of making wine were clearly described on fresco paintings that still exist today. In addition, many amphoras dating back to 3000 BC have survived.

By the golden age of Egypt, about 1500 BC, winemaking had become fairly sophisticated. Vintners now had a much better mastery of the process, especially the crucial task of keeping out air. A fresco in a tomb in Thebes from 1400 BC gives a colorful picture of contemporary viticulture. Along the back wall of the winery are rows of amphoras at various stages of winemaking. Some of the vessels are open and are probably still undergoing early fermentation. Above them are jugs with the neck containing straw or grass to let off carbon dioxide while keeping air out, a process similar to the one used today in wineries around the world. Off to the side are rows and rows of wine in amphoras with flat or cylindrical tops on them, where fermentation has been completed.

Colin Hope of Monash University in Australia has done extensive studies of Egyptian stoppers. These show that after fermentation finished, chopped-up organic material such as leaves and reeds was stuffed into the neck of the amphora, a piece of pottery was placed on top of that, and finally moist clay went over the opening to create a totally sealed container.

The Egyptians also discovered that by closing amphoras tightly after fermentation was completely finished the wine usually became much better over time. Thus the Egyptians first developed a taste for aged wines. An Egyptian prisoner named Onkhsheshonqi in the fourth century BC scribbled winemaking notes on pieces of clay to his son, writing on one, "Wine matures as long as one does not open it."

Egyptians are believed to have used cork as early as the fourth century BC for fishing buoys, but there is no evidence that they used it as a stopper for amphoras or in other wine containers.

The rise of Greek city-states as the major political powers of the Mediterranean beginning about 800 BC resulted in the shift of viticultural innovation to that area. Tree resins had been used to seal wine containers before the Greeks, but they developed the practice into an art form. One of the most popular resins came from terebinth trees, which are part of the cashew family and grow widely in the Mediterranean basin. The resin became a standard way for the Greeks not only to seal the inside of amphoras to make sure no air seeped through porous jar walls, but also to fix in place the clay stoppers at the top of jars. In addition, the Greeks added resin to the wine to impede the growth of bacteria and for flavoring. The result was retsina, which is still drunk today in Greece.

Grape cultivation spread to Italy with the rise of Rome, and the

Romans loved their wine. As one epitaph of the day said, "Baths, wine, and sex ruin our bodies. But what makes life worth living except baths, wine, and sex." The Romans left the world the most detailed evidence of ancient viticulture. Pliny the Elder, who wrote in the first century of the modern era, dealt extensively with wine in his thirty-seven-book treatise *Natural History*, going into detail about various ways of dealing with what he called "wine disease." He offers plenty of practical advice: "It is a proof that wine is beginning to go bad if a sheet of lead when dipped in it turns a different color."

Pliny credited the Celtic tribes in the Alpine valleys of what is now Switzerland with introducing the wooden barrel as a replacement for amphoras. Barrels were easier to both make and transport than the earlier jugs, although unfortunately for archaeologists they disintegrate and are lost over time. Pliny called them "wooden casks" and noted the use of cork stoppers to keep air out of them. He also gave a detailed account of harvesting a cork tree and wrote that its bark was "used chiefly for ships' anchor drag-ropes and fishermen's drag-nets and for the bungs of casks, and also to make soles for women's winter shoes."

The Bible has numerous references to viticulture and winemaking. The gospel of Luke 5:37 notes, "No one puts new wine into old wineskins, or else the new wine will burst the wineskin and be spilled, and the wineskins will be ruined." Wineskins, which were stoppered with a plug to keep out air, were a popular method in the ancient world for short-term wine storage and for transferring it into larger containers. Pictures of them remain in frescoes and on ancient jars, but the skins disintegrate over time and no remnants remain.

Corks have been found in Roman shipwrecks dating from the fifth century BC to the fourth century AD. Professor Vernon Singleton of the University of California, Davis, believes the Romans first used cork as a way to protect wine from air. Amphoras dating from 500 BC show cork being used to seal the containers, but Singleton says, "This does not appear to have been the usual ancient method of closure." He adds that old corks were very different from the ones we know today. In ancient times the cork was a large piece of raw bark, which might be an inch or two thick, and was fit into the mouth of an amphora and fixed in place with resin. These, however, still let some air into the vessel through lenticels, thin, horizontal slits in the bark. Today's smooth corks are made by punching plugs parallel to the bark, which cuts across the lenticels and provides a much tighter seal.

Resin discovered in the necks of amphoras indicates that ancients realized the cork alone was not sufficient to seal the jar properly. Archaeologists found fifteen jars dating back to the third century BC on a sunken ship off the east coast of Sicily that had cork stoppers sitting flush with the top of the container. They had been sealed tight to the jar with pitch. The Roman poet Horace, who lived in the last century of ancient times, writes in Ode VIII of having a joyous banquet for Bacchus, the god of wine, where they "remove the cork fastened with pitch." Rome's ruling class was fond of aged wines, and Falernian, a wine from near Naples and the First Growth of its day, was aged for ten to twenty years in amphoras with cork stoppers covered with clay or cement.

Corks, however, fell into disuse after the fall of the Roman Empire in the fifth century when the Dark Ages descended upon Europe. There was much less trade in the millennium between 500 and 1500, and cork farmers from the Iberian Peninsula had difficulty selling their product in other parts of the continent. An additional blow to the use of cork with wine was the rise of the Moors, who were forbidden by their holy book—the Koran—from drinking alcoholic beverages. They began conquering Europe from the south starting in the eighth century, an invasion that reached its apogee at the Battle of Tours on October 10, 732, when the Franks led by Charles Martel defeated the Moors only 130 miles southwest of Paris. It would take another seven centuries before the invaders were expelled from Iberia and a wine culture—and cork—returned to that area.

Although barrels were the main vessel for making and transporting wine during the Dark Ages, the containers no longer had a stopper made of cork as in Roman times. In its place were a variety of inferior substitutes such as wooden plugs, which were pounded into a barrel and generally provided a leaky closure at best. Rags made of hemp or other textiles were also soaked in olive oil and stuffed into the bunghole of a barrel to keep out air. Sometimes pieces of leather were similarly used. Often the stoppers were held in place by pieces of string that were tied down onto the container, and sometimes sealing wax was poured over the plug to reinforce the seal.

German winemakers used large wine casks to reduce the amount of air in the barrel in relation to the level of wine and thus lessen the danger of its going bad. In some cases they put rocks into barrels to keep the level of liquid high and reduce the amount of air.

A popular peasant solution for keeping air away from wine was to pour a little olive oil in the container. The oil floated on top of the wine and blocked any contact with air. When the wine was served, a small amount of liquid was poured off the top to remove the oil. The custom of tasting wine before serving it actually started as a way of making sure all the oil was gone and goes back to before the birth of the modern cork.

During its millennium without cork, wine had to be consumed quickly, and there was a constant race to drink it before it went bad. The value of wine decreased inexorably after it was made, and it was considered worthless once the next year's vintage was available. Without exception, from 500 to 1500 old wine meant bad wine.

Cork was first exported to England in 1307. Its most popular use in medieval Europe was as soles for footwear because it provided insulation against bitterly cold castle floors in winter. Not until the late 1500s was cork used as a stopper for bottles holding liquids, in particular wine. One of the first known uses of the word *cork* as a stopper in English was in Shakespeare's play *As You Like It*, which is believed to have been written in late 1599 or early 1600. The character Rosalind at one point says to Celia, "I pray thee, take the cork out of thy mouth, that I may drink thy tidings."

The serendipitous union of corks and inexpensive glass bottles took place first in England and then spread to the Continent starting in the seventeenth century. Ancient Egyptians and Romans made glass containers, and the Venetians had been producing them since the early thirteenth century. But that glass was both expensive and fragile. The most commonly used bottles at the time were made of heavy pottery or stoneware. Wine in those days was shipped in wooden barrels and served to customers in decanters that didn't need a stopper since the wine was quickly consumed.

In 1632, Kenelm Digby, the eccentric owner of a glassworks and a sometime privateer, introduced a bottle-making technology that produced both a strong and much less expensive glass container. The bottles were manufactured in a furnace heated with coal, rather than wood, resulting in a much hotter fire. In addition, the glass contained a higher ratio of sand to potash and lime than previously. There was later a patent fight over Digby's role in developing the new bottles, but a court ruled in his favor. The vessels became known as English Bottles, and the technology was quickly copied elsewhere. The dark green or brown containers had a so-called string rim on the neck so that a piece of twine could be tied over the cork to hold it in place. Corks were left sticking out of the bottle so they could easily be removed.

Early bottles were individually blown, and the size was determined by the glassblower's lung capacity. This led to a great disparity in the capacity of containers and the widespread practice of claiming that more liquid was in the bottle than was actually the case. Sir Boyle Roche tried to rectify that problem with the straightforward proposal to the Irish House of Commons that "every quart bottle should hold a quart." Nonetheless, for many years it was illegal to sell wine in bottles because of misrepresentations about their contents.

The English upper class bought wine in barrels and then moved it to bottles, which carried the family name or seal on the front and had a cork in the neck. In the most privileged manors, the top servant was charged with going to the wine cellar and bringing back one of the glass bottles filled with wine. He was called the bottler, but over time his title evolved into *butler*.

The quality of cork, though, was often questionable. John Worlidge, an early English agronomist, wrote in his 1676 book *Vinetum Brittannicum or A Treatise of Cider*, "Much liquor being absolutely spoiled through the only defect in the cork."

In about 1700, inexpensive bottles appeared in France. The first encyclopedia of Denis Diderot in 1751 included a drawing of a man carving a cork into the shape to fit a bottle as well as a detailed description of cork making. It said corks were used for shoes and slippers "but above all to close jugs and bottles."

One bit of cork folklore is that the French Benedictine monk Dom

Pérignon rediscovered corks for the Western world as a perfect closure for the Champagne that he had just invented. According to the story, two Spanish monks on their way to Sweden stopped at the Abbey of Hautvillers in northern France, where Dom Pérignon was the cellar master from 1668 to 1715. The French monks asked the visitors about the cork stoppers they had in the necks of their water gourds. The Spaniards explained they came from the bark of a tree that grew in Catalonia and were a wonderful way to seal a container hermetically. Dom Pérignon supposedly immediately saw this as a superior way to close Champagne bottles and ordered a supply of corks. At the time he was sealing his bottles with wooden pegs wrapped in hemp soaked in olive oil.

Like many other stories about Dom Pérignon, this one is false. André Simon, the British wine merchant, connoisseur, and historian, writes that the wine from Champagne was "first bottled, sold, and drunk as a sparkling wine in London during the sixties and seventies of the seventeenth century." The Duke of Bedford's household accounts for March 25, 1665, showed expenditures for "Champaign [sic] wine, also 2 dozen glass bottles and cork." That was three years before Dom Pérignon entered the monastery. The story about how Dom Pérignon invented Champagne is likewise false, but that's a tale for another book.

Corks and the new bottles got a major boost in 1703 with the signing of the Methuen Treaty between Portugal and England. This was both a military and a commercial accord that gave privileged trade access to both countries in the other's market. Portuguese wines, especially Port, which improved with years of aging in corked bottles, were taxed less than French imports and were soon popular in English manors. The Portuguese often put wax or pitch on top of the cork to make the seal even more airtight.

The original English bottles were almost pear-shaped with long necks and a wide base. That made them stable when sitting on a table, but inconvenient for storage in bins. So in the early eighteenth century, bottle design changed, with the neck becoming shorter and the sides narrower and flat, much like today's bottles. This made it much easier to stack them on their sides. An added advantage was that it kept the cork moist, thus protecting its seal. If a bottle is stored standing up, the cork quickly dries out and air can leak into the container.

The English bottles were used for much more than just wine and were soon the container of choice for medicine, perfume, liquor, cider, and other liquids. The closure was usually a cork.

The only thing left to do once a better bottle had been developed and cork had been rediscovered was to find a better way of getting the cork out of a bottle. For many decades there were only two ways to remove the cork, and both of them were bad. The first was to leave it sticking out of the neck, but that made it harder to store and decreased the effectiveness of the seal. The second solution, if the cork had been pushed entirely into the bottle, was to slice the glass off below the end of the cork with a special set of prongs. An anonymous poem printed in London in 1732 relates the heroic attempts by one wine enthusiast to get the cork out of a bottle: "Sir Roger set his teeth to work / This way and that he ply'd / And wrench'd in vain from side to side." Sir Roger then burned the cork from the top and pushed the remainder into the bottle—only to get his thumb stuck in the neck. Some modern wine consumers might commiserate with Sir Roger.

Fortunately the English soon came up with better ways to remove a cork, which also allowed it to be put in flush with the bottleneck. Initially they used a tool called a steel worm or gun worm, which was designed to pull unspent bullets out of a gun barrel. Later devices for pulling a cork carried a variety of names, including cork drawer, bottle screw, and bottle worm. The first English patent for a corkscrew (#2061) was given to Samuel Henshall, a clergyman, on August 24, 1795. Ever since, inventors around the world have spent endless hours developing new contraptions for getting a cork out of a bottle.

By the end of the eighteenth century, the bottle, the cork, and the corkscrew had opened a new age in wine history. For the first time since the Romans with their tightly sealed amphoras, it was possible to enjoy aged wine. Consumers no longer had to drink wine in a hurry before it spoiled. Wrote Britain's Hugh Johnson in 1966, "The invention of the cork is the most important event in the history of fine wine. . . . However well our ancestors may have been able to make their wine . . . it could never have reached anything like the point of soft, sweet perfection which a claret or burgundy can, if it is given the chance, today."

In the entire world, only a few sounds bring joy to all but the most jaded. One is the purring of a kitten. Another is the thwack of a well-pitched baseball hitting a perfectly swung bat. And a third is the pop of a cork being pulled from a bottle of wine.